The Nuts
and Bolts *of*
Church
Planting

Also by Aubrey Malphurs

Advanced Strategic Planning

Being Leaders

Biblical Manhood and Womanhood

Building Leaders (coauthor)

Church Next (coauthor)

A Contemporary Handbook for Weddings, Funerals, and Other Occasions
   (coauthor)

Developing a Dynamic Mission for Your Ministry

Developing a Vision for Ministry in the 21st Century

Doing Church

The Dynamics of Church Leadership

Leading Leaders

Maximizing Your Effectiveness

Ministry Nuts and Bolts

Money Matters in Church

A New Kind of Church

Planting Growing Churches for the 21st Century

Pouring New Wine into Old Wineskins

Strategy 2000

Values-Driven Leadership

Vision America

The Nuts and Bolts *of* Church Planting

A Guide *for* Starting Any Kind of Church

Aubrey Malphurs

BakerBooks

a division of Baker Publishing Group
Grand Rapids, Michigan

© 2011 by Aubrey Malphurs

Published by Baker Books
a division of Baker Publishing Group
P.O. Box 6287, Grand Rapids, MI 49516-6287
www.bakerbooks.com

Printed in the United States of America

Library of Congress Cataloging-in-Publication Data

Malphurs, Aubrey.
    The nuts and bolts of church planting : a guide for starting any kind of church / Aubrey Malphurs.
        p. cm.
    Includes bibliographical references (p.   ) and index.
    ISBN 978-0-8010-7262-8 (pbk.)
    1. Church development, New. I. Title.
BV652.24M35 2010
254′.1—dc22   2010030444

11   12   13   14   15   16   17   7   6   5   4   3   2

Contents

Introduction

Why write a book on church planting? In 1992 I wrote *Planting Growing Churches*. One of the reasons I wrote it was that there were very few books in print on this important topic and most addressed it from an international missions perspective—not as something that necessarily needs to take place in North America.

The Best Solution

Today, however, I felt compelled to write this book for two reasons. First, church planting is the best solution to the current state of the church in America—a church in crisis. Early in the twenty-first century, 80 to 85 percent of the churches sprinkled across America are either plateaued or in decline. If the typical traditional church in America went to the local emergency room, the doctors would quickly put it on life support. David Olson, director of the American Church Research Project, writes, "17.5 percent of the population attended an orthodox Christian church on any given weekend in 2007."[1] This means that an astounding 82.5 percent didn't attend an orthodox Christian church. And as the population continues to grow, the church loses more ground.

Another important detail that some could miss is that the number of Americans who profess no religious affiliation has practically doubled since 1990 and, most important, their central location has shifted from the Northwest to the Northeast. Why is this important? Writing in *Newsweek*, Jon Meacham quotes Albert Mohler as to the significance of all this for the church and its faith:

> It was a small detail, a point of comparison buried in the fifth paragraph on the 17th page of a 24-page summary of the 2009 American Religious Identification Survey. But as R. Albert Mohler Jr.—president of the Southern Baptist Theo-

logical Seminary, one of the largest on earth—read over the document after its release in March, he was struck by a single sentence. For a believer like Mohler—a starched, unflinchingly conservative Christian, steeped in the theology of his particular province of faith, devoted to producing ministers who will preach the inerrancy of the Bible and the Gospel of Jesus Christ as the only means to eternal life—the central news of the survey was troubling enough: the number of Americans who claim no religious affiliation has nearly doubled since 1990, rising from 8 to 15 percent. Then came the point that he could not get out of his mind: while the unaffiliated have historically been concentrated in the Pacific Northwest, the report said, "this pattern has now changed, and the Northeast emerged in 2008 as the new stronghold of the religiously unidentified." As Mohler saw it, the historic foundation of America's culture was cracking.

"That really hit me hard," he told me last week. "The Northwest was never as religious, never as congregationalized, as the Northeast, which was the foundation, the home base, of American religion. To lose New England struck me as momentous." Turning the report over in his mind, Mohler posted a despairing online column on the eve of Holy Week lamenting the decline—and, by implication, the imminent fall—of an America shaped and suffused by Christianity. "A remarkable culture-shift has taken place around us," Mohler wrote. "The most basic contours of American culture have been radically altered. The so-called Judeo-Christian consensus of the last millennium has given way to a postmodern, post-Christian, post-Western cultural crisis which threatens the very heart of our culture." When Mohler and I spoke in the days after he wrote this, he had grown even gloomier. "Clearly, there is a new narrative, a post-Christian narrative, that is animating large portions of this society," he said from his office on campus in Louisville, Kentucky.[2]

The current crisis represents what has become an ongoing problem for a church in decline. The important question is what can be done about this? Is there a solution to the problem of the decline of Christianity in general and the American church in particular? The answer is a resounding yes. The solution is twofold. First, the 80 to 85 percent of the churches that are plateaued or in decline need to pursue and undergo congregational revitalization or renewal. Most have wandered far from what Jesus called them to do in such notable passages as Matthew 28:19–20 and Acts 1:8. If the church is to recover and have an impact on what is becoming a post-Christian culture, it will need to return to what Jesus has called it to do—"Make disciples" (Matt. 28:19)!

Second, it's imperative that our churches plant more churches. In the mid-twentieth century, churches and denominations were doing reasonably well and saw little need for church planting, so they "dropped the ministry ball" in starting new works. For example, every other year at Dallas Seminary, I would host a church-planting week when I would invite several speakers to come and cast the vision for church planting as a viable ministry option for our students. I would also invite various denominations as well as others to come on campus during the week and recruit our students. Few denominations and organizations showed any interest.

Today all this has changed. The end of the twentieth and the beginning of the twenty-first century has been marked by a steady decline of the church, and the denominations in particular have begun to realize that their very survival is dependent on church planting.

Of the two solutions—congregational renewal and church planting—church planting is by far the better solution. There are at least four reasons for this. One is best summarized in the words of missiologist Peter Wagner. In response to the question, What is the difference between church planting and church revitalization? Wagner said that it's the difference between having babies and trying to raise the dead. As one who has trained leaders to plant and revitalize churches all across North America and beyond, I would attest that the latter has proved much more difficult than the former. Struggling, established churches are steeped in complacency and the status quo and thus tend strongly to resist needed change, whereas church plants see this evident problem of established churches and are most open to embracing the kind of healthy change that will make a difference for Christ in their communities.

Another reason is that newly planted churches evangelize better than older, established churches. Bruce McNicol, cofounder and president of Truefaced, writes that among evangelical churches, those under three years old will win ten people to Christ per year for every one hundred members. Those ranging from three to fifteen years old will win five people per year for every one hundred church members. But once a church reaches fifteen years, the figure drops to three people per year for every one hundred members.[3]

Church's Age	People Won to Christ per Year	Number of Members
3 or less years	10	100
3 to 15 years	5	100
15-plus years	3	100

A third reason church planting is more effective is that church planters gain credibility with their members as leaders faster than those who assume the pastorate of established churches. Few established churches are willing to hand over the reins of leadership completely to a new pastor. Before these pastors can become leaders in the church, they must build credibility and win the trust of the congregation. This can take anywhere from four to eight years, and some churches will never let the pastor lead. In a sense new pastors are like new members; they're joining the congregation and it will take time for them to prove themselves. However, the church-planting pastor has the advantage of assuming the leadership role from the very beginning. He is there first, and new congregants are joining him. Thus from the start most will grant him the credibility and trust necessary for him to lead them.

A final reason church planting is an effective solution is what I refer to as the problem of acquired baggage. In this context, "baggage" refers to the mistakes or snafus that pastors make during their tenure in the church. Pastors are people and, like all people, they make mistakes. However, today's culture has seen too many pastors fail for numerous reasons and we are hard on pastors. The problem for leaders who assume the pastorate of established churches is that often much if not all of the "baggage" is shifted from the shoulders of the former pastor to those of the new pastor. Thus they inherit the fallout from the mistakes of the former pastor.

Church planting, however, doesn't work this way because there's no former pastor and thus no acquired baggage. Certainly the planting pastor will make mistakes and acquire his own baggage, but he doesn't have to carry the added weight of another's missteps in the process.

Key to the Future of the Church

A second reason I wrote this book is because starting new churches is vital to the future of the church in America. The point is simple. No church plants—no church. Like all organizations, churches have an organizational life cycle. They're born or planted and experience early growth due to a natural emphasis on outreach. However, problems begin to arise along the way, and far too many churches shift from an outreach to an in-reach mentality as they attempt to solve their problems. This, in turn, slows growth. Should churches ignore or fail to correct the situation, their growth stymies and they plateau. If they continue in failing to correct the situation, they experience early decline that if ignored will turn into later decline and ultimately death.

The bad news is that in time all churches will fail and die. This is hard to comprehend as I consider the church that I attend—Lake Pointe Church in Rockwall, Texas. Lake Pointe is a megachurch, celebrating its thirtieth year, with around seven thousand people in attendance. However, someday we'll not be here, and the evidence for this is the many viable churches in the first century that died long ago. Take for example the Jerusalem Church found in the early chapters of Acts. This was clearly a megachurch due to its approximate size of ten thousand attendees (Acts 2:41; 4:4). It was also a biblically based, spiritually minded church (Acts 2:42–47). But where is this church today? Should you fly to Jerusalem and attempt to visit this church on a Sunday morning, you would discover that it no longer exists, as is true of the first-century churches of Corinth, Ephesus, Galatia, and others. Organizations aren't perpetual. Because they are made up of people, in time they will die. It's imperative that we keep in mind the fact that the church has always been and is still only one generation away from extinction.

The Cycle of a Church

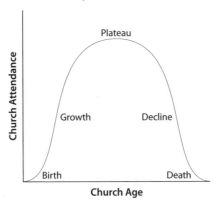

The good news, however, is that we can start new churches. And because churches in the first century and throughout history planted vibrant churches, Christ's church is still alive today. Through church planting the church has survived. In Matthew 16:18 the Savior promised that he would build his church, and one of the chief ways he's accomplished this is through starting churches that are in touch with the culture and are reaching new generations for Christ.

Why Another Book on Church Planting?

The first question was, Why write a book on church planting? The second is, Why write *another* book on church planting? There are a number of good books out on church planting, which wasn't the case when I wrote my first book in 1992. And for this I'm delighted. So why another book? The reason is that most current books endorse a particular model or way of doing church. These models are reflected by various labels, such as emergent churches, Next Generation churches, megachurches, seeker-driven churches, seeker-sensitive churches, purpose-driven churches, cell churches, connecting churches, multi-ethnic churches, contemporary churches, house churches, organic churches, new-paradigm churches, postmodern churches, and missional churches. I suspect that with the emphasis on the environment (a move that I favor), eventually we'll be hearing about green churches. In this book I will use the new term *Great Commissional churches* for churches that combine the Great Commission mandate with the church missional concept.

It is obvious that some of these models target a particular group of people, such as the Emergent or Next Generation (people born after 1982), seekers, postmodern people, and others. Other models focus on size, such as house churches, cell churches, and megachurches. Still others address an approach to ministry, such as purpose-driven and organic churches.

This book, however, isn't an endorsement of a particular model of church, though there are many good ones out there. I'm not trying to encourage a particular way of doing church as most books on church planting and some church conferences do. The problem is that what works in one part or region of the country may not work in another. There's no guarantee that what is effective on the West Coast will be effective on the East Coast, or what is meaningful in the South will be meaningful in New England. What is relevant to one generation or group of people may not be relevant to another.

This book is what the title says. It addresses the nuts and bolts of church planting. It's a guide for church planting in general, regardless of the model. Most important, I'm arguing for following a *process* for building Christ's church (Matt. 28:19–20) not a particular *model*. The important term here is *process*. By following the fourfold process outlined in this book, the result will be a church model—a fresh, new church that's relevant to who you are, where you are, at this time in your life.

This Book Is for You

If you plan to start a new church or be on the staff of a new church, or if you're the pastor of an established church that wants to sponsor a church plant, this book is for you.

In it I will examine what the Scriptures say about various issues associated with church planting, such as, What is a church? What is the church's mission? Who were the first-century pastors? My assumption is that you want to know what the Bible teaches about these topics. If that's the case, this book is for you. I mention this because I see an alarming trend on the part of some publishers to move away from those of us who stress what Scripture teaches. It's not that they oppose Scripture, they're simply more interested in what a particular leader thinks or says than Scripture. For me the first question is, What does the Bible teach about the principle I'm addressing? For these publishers, however, this isn't the first question, nor is it the second or third. Thus I really appreciate Baker Books for its willingness to stay the course and publish the works of people like me who are vitally interested in the teaching of Scripture on doing church.

Where Is This Book Going?

I've divided *Nuts and Bolts* into two parts—the preparation for church planting and the process of church planting. The process that I briefly mentioned above is at the very core of this book. However, the process likely won't happen if the church planter doesn't prepare for it. Those of us who are football fans look forward every year to the month of August. Why? Because August is when our teams begin preparation for the new season that begins in late August or early September. This preparation involves a heavy physical and mental regimen. First, the players have to condition their bodies for the season. This involves lots of running and some weight lifting. Second, they have to prepare their minds, which involves learning the plays and listening to motivational messages.

There are certain steps that church planters must take if they are to prepare themselves for a season of church planting. These steps align with each of the book's chapters. To make sure we know what we're talking about, the first chapter defines the church, church planting, and the church planter. The second helps church leaders discover where they fit in the church-starting process. It helps them determine if they should lead or minister from a support position. Chapter 3 provides some practical approaches to raising the funds necessary for starting churches. Chapter 4 addresses a number of assumptions that undergird this book and the planting process, such as the importance of Scripture and hermeneutics, the necessity of change and innovation, and, finally, the stages of church planting from conception through birth.

Part 2 addresses the important fourfold process that all church planters must work through to build a church that is relevant to who they and the people they will attract are and where they are and that honors the Savior. I've addressed each of the concepts that make up the process—values, mission, and vision—in separate chapters. Next, I break the last concept—the church's strategy—down into seven steps that are located in the last seven chapters.

The Fourfold Process

Core Values

Mission

Vision

Strategy

I have included an appendix that provides a rich source of information for church planting. In it you will find a number of tools to aid you as you seek to determine if God would have you plant churches. Other tools are sample mission and vision statements, a core values audit, and much more.

Finally, I will use the masculine pronoun almost exclusively when referring to a pastor or church planter in spite of a number of women who are pastors and church planters. The reason is simply to avoid using "his or her" throughout this book.

PART 1

Preparation *for* Church Planting

1

What Is Church Planting?

The Definition

Over a number of years of teaching at a seminary and consulting with numerous churches, I've discovered that I must define my terms. I've heard or been involved in a number of discussions where everyone assumed they knew what others were talking about only to find out later that wasn't the case. For example, when some popular, well-known person is speaking at a conference on leaders and leadership, the speaker and we assume we all know what is meant by these two terms. Right? Wrong! Very few define *leaders* and *leadership* in the same way. Simply take time to thumb through several books on leadership at the local bookstore, and you'll see what I mean.

The purpose of this chapter is to define terms or concepts in such a way that you will be clear about what I mean. I want us to be on the same page from the start. My focus is on the definition of *church planting*. However, for even further clarification, I'll also address the definitions of the *church* and *church planters*.

Church Planting

First, I want to define *church planting*, which is what this book is all about. A mistake in understanding at this early stage could affect how you comprehend the rest of the book. I define *church planting* as an exhausting but exciting venture of faith, the planned process of starting and growing local churches based on Jesus's promise to build his church and in obedience to his Great Commission.

In this section I will break down this definition into its various components for further clarification.

Exhausting

I suspect that few who have been involved in any kind of church ministry would be surprised to hear me say that church planting is exhausting, as are church revitalization, interim ministry, and other forms of church ministry. And the same could be said about parachurch ministry. The reason I need to say this is that some embrace the mistaken idea that starting churches is easy. After all, how difficult is it just to teach the Bible and love on new people? However, church starting involves so much more than this, as you'll discover in the pages that follow, and at times it will drain you of strength.

Church planting involves long hours, perhaps longer than those put in by pastors of established churches. There's so much to do when starting from scratch and never enough time to do it all. There will always be one more visit that needs to be made or a phone call to be returned. Church planters need forty-eight-hour days, not twenty-four-hour days.

Most disappointing is that people of the faith, especially pastors, will criticize church planters rather than encourage them. Other churches may not be excited to see a new church planted anywhere nearby. They view the new church as competition and may say cruel things to dissuade the planter. Then there are those who'll attack a church planter because he's planning a church that's contemporary and different from the norm. This is emotionally draining and can take a toll that's far worse than physical exhaustion.

Exciting

One emotion that counteracts the exhaustion of starting a church is the excitement it engenders. I make a point of telling the church planters I train that, if there's no excitement, then something is wrong. I've never encountered a viable church-planting situation where the people weren't excited about what they were doing. Therefore, if you plan to start a church but notice that people aren't excited about it, then call it off—go no further. Something is seriously wrong. Stop what you're doing and reevaluate the entire project. It's likely that now isn't the time to plant such a church. The people simply aren't ready. Note that this is the case in far too many established churches. Somewhere along the way, they've lost the excitement of being involved in Christ's church, which doesn't bode well for the future.

Church planting is exciting for a number of reasons. First, church planters are pioneers. That's another way of saying most of them are entrepreneurs. They're wired from the beginning to start new works, and this helps them realize who God has made them to be. There's an excitement about being who God wants you to be and doing what you know God wants you to do. There is also the excitement of anticipating what God could accomplish through you and the new ministry. God might use you to reach thousands, as he has Billy Graham, or he may use you to reach a neighborhood. Regardless, God will use you to accomplish his will and build his church. Church planters are excited because they expect God to do something special through their ministry. Not only do they know that God can use them wonderfully but they believe he *will* use them. They can feel it in the depth of their soul. Now is their time in history to be used of him to do something special. They expect to serve God's purpose in this generation—their generation (see Acts 13:36).

A Venture of Faith

Church planting is both an exhausting and an exciting faith venture. Hebrews 11:6 tells us that nothing of spiritual significance is accomplished without faith. Indeed, "without faith it is impossible to please God" (NIV). And church planters are men and women of authentic faith who desire more than anything to please God, and they do this, much like the patriarch Abraham, through believing and obeying him. What does that mean? You'll find the answer in Hebrews 11:8 (NIV): "By faith Abraham, when called to go to a place he would later receive as his inheritance, obeyed and went, even though he did not know where he was going."

You may or may not know where you're going to minister—at least initially. Regardless, if God is in it, he'll let you know in good time. Proverbs 3:5–6 (NIV) is key to this faith and direction. The sage writes, "Trust in the Lord with all your heart and lean not on your own understanding; in all your ways acknowledge him, and he will make your paths straight." The statement "he will make your paths straight" indicates that God will make your direction clear when the time is right. Our job is to trust and acknowledge him.

A Planned Process

Starting a church is a dynamic, planned process. It has a beginning but ideally no ending. Starting a church is just that: beginning a ministry that was not already in existence, with the goal that it continue for as long as God is pleased to work through it.

I depict this process in two ways. The first is the organizational life cycle that I presented in the introduction to this book. That cycle instructs us that organizations begin and grow but in time they plateau and eventually die. The idea is for the church to begin and continue to grow with no end in sight. We know that someday God will close the doors of a church, as we discovered in the introduction when we looked at several first-century churches. However, we don't begin with the church's demise in mind. Our focus is on its beginning and growth, not its death.

Another way to think of the process of church planting is focusing on the life stages of a church. Every church works through five stages: conception, development, birth, growth, and reproduction. Here the process is evident, beginning with conception—the idea of starting a church—and continuing through the stages, with the ultimate goal of reproducing other churches or church plants. The plan should be to promote the planting of other church-planting churches.

Occasionally I come across believers who are opposed to planning. The thinking is along the lines that it isn't spiritual to plan. Nothing could be further from the clear teaching of Scripture. For example, Jesus reveals his plan for the disciples and his church in Matthew 28:19–20 and Acts 1:8. Also look up the following passages on planning: Proverbs 14:22; 15:22; 16:9; 19:21; 20:18; 21:31.

Starting and Growing the Church

The goal of church planting is not only to start a church but to see it grow. Churches grow in several ways.

BIOLOGICAL GROWTH

Churches grow biologically—people having babies. This is good because it signals that the church has young couples that are having babies who are the future of the church. It means the church has a future.

TRANSFER GROWTH

Churches grow through people transferring from another church. This can be good or bad. Some people leave one church and attend another because their expectations are too high or they've been disciplined and asked to leave. On the other hand, some people leave a church because it is toxic and is doing harm to their faith.

EVANGELISM GROWTH

Evangelism growth results when a church is reaching unbelievers with the gospel of Christ. They are saved and join the church. Evangelism is an imperative and key to fulfilling the Great Commission. Unfortunately, few churches are evangelistic, which is one of the major reasons the American church is in crisis.

SPIRITUAL GROWTH

We can also view church growth from the spiritual perspective. According to Christ's Great Commission, his church is to grow both numerically and spiritually. It is Christ's desire that his church grow numerically as people come to faith in Christ. But the ultimate objective of the Great Commission is that the church grow spiritually as believers mature over time.

I've noted over the years that some people tend to emphasize one type of growth over the other. For example, some small, struggling churches state that they may not be growing numerically but are growing spiritually. This viewpoint is unfortunate because numerical and spiritual growth should work together. In most cases, churches that aren't growing numerically by reaching lost people aren't growing spiritually either. And some churches grow numerically but not spiritually. Again, spiritual and numerical growth must complement one another and are not opposed to one another.

Scripture presents a clear theology of numerical growth. Luke records the results and ensuing growth of the church in a number of places in Acts (2:41, 47; 4:4; and many other passages). He uses these numbers to signal that God is at work in and through the Jerusalem Church.

A key question to ask here is what is success, or how should a church plant view success? As stated in this section and depicted in Acts, success is seen in both spiritual and numerical growth, and the latter in most cases reflects the former.

Resting on Jesus's Promise

Church planting rests on Jesus's promise in Matthew 16:18 (NIV) that he would build his church: "And I tell you that you are Peter, and on this rock I will build my church, and the gates of Hades will not overcome it." What is the promise in this passage? It's that Jesus is in the church-building business. He is the builder of churches, not us. However, he's assigned us the pleasure of being a part of the process. Note also that it's his church that he's building, not ours. At times we've all referred to the church we attend as "our church." Hopefully, we don't really mean that. But some do, and that's where the church gets into trouble. A former student told me of an established church that he pastored in the Northwest where the people had taken ownership of Christ's church with disastrous results. Thus one Sunday he preached on Matthew 16:18, invited all who would give the church back to Jesus to come forward, and God blessed them.

I must confess that Matthew 16:18 troubled me for a number of years. It says that Jesus will grow or build his church. My problem was how does this square with the declining state of the church in America? I knew that Jesus wasn't falling down on the job but still I struggled with the promise. Then I was part of a conference where Tony Evans, the pastor of Oak Cliff Bible Fellowship in Dallas, Texas, was the main speaker. He preached on Matthew 16:18 and explained that maybe the majority of our struggling churches aren't Christ's church, at least not the one that he's building. I believe that Tony is correct and that this should cause these churches to pause and reflect on what they're really all about.

Implementing Christ's Great Commission

Church planting is an exhausting but exciting venture of faith, the planned process of starting and growing local churches based on Jesus's promise to build his church and in obedience to his Great Commission. The Great Commission is Jesus's mandate for his church. We're not to start just any kind of church; they should be Great Commission churches. These are churches that take most seriously Jesus's command to make disciples! Making disciples begins with evangelism and continues with edification or the building up of the saints in the faith with the ultimate goal of their attaining spiritual maturity (Col. 1:28–29; Heb. 5:11–6:1). As I have said, I believe that the failure to pursue Christ's mandate for his church is one of the primary reasons the American church is in crisis. And when I work with churches that desire revitalization, which is almost every weekend, one of my primary goals is to call them back to what Scripture says they're supposed to be doing, because so many have wandered from his mandate.

While I'll address this fully later in chapter 6 on mission, this is obviously the mandate for new churches as well. Of course, new churches don't have to attempt to woo their people back to the mandate. Instead, they begin with the mandate and encourage those who are responding to some other mandate to find another church that's more in line with their thinking, as there are plenty of them out there. I argue that a major role of the senior or point pastor of the new church will be to keep the main thing the main thing and not to stray from Christ's mission for his church.

The Church

Most of this chapter is devoted to defining the term *church planting*, but I must also define the *church*. If we're starting churches, it's imperative that we know what a church is. Scripture speaks of several kinds of churches, such as the universal church made up of all believers and the local church made up of a number of believers who live in a particular geographic locale. It's the latter concept that I will address here. My definition of the local church is that it's an indispensable gathering of professing believers in Christ, who, under leadership, are organized to obey Jesus's Great Commission by accomplishing certain functions to the glory of God. This is a long but important definition, so I'll break it down into two broad categories and then address the various components that make up each one.

What Christ's Church Is

First, I will address the essence of the church—what it is—and then I will address what it does. *The local church is an indispensable gathering of professing believers in Christ, who, under leadership, are organized.*

INDISPENSABLE

The essence of Christ's church is that it is indispensable. Bill Hybels articulates it best when he states that the church is the hope of the world. It's God's divine institution or organization that he's chosen to work through to reach out to and impact our fallen world. As we study the various beliefs and worldviews of those who make up this country, we quickly realize that there are a number of different ideas as to what is the hope of our world as well as our country. Many felt that when the country elected its first black president, Barack Obama, he was the hope of the world. Others believe that politics is the hope of our nation as well as the world. And many people run for political office, hoping to bring broad, sweeping changes to Washington. Still others feel that education, science, or various causes are the hope of the world. The Christian church planter can state without equivocation that Christ and his church are the hope of the world. Again, according to Matthew 16:18, Christ is building his institution—the church—because it's the only real hope for a lost and dying world.

A GATHERING OF PROFESSING BELIEVERS IN CHRIST

Christ's church exists as an intentional gathering of people who are "called out" (*ekklasia*) by God. This means that people have sensed the calling of God and have purposefully come together to seed a new church. Some of these people may be unbelievers as well as believers in Christ. I say this because, in a doctoral class that I took at Dallas Seminary under the leadership of Dr. Charles Ryrie, he challenged us with the question: Is a church not a church if there are unbelievers present in it? He was responding to the students' definition of the church that included only believers in Christ. As we pondered his question, we realized we needed to include lost people, because it makes sense that most churches likely have a few unbelievers present who profess Christ, but their presence doesn't change the fact that the organization is a church.

UNDER LEADERSHIP

Scripture indicates that the New Testament churches were under leadership. The most obvious leaders were the apostles (the Twelve) whom Christ trained to be the pillars and leaders of the first-century churches. They and their leadership are prominent throughout the book of Acts (in particular see Acts 6:1–4; 15:1–29; and 15:36–41). Both 1 Timothy 3:1–7 and Titus 1:5–9 provide the qualifications for elders who were the first-century house church pastors and leaders.

Scripture also mentions deacons, as found in 1 Timothy 3:8–10. This passage presents only their qualifications but doesn't address what they do. I suspect that according to the meaning of the term *deacon* (*diakonos* means "servant"), they served the early church. It is likely this involved leadership, as they appear to have been elected to their office, hence the necessity for the list of qualifications. Some believe there was a special church office that consisted of women leaders called deaconesses, such as Phoebe in Romans 16:1. Others believe they were simply the wives of deacons (1 Tim. 3:11). Regardless of their role, the fact these women are singled out may indicate that they had some type of leadership role in the church.

ORGANIZED

Because I consult with churches and teach at a theological seminary, on occasion I come across well-meaning Christians who believe it's unspiritual to be organized. Instead they would argue that we should "let go and let God" or "go with the flow" of the Holy Spirit. However, Scripture teaches otherwise. Yes, we are to be led by the Spirit (Rom. 8:14), but that doesn't mean we can't be organized. Several passages indicate that the early churches were organized for ministry. For example, in 1 Corinthians 14:40 Paul addresses the church's public assembly and says that it's to be accomplished in a "fitting and orderly way." That implies organization. In Acts 6:1–6 the Jerusalem Church was facing a potential split in the ranks between the Hebrew and Grecian Jews because the widows of the latter were being neglected in the daily distribution of food. So how did the apostles handle the situation? They organized. The problem seemed to be lack of organization rather than willful disobedience or racial intolerance.

What Christ's Church Does

The first part of my definition of the church is that it is *an indispensable gathering of professing believers in Christ, who, under leadership, are organized.* The rest of the definition is just as important. It addresses what the church does: *The church is to obey Jesus's Great Commission by accomplishing certain functions to the glory of God.*

OBEYS THE GREAT COMMISSION

As I said earlier, the church's mandate from Christ is the Great Commission as found in such passages as Matthew 28:19–20; Mark 16:15; Luke 24:47–48; and others. While I'll devote an entire chapter (chapter 6) to this mandate, the gist of the *mission* is to make disciples according to Matthew 28:19–20. This is twofold and includes evangelism and edification, the latter leading to maturity.

ACCOMPLISHES CERTAIN FUNCTIONS

The church has five primary functions that may be found in the Jerusalem Church (Acts 2:41–47, and supported by other passages as well). They are *biblical teaching* (2 Tim. 4:2); *fellowship* (Heb. 10:25); *worship* (Rom. 12:1; 1 Peter 2:9), which includes prayer, the ordinance of the Lord's Supper, financial giving, praise, and so on; *evangelism* (Matt. 28:19; 2 Tim. 4:5), which includes the ordinance of baptism; and *service or ministry* (Romans 12; 1 Corinthians 12).

GLORIFIES GOD

The purpose of the church is to glorify the Triune God (Rom. 15:6; 1 Cor. 6:20; 10:31). But what does that mean? The term *glorify* ranges in meaning from honoring God to valuing him for who he is. While the church is to glorify God within the congregation, I believe that it's most important that it glorify God in its community before a lost but watching world. The new church is to present Christ and live in such a way in its community that unbelieving people want to know God or at least know more about him.

Church Planters

I've defined church planting and the church. However, one more definition is needed for the sake of clarity. Who are church planters? Church planters are those who are involved in church planting as defined in this chapter. They're men and women who have in some way committed their lives to the exhausting but exciting venture of faith that includes the planned process of starting and growing local churches, based on Jesus's promise to build his church and in obedience to his Great Commission.

Broadly speaking, this definition would include a number of people. First and most obvious, it describes the individual whom God directs to take the lead in starting a church. Second, it would include the team that the individual recruits to plant a church with him. It would also include those leaders who pastor established churches and have used their churches to train church planters and sponsor church planting.

I'm convinced that the best way for a church planter to launch a church—especially if he doesn't have a lot of experience—is for a gifted, talented, established church pastor to bring him on staff for a couple of years. During this time, the church planter gains valuable ministry experience, the church covers his salary, and usually he is free to recruit a team of people who will go out from the church and launch a new church with him.

A great example of one who puts this into practice is Leith Anderson, who is the senior pastor of Wooddale Church in Minneapolis. He so wants to encourage church planting that he gives future church planters what he refers to as a "hunting license." This means they are free to recruit anyone from the church to be part of the team. This speaks volumes about Leith and indicates that he is not threatened by such an approach, as some pastors would be.

Those who train church planters to start churches are in a sense also church planters. This would include those of us who teach church planting at a seminary or Bible college. It would also include those who train church starters within a particular denomination or network.

Questions for Reflection and Discussion

1. What is your definition of church planting? Does it agree or disagree with the author's definition? If the latter, how does it differ?
2. If you are currently involved in a church plant or considering becoming involved, are you experiencing a sense of excitement over the prospect? If not, why not? If not, how would the author advise you to proceed?
3. Are you a person of strong faith? Do you find it easy to trust God? Do you trust him for your finances? How do you respond to the idea that church planting is a venture of faith? Does this frighten you, energize you, or a little of both?
4. Do you agree with the author's definition of the church? If not, explain how you disagree.
5. Which definition of a church planter fits what you believe God has in mind for you? Why or why not?

2

Who Plants Churches?

A Church Planter Profile

In the early to mid-twentieth century, those who were attracted to the idea of starting a new work, especially under a denominational label, would let those responsible for new church starts know of their desire and would request their help, specifically in the form of finances. However, far too often a year or two later, the new church had gone nowhere and the so-called church planter had moved on to other matters. The money that had been invested was depleted along with the energy of those who had given their time and other resources to the new work.

So what went wrong? While there are exceptions, more than likely the so-called church planter wasn't a church planter. That is, God didn't design him to start churches. Those in positions of responsibility, however, had no way of knowing this.

Now all this has changed. Instead of simply supporting and sending just anyone out to plant a church, most denominations, networks, and church planting churches wisely insist that prospective church planters go through an assessment process to determine if they are church planter material. We have discovered that church planters pattern a certain way when they work through the assessment process, and this information pays rich ministry dividends for those who are open to it.

The purpose of this chapter is to assist prospective church planters in answering the question, Am I a church planter? I've divided this chapter into two sections: the preparation for and the process of discovering one's divine design. Before I launch into the chapter, you need to understand that much of it applies to the lead church planter, not necessarily to those who are part of his core team.

Preparation for Assessment

To prepare to discover one's divine design—the assessment process—we first must understand the purpose for assessment.

The Purpose for Assessment

The purpose for assessment is to determine how God has designed a person for ministry. While the emphasis in this chapter is on church planting, leaders who do an assessment will discover their divine design and where they fit best in the bigger ministry picture. It may be church planting, but it could be revitalization, interim ministry, the chaplaincy, or some other form of ministry. This is the reason assessment is never a waste of one's time. Suppose you go through the assessment process and discover that you aren't wired to be a church planter. That's really to your benefit for at least two reasons. First, you won't attempt to lead a church planting venture, which most likely would end up in failure. Second, a good assessment process will help you get an idea of what God has wired you to do and thus will point you in the right ministry direction.

A Good Formal Assessment Process

There are several organizations that provide formal assessment for prospective church planters. They consist of such groups as the Evangelical Free Church of America, Stadia New Church Strategies, Church Planting Assessment Center, Dynamic Church Planting International, New Church Initiatives, and a number of others. Some are denominationally based while others are not. Go to their websites if you desire to know more about them. You could also Google the topic "church planting assessment" for other organizations.

A good formal assessment process would consist of the following.

1. There should be several interviews. The purpose of the first interview is to find out as much as possible about the prospective planter and get to know him. The final interview at the end of the assessment period is for advising the prospective planter whether to pursue church planting or go in a different ministry direction. In some cases the interviewer may encourage the candidate to get some general ministry experience before pursuing church planting.
2. The candidate will likely take a number of audits or assessment tools, such as a spiritual gifts inventory, the DiSC profiles, the Myers-Briggs Temperament Inventory (MBTI), and others.

3. The assessment center will likely divide the prospective planters into teams and assign them various group exercises to see how they interact with one another. Other exercises might be the following: preaching a sermon, explaining why they feel God wants them to plant a church, putting them in common church plant situations to see how they respond, assigning them a demographics exercise, and asking them to prepare a church-planting proposal.

Keys to Good Assessment

I believe that there are at least three keys to a good ministry assessment: self-knowledge, experience in ministry, and past experience.

SELF-KNOWLEDGE

One vital key to good ministry assessment is how well potential church planters know themselves. The reality is that some know themselves better than others. The divine discovery process should encourage each to look deeply into himself and be as honest and forthright as possible regarding his discoveries. If a person finds that he doesn't know himself very well, often he can rely on the help of another person who has known him and has been able to observe him over several years.

A spouse should know her partner well, and I have a bias here. My experience has been that wives know their husbands better than husbands know themselves. This is the reason it's wise for the prospective church planter to go through the assessment process with his spouse. Others who might know the planter well could be family members, such as parents or siblings. I would also add to this list a person's best friends who, over a period of time, have come to know him well.

EXPERIENCE IN MINISTRY

A second key to a good assessment is experience in ministry. It's within the context of ministry that we come to discover and understand our divine design. It's the doing of the ministry that tells us about ourselves. For example, we can take various spiritual gifts inventories but we really don't know if we have certain gifts until we try them. You may believe you have the gift of teaching, but until you attempt to teach, you really won't know for sure. Therefore you would be wise to attempt to minister in a number of different areas to further discover your giftedness.

PAST EXPERIENCE

A third key is past experience, which is a very good predictor of future ministry potential. This means that prospective church starters should review the kinds of ministries and other jobs they've been attracted to and enjoyed in the past. For example, a potential church planter may have been an entre-preneur—having started a business or possibly a number of new ministries at his church. This speaks volumes about this individual's design and what God has in mind for him.

**Three Keys
to Good Assessment**

- Self-Knowledge
- Experience in Ministry
- Past Experience

The Process of Assessment

Good assessment is built on what I refer to as the 3Ds. The first D stands for *design* or *divine design*. The second D is for *direction* or *divine direction*, and the third for *development*. I believe this is the proper order and approach to determine what God would have us do in terms of ministry.

First, the potential church planter must discover his divine design, which we will explore further in the rest of this chapter. After a person has dis-covered his divine design, it will lead to God's direction for his life. For example, if he has the gifts of teaching and of leading, I would argue that it's obvious God wants him involved in a teaching ministry where he can also exercise his gift of leadership. Based on his gifts, I would identify this as God's will or direction for his life or his ministry calling. It seems obvi-ous to me that, if God has given us certain gifts, we are to use them for his service and glory.

When a person knows the direction he is to go in, the next step is to pursue the third D, development. He must determine how he will develop his gifts. He may decide to go to school, join a church staff, read books, and so on.

3Ds

- Design
- Direction
- Development

Divine Design

One's divine design consists of a number of factors. For brevity's sake I will focus on three, along with some general characteristics based on observa-tion. Three important factors in a person's divine design are his gifting—both spiritual and natural—his passion, and his temperament.

THE CHURCH PLANTER'S GIFTING

The Bible is very clear that God has given every believer various spiritual gifts with which to serve him and others (Rom. 12:3–8; 1 Corinthians 12; Eph. 4:7–13; 1 Peter 4:10–11). I would define a spiritual gift as a unique, God-given ability for service. Note the various characteristics of a spiritual gift. First, a spiritual gift is unique. Not every Christian has the same gift, although some may. Second, gifts are God-given. God, not us, sovereignly determines who gets what gifts. I like to put it this way—if you don't like your gifts, take it up with God, the giver of gifts. Third, the gifts are to be used for service. Peter writes, "Each one should use whatever gift he has received to serve others" (1 Peter 4:10).

Scripture mentions a number of spiritual gifts, including administration, apostleship, evangelism, encouragement, faith, giving, helps, leadership, mercy, pastoring, and teaching. I have included a Spiritual Gifts Inventory in appendix A of this book. Either now or when you finish this chapter, take the gifts inventory. In regard to starting churches, I believe that a lead church planter will usually have most of the following gifts: apostleship, leadership, evangelism, teaching (this includes preaching or communication), and faith.

God has also given mankind natural gifts to be used for service. This is true of believers as well as unbelievers. While I can't prove it biblically, I believe that all people are born with natural gifts, whereas Christians receive spiritual gifts at their new birth (conversion). God gives gifts to unbelievers because he is a God of grace; he gives lost people various gifts, such as the ability to sing, play an instrument, act, write, teach, lead, build, and many others. In theological circles, we refer to this as God's common grace. Regardless, church planters need to be aware of their natural gifts as well as their spiritual ones. Two natural gifts that often characterize the lead church planter are leadership and communication.

Whether a natural or spiritual gift or both, leadership is crucial to the lead church planter. It will make the difference between success and failure. Over the years as a consultant, I have worked with a number of established churches, and the difference in whether or not they prosper spiritually is the ability of the senior or lead pastor to lead the church. So a critical question facing the new planter is, Are you a leader? The Leadership Style Inventory is in appendix E and will help you address the leadership question.

THE CHURCH PLANTER'S PASSION

A second area of divine design is one's passion. Passion is a God-given capacity to attach ourselves emotionally to something or someone (a group of people, a cause, an area of ministry, and so on) over an extended period of time to meet a need. Passion is feeling strongly about something, a feeling that comes from God. The focus of our passion is what we care deeply about, what gets us up in the morning, and what we think about it during the day.

The focus of our passion might be ministry to a particular age group or an issue such as apologetics. The key is that it serves to direct the use of our gifts. You might have a gift of evangelism with a passion for children. Thus the focus of your gift is the evangelism of children.

Finally, passion develops out of a strong sense of need. While it may affect our own needs, it primarily focuses on those of others. And passion has tenure. It's not here today and gone tomorrow. It's sticky. It stays with us for an extended period of time.

I believe that several passages address passion: Acts 18:25; Romans 12:11; and 15:20 where Paul uses the term *ambition* to describe his passion to proclaim the gospel to the Gentiles.

I encourage you to take the Passion Audit in appendix B to discover your predominant passion. I use the term *predominant* because you may have several areas of passion. You should know which of your passions is predominant or primary. Often lead church planters have a primary passion for lost people, unchurched lost people, the Great Commission, preaching, or evangelism. Is your passion one of these or similar to one of them? As you can see, they relate closely to lost people and evangelism.

In my consulting work with churches, I find very few churches that value evangelism. The result is that most are weak in this vital function of the church. I find it also difficult to get them to "turn up the heat" on evangelism. However, the exception is those churches who are led by pastors with a passion for lost people or evangelism. They don't need to turn up the heat because evangelism is happening in their churches. They won't have it any other way. Therefore I look for an evangelistic passion or gift in church planters.

THE CHURCH PLANTER'S TEMPERAMENT

The third area of divine design is the church planter's temperament. I define temperament as one's unique, God-given (inborn) style of behavior. Temperament is *unique* in that not everyone has the same temperament, though some may share your temperament or a similar one. Like spiritual and natural gifts and passion, I believe that God is the source of one's temperament. The term *inborn* implies that, unlike spiritual gifts, one's temperament characteristics were present at birth. Finally, temperament concerns one's *behavior*. It's based on a person's actions or behavioral style. Each person has a unique behavioral pattern or style that involves distinct ways of thinking, feeling, and acting.

Two tools that identify temperament that I've found most helpful are the personal profile popularly known as the DiSC, and the Myers-Briggs Type Indicator (MBTI). The letters DiSC each represent a different temperament or behavioral pattern. The D stands for dominance. The I is inspirational or influential. The S is steady temperament, and the C is the compliant behavior pattern.

The MBTI seeks to determine our preference for extroversion or introversion. The former focuses on the outer world, while the latter on one's inner world. The MBTI also helps us discover how we take in information. We prefer either sensing, which involves using the senses to collect information, or intuition, which means developing ideas. The latter are natural visionaries. The MBTI helps us know how we process information. This involves a preference for thinking or feeling. The former are the more logical, facts-oriented people. The latter are more in touch with their emotions and personal values. Finally, the tool helps us understand what lifestyle we've adopted for dealing with the outer world. Some take a planned, organized approach to life and are quick decision makers while others are most adaptable and take a more flexible approach to life and ministry.

In appendixes C and D there are two temperament indicators. Temperament Indicator 1 is patterned after the DiSC, and Temperament Indicator 2 is patterned after the MBTI.

When lead or point church planters take the DiSC, they are usually one of the following: the developer (D), the results-oriented person (D), the inspirational person (D/I), or the persuader (I/D). On Temperament Indicator 1 it's one of the following: the doer, the doer-influencer, or the influencer-doer.

On the Myers-Briggs and Temperament Indicator 2, church planters are usually the inventor (ENTP), the leader (ENTJ), the people person (ENFP), or the persuader (ENFJ).

Divine Design

- Spiritual and Natural Gifts
- Passion
- Temperament

The Church Planter's General Characteristics

In addition to the material above, those of us who have worked with and observed lead church planters have noted a number of common traits or characteristics among them. I've listed them below. Place a check in front of those that are characteristic of you. You won't have all these characteristics, but you or the lead pastor should have a majority of them.

___visionary   ___strong people skills

___courageous   ___strong prayer life

___self-starter   ___flexible/adaptable

___risk taker

___resilient

___focused

___optimistic

___spouse on board

___nontraditional

___emotionally healthy

___good self-esteem

___likes a challenge

___challenges status quo

___inspirational

___people magnet (attracts people)

___healthy family

___servant's heart

___team player

___strategic thinker

___spiritually mature

___good knowledge of the Bible

___not quick to quit

___innovative

___good listener

The Church Planter's Character

I would be remiss if I didn't say something about the prospective church planter's biblical character qualifications. In 1 Timothy 3:1–7 and Titus 1:5–9, Paul lists the qualifications for first-century house church pastors, known as elders. These characteristics are different from those listed above in that they apply not just to church planters or lead church planters but to anyone pursuing pastoral ministry in general.

Following are the characteristics in no particular order. Place a check in front of those that are true of you. In addition, you should take the Men's Character Assessment for Leadership in appendix F (or the Women's Character Assessment for Leadership in appendix G).

___above reproach

___not given to drunkenness

___husband of one wife

___gentle

___temperate

___not quarrelsome

___sensible

___not a lover of money

___respectable

___manages family well

___hospitable

___not a recent convert

___able to teach

___not overbearing

___not violent

___not quick-tempered

___good reputation with outsiders

___not pursuing dishonest gain

___loves what is good

___holds firmly to the faith

___upright

___holy

The Church Planter's Call

Finally, an issue that I must address is the concept of a call to ministry in general and a call to church planting in particular. I've heard some older pastors advise younger men who are considering pastoral ministry that they shouldn't pursue such ministry without a personal call from God. Regarding such a call, Pastor Kent Hughes writes, "My call to ministry was real! And I am convinced that God calls certain of his children to this special service. To be sure, my experience of the call is not normative for anyone else, for the experience of God's call is as varied as there are people: only the reality is the same."[1] I've also heard a number of writers on church planting and church planters advise prospective church planters not to pursue such a course of action without a special call from God to start a church.

Regardless of what constitutes such a special call or how it is accomplished, here is the important question: Is the concept of God's call, which has received so much emphasis, biblical? Those who believe that it is use such examples as the Old Testament prophets (Moses, Jeremiah, and Isaiah, for example) and such passages as Isaiah 6. They also point to Paul and his call.

One major problem with this view is that it employs a questionable hermeneutic. (Hermeneutics addresses how to study and interpret the Bible.) The problem is that those who cite such passages are using descriptive passages as if they were prescriptive and normative for all. Simply because a person did something doesn't mean that others must or should do the same, unless it's a clear command from God. If Isaiah 6 is describing Isaiah's call to ministry, what makes it normative and prescriptive for all others who would pursue the ministry? Personally I doubt that Isaiah included this passage to teach that a person must have a similar call to go into ministry.

Also, as Hughes states, the experience of God's call is as varied as there are people. If there is no one experience or standard for God's call, how do we know when it *is* God's call? I'm not saying that God can't issue a special call to ministry and church planting. Of course he can, but does he always do that, and where is the biblical evidence that specifies such a call is necessary?

If you wish to dig a little deeper into the concept of God's call, I address it more in depth in *Maximizing Your Effectiveness*.[2] I believe the potential church planter is far better off discerning how God has designed him instead of waiting for and debating some mystical, subjective call. The truth that God has "wired" us a certain way speaks volumes about what he wants us to do with our life in general and ministry in particular. Otherwise, why did he design us the way he has? Thus I would advise you to consider your divine design above and beyond a subjective call to the ministry, specifically to church planting.

Questions for Reflection and Discussion

1. Do you agree with the author's position that assessment is a key factor in helping you decide whether you should pursue church planting or some other ministry? Why or why not?
2. Have you considered going through a formal assessment process? If not, why not? If so, which process will you use?
3. How well do you believe you know yourself in terms of your divine design? Do others, such as your spouse or good friend, agree with your self-assessment of who you are?
4. What does your past ministry or work-related experience tell you about what God might have in store for you in the future? How might your past experience point to church planting?
5. Do you understand and find helpful the author's concept of the 3Ds (design, direction, and development)? Why or why not?
6. Based on the results of your using the tools in the appendix and your own self-knowledge, what is your divine design (gifts, passion, temperament)? In what ministry direction(s) does it point you? Does it include church planting? How might you pursue this direction?
7. From the list in this chapter, what did you discover about your general characteristics? Did they indicate that you would make a good church planter?
8. What did the character checklist in this chapter reveal about you? Are most of the items part of your character or are there some serious issues to face?
9. Do you agree with the author's view of a divine call? Why or why not? If you disagree, do you feel a special call to church planting? How do you know?

3

How Much Will It Cost?

New Church Funding

Most pastors know that ministry costs money, and church planting is no exception. When an established church calls a pastor, most have a salary package in place for him as well as a budget to cover the costs of doing ministry. However, this isn't the case with starting churches. The lead planter and his team will need to raise funds for both their salaries and ministry expenses. For some, raising the necessary finances for ministry can be a daunting, frightening task. And I believe that far too many don't pursue international missions as well as church planting because of this challenge.

It's my view that if the church planter believes in his ministry and the need for it, he will be willing to do whatever it takes to see God provide the necessary funding. Most likely he finds that the funding part is simply another of the many challenges that face church planters. I suggest that church planters relax and enjoy the experience as they observe the sovereignty of God in action. It can be exciting to see whom God brings along to be a partner in funding a new work.

The purpose of this chapter is to address the financial side of church planting. I've arranged the contents of the chapter around four financial Ps: the financial promise, financial providers, financial principles, and financial provision.

The Financial Promise

It's imperative for church planters to understand that they're not alone when raising the necessary monies for ministry. God is on their side and will supply their needs, though not necessarily their wants. How can we know this? The answer is found in Matthew 6:25–34, where Jesus makes a promise.

The Promise

Jesus's promise in Matthew 6:25–34 is that he'll take care of the basics of life for those who serve him. The problem in context is that of worry. Jesus doesn't want his disciples to worry about their needs, such as food, drink, or clothing (vv. 25, 28), in the midst of ministry. His reasoning is that there is more to life and that our body is more important than what we eat, drink, or wear. He uses the birds (v. 26) and the flowers (v. 28) as examples and argues that, since God takes care of these, he'll take care of us, because we're far more valuable to him than they are. We must not miss this truth. God knows we have these needs, and he'll take care of them.

The Condition

Jesus does attach a condition to his promise. It's found in verse 33: "But seek first his kingdom and his righteousness, and all these things will be given to you as well." The promise isn't just for anyone, but for those who are kingdom seekers and righteousness pursuers. And while he does promise to meet our basic needs in life, he's not necessarily promising to supply our wants. This is particularly important for those who live in America. As a nation we have been indulged to the point that we expect our wants to be met. Perhaps the hamburger commercial that encourages, "Have it your way," best summarizes where we are. It appeals strictly to our wants, and we've become used to gratifying them. When applying Jesus's teaching to our lives, we must distinguish between wants and needs or risk misunderstanding and therefore misapplying the passage to our individual life situation.

The Problems

Having said all the above, we're not yet done with the passage. There is still the matter of how we respond to the promise. We may have a couple of problems.

THE PROBLEM OF OUR FAITH

First, there is the problem of our faith. Do we really believe Jesus's promise? When the proverbial "push comes to shove," will we trust him and step out in faith to plant churches? It's one thing to think we'll trust him before getting out there; it's another to trust him when we're up to our elbows in the church plant itself and all the problems that accompany it.

THE PROBLEM OF OUR FEELINGS

There is also the problem of our feelings. Are we willing to set aside our personal wants to pursue God's kingdom and righteousness? Over time we become used to what for most Americans is a lifestyle of extravagance. And far too many believe that someone—the government, an employer, parents—owes them such a life. On a number of occasions, I've heard people say that the most important thing in life is that we're happy. Unfortunately, this view has been used to justify all kinds of practices, such as divorce, abortion, cheating, and others.

Actually the most important thing is that God is happy. The Matthew passage teaches that our pursuit of God's kingdom and his righteousness is more important than pursuing material things, because it makes God happy.

It's imperative that potential church planters and their spouses consider their past lifestyles as well as their current one, because the lifestyle they're asked to live as church planters can have a subtle emotional impact on them. We've become used to having it our way to the point that we feel something is missing in our lives—that we're coming up short—when we don't get everything we want. And this leads easily to discontent with our circumstances while we're planting a church. So the questions for church planters and spouses are, Have you considered these lifestyle issues? Can you give up or put aside your current lifestyle for the cause of Christ's kingdom and the pursuit of his righteousness?

The Financial Promise

The Promise: Jesus's promise of Matthew 6:25–34 is that he'll take care of the basics of life for those who serve him.

The Condition: "But seek first his kingdom and his righteousness, and all these things will be given to you as well."

The Problems: Our faith and our feelings.

The Financial Providers

Next we must focus on the financial providers—the second P. Who might God use to provide for the personal and ministry needs of the church planter? Our Lord wants us to plan wisely when it comes to our finances. In Luke 14:28 he teaches: "Suppose one of you wants to build a tower. Will he not first sit down and estimate the cost to see if he has enough money to complete it?"

God may use any or all of the following as funding sources.

A Sponsoring Church

I'm convinced that one of the best ways to start a church is under the direction of a sponsoring church. One of the most successful church planters I've ever trained (Pastor Tim Armstrong, whose church was awarded Saddleback's "church of the year" award) did so under the auspices of a sponsoring church. A sponsoring church can bring the prospective church planter on staff where he can gain valuable experience. The church may provide people who are willing to become a part of the core leadership of the new church. They can pray for the new work, and they provide needed accountability for the church planter.

Another advantage of a sponsoring church is funding. This can take a number of forms. If they bring the church planter on staff, they provide his salary while he's in training and recruiting others for the new start. They might make a large, one-time financial gift to the work. They might add the church plant to the mission budget until the church becomes self-supporting. They might encourage their people to support the church individually, over and above their normal giving to the church. They could do a combination of the above.

A Core Team

Another source of needed funding is the church plant's core or launch group, who are all the people who make up the initial congregation. As the church planter recruits the launch team, he must make them aware that in time (usually one to three years), they with others will become the primary financial supporters of the new plant. This is a discussion that must take place as the planter recruits people to be a part of the launch team.

This group can be a vital source of funding. I worked with a core group of people in Oak Cliff, Texas, a suburb of Dallas, who were able to come up with most of the funding for the pastor's salary and much of the ministry expenses. They were so committed to the church plant that they were willing to dig deep into their pockets to see it happen. And I would argue that this ought to be the attitude of any launch team. It's what some would call "putting their money where their mouth is." You see, membership has its obligations, one of which is financial.

A Home Church

Many church planters have a home church—a church where they came to faith and became involved in ministry, a church that they attended for a long time while growing up or while establishing a business, or the church where they're serving on staff. The church planter should make the pastor of his home church aware of his belief that, based on his divine design, God is leading him into church planting. If the pastor doesn't immediately volunteer support, then eventually the planter could approach him again. This is a good reason not to lose contact with your home church, even if you are away from the area for job-related reasons, military service, or further training.

A Prayer Team

I believe that once a leader believes that God wants him to plant a church, he should recruit a prayer team to pray regularly for wisdom and God's direction in this matter. This team could consist of individuals located in one church, or they could be people who don't even know one another. Regardless, their commitment would be to hold the prospective planter up in prayer before God.

The church planter must be willing to take the time necessary to keep these people informed of what is taking place and what they specifically need to be praying for. This could involve regular phone calls, emails, and even snail mail.

Eventually the planter could determine if anyone would be willing to support the new work financially as well as with prayer. However, he must keep in mind that the first objective of such a team is prayer and not finances.

The Leadership Core

The leadership core consists of those who will make up the staff of the new church. I strongly encourage lead planters to recruit and train a staff planting team before launching a new work. The research tells us that 90 percent of struggling plants started with only a single paid person, whereas 88 percent of fast-growing church plants have teams.[1]

Not only would the leadership staff likely need to raise support for themselves, but the lead planter should expect them to give to and support the new work as well. I've heard of staff who feel that because they're on a church's staff they don't feel obligated to support the church financially. I would argue that this is fallacious reasoning and indicative of those who aren't really committed to the ministry of the church.

A Denomination or Organization

There was a period of time in the twentieth century when the church was doing well, specifically in the South and Midwest. Thus there seemed to be less interest in church planting on the part of denominations and other independent organizations. All that changed beginning in the late twentieth and continuing into the twenty-first century. I believe that a healthy denomination or organization of churches should see at least 20 percent of its established churches starting up new works each year. I suspect that most would agree with this figure.

The way these groups would fund a new plant varies. Some may not directly fund the church plant but recommend that their churches located near the new church lend their support both financially and otherwise. Some groups do give a percentage of funds directly to the new work. If you as a church planter are part of a particular denomination or network, you would be wise to contact the group and see what they're willing to do for your new church. I'm addressing finances specifically, but some would provide other vital services as well, such as free assessment, training, coaching, encouragement, a rich denominational heritage, and so on.

However, along with all this, keep in mind that there will be and should be "strings" attached to such services. For example, some organizations ask you to support—in turn—other denominationally or organizationally related church starts; to include the denominational label, such as "Baptist," in your church name; to make regular progress reports to them; and so forth. As long as these strings aren't too restrictive or time intensive, you would be wise to consider doing what they suggest.

Family, Friends, and Acquaintances

A great source of funding is one's family, friends, and acquaintances. These are people who know you reasonably well, so it's a good sign if they're willing to support you. They may be people with or to whom you have had prior ministry and they believe in you and are willing to put their money behind you. Also these people may be a source for other contacts who would support the new work. You never know whom God will move to get behind your new work financially.

I advise church planters and their spouses to make a list of such people. Then they should approach them, present the opportunity for involvement, and ask them about others they know who might be interested.

A Fund-Raiser

If I were to plant another church, I would recruit a fund-raiser as a vital part of the core team or planting staff. A better title than fund-raiser might be minister of stewardship, minister of generosity, minister of support, or director of support ministries..

The fund-raiser could be a retired financial planner or professional fund-raiser or someone who has been involved in a similar field. Such a person would bring to the position a wealth of knowledge that the typical pastor doesn't have.

This person's primary function is to assist the church planter in fund-raising. A job description might consist of the following:

1. Accompany the church planter when he is approaching potential donors.
2. Come up with fund-raising ideas.
3. Train the lead planter and his staff in various skills, such as how to ask a person to give to the new work.
4. Set up a banquet or special meeting and invite potential givers.
5. Though normally donors expect the lead person to follow up, there are likely situations when the fund-raiser could do some follow-up.
6. Keep the entire core leadership apprised of how financial matters are progressing as well as make wise suggestions about how each could better raise funding.

7. Establish a proactive stewardship development plan for the church plant as it begins to grow and attract new people.

I believe that having such a person on the team—especially a retired person—would communicate well to potential donors in general and especially to older ones. Where might you find such a person? I suspect that some of these people are part of an established church—perhaps a sponsoring church. You can ask around. Also contact those who are in the business of fund-raising or a similar business and assess their interest and solicit names of those who have retired from the business and might be willing to join your team.

Personal Employment

The employment of the church planter to provide funding for the church would be at the very bottom of my list of sources, because any kind of ministry—especially church ministry—is likely to be full-time and having another job would be a major distraction. However, it may work well for the planter's spouse to work.

During my first church plant, I attempted to work and found my second job most distracting and time-consuming. I was a schoolteacher, and there were times when I should have been with or contacting people for the church, but instead I was busy with my job at school.

I believe that having a second job can also give others the idea that you aren't completely committed to the new work. I realize that the apostle Paul was a "tentmaker." However, I would say the same to him, and I believe he made tents only as a last resort. Keep in mind that for various reasons some people refused to support him. Therefore he made tents to provide for himself and a number of the churches he started.

Financial Providers

Sponsoring Church

Core Team

Home Church

Prayer Team

Leadership Core

Denomination or Other Organization

Family

Friends

Acquaintances

Fund-Raiser

Employment

The Financial Principles

I believe church planters need to know at least five principles for raising funds. I've divided them into negative and positive principles.

Some Negative Fund-Raising Principles

While there will be some exceptions, there are at least three negative fund-raising principles that you should be aware of.

DONORS DON'T GIVE TO PAY THE BILLS

Donors aren't excited about paying bills, such as utilities, salaries, or the mortgage. Paying the light bill, though necessary, isn't very glamorous. And contributing toward salaries often raises questions about the planter's personal credibility and use of funds. While in some instances the church planter can raise funds to cover other salaries such as those of the staff, some people will question the use of the funds for his own salary. So be careful here.

DONORS DON'T RESPOND WELL TO NEGATIVISM

It's likely that you have observed some Christian ministries that attempt to appeal to their constituency through the use of guilt and negativism. I recall that a number of years ago a well-known figure used his healing ministry to support a university and a hospital. People were shocked when this person announced that God had revealed to him that if a certain amount of money didn't come in from his donors within a particular time, that he (God) was going to take the leader home. I believe this was a breaking point in the man's ministry. Only a faithful, trusting constituency supported this approach, and the ministry never completely recovered from this blatant use of guilt to raise money.

Paul warns us in 2 Corinthians 9:7: "Each man should give what he has decided in his heart to give, not reluctantly or under compulsion, for God loves a cheerful giver." We should never attempt to make people feel guilty so they will give.

DONORS DON'T RESPOND WELL TO NEEDS

Perhaps someone or some ministry regularly sends you appeals for money based primarily on needs alone. While these are most likely legitimate needs, they don't generally motivate people to give and support the ministry. Instead, they leave the recipient with the distinct impression that the ministry is in trouble. In such a case people may give once or twice but no more. We want to hear good news and that our gifts are going for more than just the ministry's needs. As someone once said: "If need motivated giving, then everyone would be givers."

Some Positive Fund-Raising Principles

There are at least two positive principles that will aid you in your fund-raising.

Donors Respond to Visions

If people tend not to give to pay a ministry's bills, to assuage their guilt, or to meet needs in general, to what will they give? The answer is vision—a clear, compelling vision. A well-cast vision brings to a ministry a sense of significance. It casts a clear, compelling picture of an exciting Christ-honoring future, showing that what the organization is doing is making a difference in a profound way. People who give to Dallas Seminary, for example, would not give because the school needs to pay the light bill or even my salary. But they might give to a seminary that is raising funds for scholarships for international students who, when they return to their country, will be in high positions where they can exert much influence for the Savior.

Donors Respond Well to Big Visions

It's interesting that donors give not only to organizations that cast vision for their ministries, but to churches and parachurch organizations that cast *big* visions. Paul in Ephesians 3:20 writes, "Now to him who is able to do immeasurably more than all we ask or imagine, according to his power that is at work within us. . . ." I believe that here Paul is slapping the wrists of the church at Ephesus for not asking and imagining big enough. While the "asking" refers to their prayer life, the "imagining" is a reference to their vision for ministry. A number of years ago J. B. Phillips wrote the book *Your God Is Too Small.* I believe that God was writing the same book to this church.

If I were to plant a church again, say in Dallas, Texas, where I now live, my vision wouldn't simply be the planting of another church where there already are numerous churches. Instead, I would plant a church with a vision for reaching Dallas County. I would likely plant in the suburbs and then expand into the inner city and out into the rural parts of the county. And I'm convinced that more people would support this vision than just the planting of another single church in Dallas.

Fund-Raising Principles

Negative Principles
- Donors don't give to pay the bills.
- Donors don't respond well to appeals based on guilt and negativism.
- Donors don't respond well to needs.

Positive Principles
- Donors respond to visions.
- Donors respond well to big visions.

The Financial Provision

Not all on the church-planting team will be good at or eager to develop funds for church planting. However, if this is the case, the lead church planter must develop skills in this area. Many find it a challenge that they readily accept, especially those who have been successful at it in the past. If you really believe that God is in what you're doing, then you'll find it easier to raise funding. In this final section, I will address the problems and practices of raising money for a church plant.

The Problems of Raising Money

My experience is that there are two particular problems that you'll face when raising money for God's ministry.

THE PROBLEM OF OUR PRIDE

The first problem is pride, especially for those of us who have grown up in America. So many Americans are middle class, white-collar professional types who have never had to ask anyone for money. And we tend to react negatively to asking for help.

The real culprit here is personal pride and perhaps a failure to humble oneself and depend on God. Before a person begins to raise money for ministry, he needs to address this issue of pride.

THE PROBLEM OF OUR FEAR

The second problem is fear. Many people fear being turned down, and this is an emotional problem. Being turned down would be perceived as rejection, which strikes a blow at their self-esteem. Before a person begins any fund-raising, he must first deal with this issue and perhaps other emotional baggage as well. Otherwise, he won't last very long.

Our self-esteem or worth as a person is wrapped up not so much in *who* we are but *whose* we are. According to Paul, we are "in Christ" and must see ourselves as such because that's how God sees us. Once we truly understand and accept this concept, we are ready to handle the rejection of being turned down for support.

The Practice of Raising Money

Next, we need to examine the actual practice of fund-raising. This involves both the contacts with prospective donors and the conversation when we ask for their support.

CONTACTS WITH PROSPECTIVE DONORS

We never know whom God will move to support us. The very people you think will rally to your support don't. And those whom you question even approaching for help come through. We simply don't know whom God will move to be a financial partner with us. Regardless, the more contacts we have the better. And the key to lots of contacts is networking. The Savior developed an extensive network (see, for example, John 1:40, 43–45), and we would be wise to do the same.

I advise church planters to begin early in the planting process to collect the names of prospective donors, encouraging them not to forget their spouse's network as well. And as we have opportunity, we should develop relationships with all our contacts, letting them know what God is doing and asking for their prayer support. Then let the adventure begin.

Be sure to understand that God will use you to raise the necessary funds for your venture. This is all part of his sovereign work. So be patient with the process and be sure to follow up on every possibility. Having someone on staff as a fund-raiser to assist and accompany you in the work is wise.

THE COMMUNICATION WITH PROSPECTIVE DONORS

So what do you say to a contact? How do you ask him or her to be part of your ministry? This will likely involve at least a telephone call and a personal meeting. There are several procedures outlined in appendix H to help the fund-raiser think through what to say to these people.

Financial Provision

The Problems of Raising Money
• The problem of our pride
• The problem of our fear
The Practice of Raising Money
• The contacts with donors
• The communication with donors

Funding New Churches
The Four Financial Ps

• The Financial Promise
• The Financial Providers
• The Financial Principles
• The Financial Provision

Questions for Reflection and Discussion

1. Are you convinced that God will provide for your basic needs as you start a church? Why? What about your wants?

2. Are you a kingdom seeker? Are you in pursuit of God's righteousness? Why or why not?

3. How might your lifestyle keep you from pursuing God's kingdom and trusting him for your needs? Have you discussed this with your spouse?

4. Briefly review the various funding sources covered in this chapter. Did the author miss any? Which ones look like possible funding sources for you?

5. Would it be possible for you to have a fund-raiser as part of your team? Why or why not? Have you looked for one?

6. Do you agree with the negative fund-raising principles? Why or why not? Can you think of any others? Are you trying to use one of these approaches?

7. Do you agree with the positive fund-raising principles? Why or why not? Are you a good vision caster? Is your vision big enough (Eph. 3:20)?

8. Do you see yourself as struggling more with pride or fear or both in asking people for money? Why?

9. Have you started a list of potential funding contacts? Why or why not? If so, is it extensive? If not, when will you begin to collect these contacts?

4

What Are the Foundational Assumptions?

Important Concepts

All Christians carry with them certain practical and theological assumptions about Christ's church and its ministry. The problem is that the majority aren't aware of these assumptions, though they affect how they view and even conduct their church's ministry. One interesting and important example is the role of the pastor. A common assumption, particularly of the Builder Generation, is that the pastor (in his role as pastoral caregiver) is supposed to visit them, especially when they are in the hospital. Many people believe this assumption is biblical, but it's not anywhere in the Bible.

Where do such assumptions come from? Most often they're simply passed on from generation to generation. And most are accepted without being examined. We've become so used to them that we don't even question their practice. If you asked about them, many church members would simply say, "We've always done it this way."

These assumptions affect people's expectations of the church and its pastor. For example, should the pastor fail to visit people in the hospital, his ministry to some of these people would no longer be effective. Often the same assumptions are made of a church-planting pastor. In the world of church planting, it's most important that the leadership core and the launch team be aware of their general assumptions about how they'll do church. Using the example of the pastor's role above, some might expect him to visit them in the hospital, while others feel there are more important things that he should be doing, such as developing leaders, studying the Bible, and so on. Either way, a lack of clarification could prove costly.

Seven assumptions will undergird the rest of this book and will likely serve to formulate your assumptions as well:

1. It's important how we interpret the Bible.
2. Numerical growth is important.
3. The pastor's primary role in the church is not pastoral care.
4. Business principles can be applied to the operation of the church.
5. There is no exact biblical model for doing church.
6. Innovation is important.
7. It's important to understand the stages of development of a church.

The Importance of How We Interpret the Bible

The first assumption is that it is important how we interpret the Bible. It's imperative that we base all that we do squarely on the Scriptures, because they are the source of truth for all Christians. We must consult the Scriptures in particular on what they say about *ecclesiology* (the theology of the church) and doing church. For example, we must know the purpose, mission, and vision of the church. My argument is that pastors need to know what the Bible says about doing church so they can base their ministries on the Scriptures. I suspect that if you're evangelical in your Christian belief system, you would grant me this point.

However, committed Christians differ on how they interpret the Bible and what it says about doing church. Therefore church planters and pastors must understand hermeneutics—methods of interpreting the Bible. I want to address two important hermeneutical principles that I believe have been violated by a number of churches, even though they seek to interpret the Bible accurately.

The Descriptive versus the Prescriptive Hermeneutic

In the introduction I touched on the issue of the descriptive versus prescriptive hermeneutic. There are some biblical passages that describe how the early church did some ministries, but they are not necessarily prescriptive for the church today. An example is found in Acts 20:7–12. Though not entirely clear, it seems that the context of this passage is a local church at Troas. Let's assume this context for the sake of the principle. In verse 7 Luke mentions that the church came together to break bread. A second assumption on my part is that this is a reference to the Lord's Supper. With these two assumptions in mind, there are those who would argue from this passage that because Troas partook of the Lord's Supper on the first day of the week, we should do so as well. They believe it's imperative that we follow the example of this church in Acts 20.

Initially this would seem to make sense. The problem with this interpretation, however, is that nowhere in this passage or in any other in the Bible does it prescribe or command that we partake of the Lord's Supper on the first day of the week. This is simply a descriptive passage of what the church at Troas practiced. There is no command attached to it. Thus the local church today has freedom as to when to celebrate the Lord's Supper. It could be on the first day of the week, in the middle of the week, or on the last day of the week.

The Negative versus the Positive Hermeneutic

The second hermeneutical principle that many churches violate is what I refer to as the negative versus the positive hermeneutic. There are some who say that the Bible must address what we do before we can do it. I refer to this as the negative hermeneutic. They articulate this view with the following: "Where the Bible speaks, we speak; where the Bible is silent, we're silent." An example would be the use of musical instruments in a worship service. Some forbid their use simply because the Bible doesn't mention them.

Initially this would seem to make sense. However, on closer examination it really doesn't. Simply because a practice isn't mentioned in the Bible doesn't mean the early church didn't do it or that the church today shouldn't do it. Absence of proof isn't proof of absence. In actuality, much of what these churches—who espouse a negative hermeneutic—do isn't found in the Bible, for example, using hymnals, serving grape juice instead of wine at communion, and meeting in a special building instead of a house (the early church met in houses).

The positive hermeneutic, as I refer to it, makes more sense. It teaches that just because a practice isn't mentioned in the Bible doesn't mean we can't do it. As long as it doesn't violate some clear, biblical principle, then God gives us the freedom to do it or not.[1]

The Importance of Numerical Growth

My second assumption is that numerical growth is important to Christ's churches, particularly in church plants. Christ wants his church to grow numerically (Acts 2:41, 47; 4:4; 5:14; 6:1, 7; 9:31, 35, 42; 11:21, 24; 14:1, 21; 16:5; 17:12) and, if it isn't, something is wrong. On occasion numbers and/or numerical growth surfaces in my conversations with people. And I've discovered that many are uncomfortable talking about numbers, especially when it comes to local church attendance. I can understand this because I've been at some pastor's conferences where certain pastors play "the numbers game" or push the "success syndrome." Sometimes these are pastors of growing churches who interpret such growth as their personal success as well as God's blessing on them and their ministry. Thus they may ask you how large your church is so they can make subtle comparisons of their ministry with yours. Their motive is to let you and others know that they are more successful. I've also heard pastors and members of smaller churches state that they may not have a lot of people attending their church, but the ones who do are spiritual people and that's what's most important, not the number in attendance. In light of all this, many people, especially younger people, frown on any discussion of numbers and attendance.

You may recall from the discussion in chapter 1 that legitimate church growth happens in three ways: *biological growth* occurs when young families have babies; *transfer growth* takes place when people move from one church to another; and *evangelism growth* is the result of the people of the church sharing the gospel with lost people who accept Christ and then join the church.

We see examples of the latter in the Bible—Acts 2:41, 47; 4:4; 5:14; 6:1, 7. In Acts 2:41 Luke points out that around three thousand people came to faith as the result of Peter's sermon. And in Acts 4:4 a number of men (five thousand) came to faith as well. Why does Luke go so far as to mention the number of converts? Luke uses these numbers and other references to conversion growth to send the message that the Jerusalem Church was making a powerful impact for Christ. And I would go so far as to say that the Holy Spirit might do the same today. I contend that if a church is spiritually healthy, in most situations it too will grow numerically as the Jerusalem Church did. A possible exception might be a church in Muslim-dominated North Africa where one or two converts a year is the norm.

If a church isn't growing or is in decline, something is wrong. Therefore, based on the biblical evidence, numbers are important and likely indicate that a church is blessed of God and reaching people for Christ.

The Primary Role of the Pastor

Another of my assumptions is that pastoral care is not the primary role of the pastor of a church. I want to return to my illustration at the beginning of this chapter. There I mentioned that a large number of those who belong to the Builder Generation expect the pastor to visit them, in particular when they're in the hospital. They see the role of the pastor as that of a chaplain who is there basically to take care of them. This is critical, because these people and often their families establish their expectations of the pastor on this assumption. Unfortunately no one stops to determine if it's correct or even biblical.

If people searched the Scripture, they would find that this expectation is not biblical. And while there's nothing wrong with a pastor visiting congregants in the hospital, it should not be considered the primary role of the pastor of today's church. In addition, I would go so far as to say there are many more important things that the pastor should be doing, such as developing leadership, casting vision, praying, making sure the church is in pursuit of the Great Commission, and teaching the Word of God.

I noted that in Acts 6:1 the church is facing a problem; the widows of the Grecian Jews were being neglected in the distribution of food. How would many of today's pastors handle this situation? They would assume the role of chaplain and pastoral caregiver, step in, and take care of the people and the problem themselves. Note that the Twelve turned this responsibility over to seven laymen who were chosen by the congregation, so the apostles could give their "attention to prayer and the ministry of the word" (v. 4), which are more important to the health of the church than pastoral care. I've provided a rather in-depth treatment of this concept of pastor as chaplain and primary caregiver in appendix I.

Applying Business Principles to the Church

I've observed a number of Christians who frown on reading and researching books and periodicals that come from the business world and would never think of applying their principles to Christ's church. Their reasoning is that business is simply a part of the "world" and thus has no place in the church. This is another one of those buried assumptions that needs to be exhumed.

First, it seems a little ironic that many of the people who object are businesspeople themselves. Apparently they think it's okay to apply worldly principles to worldly matters. But if these are principles that work, why shouldn't they be used for the good of the church as well, or are the principles that may be derived from business practices necessarily worldly and thus wrong?

These well-meaning people aren't aware that all truth is God's truth, and while all the Bible is true, not all truth is found in the Bible. Special revelation is found in the Bible, but general or natural revelation from God can be found in nature, history, and other sources (see Ps. 19:1–6; Acts 14:15–17; 17:22–31; Rom. 1:20–21). Thus we can find truth in medicine, physics, engineering, business, and many other disciplines, because ultimately any truth comes from God. Even lost people can stumble onto truth. Still we must discern what is truth. To spot God's truth, we must have in place a mental theological grid through which we filter all that comes our way.

Sometimes my seminary students will challenge me on this concept. Usually I respond by explaining the above. Then I move into the world of the seminary in general and exegesis and the languages in particular. I ask how many use tools such as the major Greek and Hebrew lexicons. They all raise their hands. Then I ask if Christians authored these tools. The usual response is probably not. Then I ask why they're using tools developed by unbelievers to better understand and better interpret Scripture. They get the point.

We can find God's truth in business practices and other areas as well that can benefit the church. Therefore I challenge church planters to look for truth about leadership in the Bible but not to exclude the world of business as another possible source.

No Exact Biblical Model for Doing Church

Many people in our churches—especially the more traditional churches—assume that the way their church does ministry is the biblical way. They argue, "That's why we do it the way we do." So they have a sermon from the Bible on Sunday mornings and a Wednesday night prayer meeting because they believe it's the way they did church in the New Testament. They want to follow this example.

My response to this is, "Show me where it says or even illustrates this way of doing ministry in the Bible." They can't do it because there is very little in the Bible that tells us how churches did ministry in the first century. One rare example is found in 1 Corinthians 14, where Paul reveals that the church at Corinth met together to sing a hymn, give a word of instruction, speak a revelation from God, speak in tongues, and prophesy (v. 26). However, few would follow these practices today outside the charismatic churches.

It's my conviction that God doesn't prescribe an exact model for doing church. He gives us freedom in this, leaving it up to us to design and develop specific models that are relevant to our church population and location. It takes all kinds of churches to reach all kinds of people.

There is nothing sacred about how the people in the first century did church. Actually some ministered very poorly and are held up as bad examples (see Revelation 2–3). Thus church planters are free to develop unique ways of doing ministry—doing church in the ways that will be most meaningful to their congregation.

I've observed that each generation is affected by the ways in which the previous generation did church. They either accept and mimic them or rebel and forge new paths. For example, some Boomer churches followed in the paths of the Builder churches. And some Next Generation churches are copying the Boomer Generation. But a growing number of Next Generation believers are rebelling against the way Boomer churches have ministered, especially their emphasis on large churches, and they are opting instead for smaller house churches.

The Importance of Innovation

Some people who assume that their churches mirror what the first-century churches practiced may unconsciously use this as a reason not to make changes or innovate. One old-timer put it this way: "If the piano and organ were good enough for Jesus and Paul, they ought to be good enough for us!" This is his rationale for not changing what's been done practically from the beginning of the church. And that same old-timer adds, "If you want to see what church was like around here back in the 1920s and 1930s, then come and worship with us Sunday morning."

What does the Bible teach about change? Do we have a theology of change? The answer is yes, and it can be summed up with three terms: *function*, *form*, and *freedom*.

The Church's Functions

I define the church's functions as its timeless, unchanging, nonnegotiable principles that are based on biblical mandates. Because they are mandates, all churches are to pursue them. They aren't options. Some examples would be worship, evangelism, fellowship, service, biblical instruction, as well as others. Just as they took place in the first century, so they are vital to the church in the twenty-first century and every century between.

The Church's Forms

I define the church's forms as its timely, changing, negotiable practices that aren't based on Scripture but on culture. Whereas the church's functions are principles, its forms are practices that address how the church will carry out its prescribed functions.

Worship through music is a function of the church, but it can be conducted in a number of ways or styles with different instruments. A traditional style would use organ and piano, whereas a contemporary style might include drums and guitars. Churches are free to choose the forms that work best for reaching lost people and growing their people in the faith. The key to a good form is that it connects people with the function so that they understand it.

Some churches choose to use the King James Bible with all the *thee*s and *thou*s. Others assume that most young people don't understand the King James translation and this impedes them in receiving and grasping biblical instruction. For them to better understand the Bible, these churches use a modern-day translation instead.

When a person has become emotionally attached to a function, he or she will welcome change. What matters most to this person is that a function, such as evangelism, happens, not the form it takes. However, if one is emotionally attached to a form and not the function, then he or she will resist changing to another form.

The Church's Freedom

The church has freedom as to the forms it uses but not its functions. And often in today's fast-paced world, the forms need to change quickly to meet the needs of the people in many areas of the world. The problem is that, regardless of our age, we're all somewhat resistant to change. In this regard the words of Francis Schaeffer are most instructive: "Not being able to change, to change under the Holy Spirit, is ugly. The same applies to church polity and practice. In a rapidly changing age like ours, an age of total upheaval like ours, to make nonabsolutes absolute guarantees both isolation and the death of the institutional, organized church."[2]

Change or transformation is at the very heart of the gospel. Christians who are growing in their faith will change. It's a byproduct of spiritual growth. If I'm the same person this year as I was last year, something is wrong with me spiritually. The sign of an immature Christian is one who is not willing to change or adapt to change. You'll never mature as a Christian until you learn to deal constructively with personal and organizational change. The problem is that too many churches cave in to the change resistors and over time lose their ministry and thus their spiritual edge.

Theology of Change

- The Church's Functions
- The Church's Forms
- The Church's Freedom

The Importance of the Stages of Development

The growth of the church can be compared to that of an individual. Both go through five general stages: conception, early development, birth, growth, and reproduction. The church planter should understand these stages, for this will help the church grow and protect it from an early death.

The Conception Stage

The conception stage is when the idea of starting a church is realized. It's during this phase that a number of events take place that are foundational to the church's future.

1. The assessment of the lead pastor to determine if he's wired to be a church planter.

What Are the Foundational Assumptions? 57

2. The recruitment of a core leadership team that will become the staff.
3. The raising of funds for the venture.
4. The discovery of the church's values and the articulation of a mission and vision along with a strategy to accomplish the same. (Because this is a primer on church planting, I will spend much of the rest of this book addressing strategy.)
5. The drafting of a prayer team who will bathe the newly conceived church in prayer.
6. The adoption of a doctrinal statement.

The Early Development Stage

Now that the idea of planting a church has been conceived, the next stage is to develop it, much as a child develops in its mother's womb. This involves the recruitment of a core group of people who will become the launch team and initial congregation. They are the focus of this stage. Most likely such recruitment has already taken place in the conception stage and possibly before that. People will hear about the idea and want to know more. As the team recruits the launch group, it will also begin to help them grow. This involves helping them mature spiritually, begin implementing the new church's ministry (worship and Bible study), and administer the new church's affairs.

The Birth Stage

The third stage is the birth of the church that has been conceived and begun to form.

1. The group needs to decide when they will launch the church. Some common times are Easter, the week before Easter, Christmas, and September, when the kids return to school.
2. The group assesses its size. The bigger the church is when it is born, the healthier it will be. A minimum number for birthing a church is fifty people. A much better size would be two hundred or more.
3. If the group hasn't already done so, they will need to pick a name for the church. Names should be short, recognizable, and memorable.
4. They will need to locate a place to meet. Some good choices are a school building, a theater, or possibly a church facility that's not being used at all or not used on Sundays. I'll say more about this in chapter 13.
5. The church will need to publicize its meetings, such as its worship service. Much of this is simple marketing strategy, such as using mailers, as well as word of mouth.
6. The church needs to plan these meetings carefully. I would advise them to have preview meetings that will serve to "work out the bugs" before they birth.

The Growth Stage

Once the church has launched, it's important that it grow. As discussed earlier, the characteristic of spiritually healthy, biblically based churches is that they grow numerically. This was certainly the case with the Jerusalem Church. So what are some practices that help newly established churches grow?

1. *The lead pastor.* My experience is that those whom God uses to grow churches are visionaries who have a passion to reach the lost and who have spiritual gifts, at least those of leadership, evangelism, and teaching or preaching. Should the church have a governing board in place this early in the church's development (which I would not advise), they need to let the pastor lead.
2. *A vision.* As I just said, we need visionary pastors who in casting the church's vision clarify the church's direction and what it will look like when it gets there.
3. *Staff.* The church needs the right staff and the right number of staff. The right staff are those who not only equip people to serve in the staff's areas of expertise but train leaders to lead (the staff is key to the church's development of its leaders). The ideal number of staff to promote growth is one staff person per one hundred to one hundred fifty people.
4. *Congregational mobilization.* The new church must have in place a process for equipping its people for ministry. Involved people stick or assimilate, rather than slip out the back door when no one is looking.

The Reproduction Stage

Our goal in starting churches is not simply to plant another church. It's to start church-planting churches. It's imperative that a church reproduce. We need more churches if we hope to reach more people for Christ. My vision is to start a church-planting movement that will plant churches all over America and beyond. So what might this involve?

1. Begin by praying for daughter churches.
2. Cast the vision regularly among the people for starting new churches, even before the first one is planted. People must understand up front the vision for church starting.
3. Study the community with this in mind. It involves collecting demographic and psychographic materials that should tell you all about your ministry community.
4. Select and equip a core leadership team. In particular, look for God's man to lead in the planting of another church.

5. Recruit a committed core group from the church to be a part of the new work. Start with those who have to drive far to get to your church.
6. Raise support to assist the work financially. Include the new plant in the missions budget or do special fund-raisers (capital campaigns).

I've written this last section to give you the big picture of what planting and growing a church involves. I also hope to tease you to want to learn more. You should find my book *Planting Growing Churches* most helpful in this respect.[3] In it you'll find a chapter on each of these stages.

Five Stages of Church Growth

1. Conception
2. Early development
3. Birth
4. Growth
5. Reproduction

Seven Church Planting Assumptions

1. How we interpret the Bible is important.
2. Numerical growth in the church is important.
3. The primary role of the pastor is not pastoral care.
4. Business principles may be applied to the church.
5. There is no exact biblical model for doing church.
6. Change and innovation in the church are important.
7. The stages of church growth and development are important.

Questions for Reflection and Discussion

1. Do you share the author's assumption that a knowledge of hermeneutics is important to understanding what the Bible says about doing church? Why or why not?
2. Do you agree with his emphasis on the descriptive versus prescriptive passages and the positive versus the negative hermeneutic? Why or why not? Can you give examples of how these have been violated in churches that you've attended?
3. Do you become uncomfortable when people talk about numbers and church growth? Why do you think Luke uses numbers in Acts 2:41 and 4:4? Do you agree with the author's assumption that numerical growth is important to churches? Why or why not?

4. Do you agree with the author's assumption that the pastoral care model isn't the primary or only role of the lead pastor? Why or why not?

5. How might pastoral care distract the pastor from other more important matters? What are some of those matters? Does all this mean that lead pastors shouldn't do pastoral care?

6. Do you agree with the author's assumption that it's okay to explore and apply to the church principles from the business world? Why or why not?

7. Do you agree with the statement, "All truth is God's truth?" Why or why not? How can you know what is and isn't God's truth?

8. Do you agree with the author's assumption that Scripture doesn't provide us with an exact or sacred model for doing church? Why or why not? If you disagree, can you show such a model in the Bible?

9. Do you agree with the author's assumption that change and innovation are important to the church? Why or why not?

10. Does the author's theology of change make sense? Why or why not?

11. Is change easy or hard for you? How might this affect your view of change in the church?

12. Did you find the section on the various church stages helpful? Why or why not? How might it help you grow and develop the church?

PART 2

Process *of* Church Planting

5

What Drives a New Church?

Core Values

As stated in the introduction, church planters work through a process during the conception stage that produces a unique church model that is endemic or relevant to the people of the new church, their particular locale, and their culture. The problem with copying existing church models is that there is no universal model that fits all churches. What works in one part of the country may not work in another. And what works with a particular ethnic group, stratum of society, or culture may not work for another.

In the rest of this book I'll present and develop the fourfold process for church planting: developing core values, ministry mission, ministry vision, and a strategy. You would be wise to follow this process in developing your unique model.

The Fourfold Process

Core Values

Mission

Vision

Strategy

Before examining the process, I'll introduce an illustration that should help make it clear, one that Rick Warren uses for his church model. It's an illustration of the bases of a baseball diamond. First base represents the new *church's core values*, where the process starts. Second base represents the *church's mission*. Third base depicts *its vision*, and home plate is the *church's strategy*.

There are three critical questions that the process for church planting asks and answers. The first question is, Where are we? or Who are we? This questions the status or identity of the church and relates to established churches as well as to new plants. The answer to either question reveals the church's core values.

The second question is, Where do we want to go? The answer provides the church's mission and vision. The third question is, How will we get there? The answer to this question is the new church's strategy.

Three Critical Questions

1. Where are we? (Who are we?)
   Core values
2. Where do we want to go?
   Mission
   Vision
3. How will we get there?
   Strategy

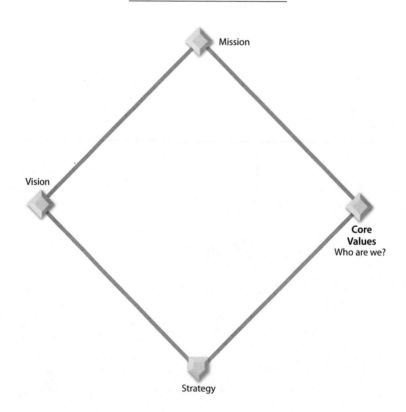

So the process begins at the conception stage with the discovery of the new church's core values. The core values are important to the ministry because they make clear the reason the church does what it does. Also the core values make up a vital part of the church's DNA, which affects the accomplishment of the other three process concepts. The wrong values result in the wrong mission, vision, and strategy. The purpose of this chapter is to explain the importance, the definition, the theology, the kinds, the discovery, and the communication of the planted church's core values.

The Importance of Core Values

Lyle Schaller, who is probably the foremost consultant to church consultants, writes, "The most important single element of any corporate, congregational, or denominational culture, however, is the values system."[1] Why are values so important to the church planter and the future church?

The Church's Ministry Distinctives

While some churches are similar to each other, no two churches are exactly alike. Each has its own unique thumbprint or DNA. And one of the distinctives is the church's core values. This is important because, as you'll see later, core values drive the ministry or new church plant toward some kind of mission, hopefully the right mission. Most churches will share some values with other churches and differ on some values. For example, a driving core value in a Bible church is biblical instruction. This means that the Scriptures are central to all it does. This isn't the case with churches that don't believe in the Bible or do not hold to biblical teaching. So a church's values determine its ministry distinctives.

Ministry Alignment

You don't want to plant a church whose congregants hold to values that differ from yours. This situation could best be described as ministry chaos and a nightmare for the church planter. This is one of several reasons I recommend that every church have a new members or visitors class. The wise church planter-pastor will lead this class and make sure that all understand the church's core values. He should advise those who differ to look for another church, because they won't be happy in the church plant. This doesn't mean they hold to bad values, just different values, and this will eventually prove most problematic, because values dictate personal ministry alignment.

The same would be true of the church's staff. One characteristic of staff that have not been with the church for very long is a lack of values alignment with the church. So as the church planter puts together a staff team, he must be diligent in the selection of who will accompany him on this exciting venture of faith. Where values align, they'll pull together. Where they don't, they'll pull apart.

Determine What's Important

Values signal the new ministry's bottom line. They communicate what really matters. They drive a stake in the ground that announces to all: *This is where we stand and what we believe.* Thus if a church says they value evangelism, they will expect the people to share their faith with others and lead them to Christ.

We've looked at the problem the Jerusalem Church was having, recorded in Acts 6:1–7, when some widows were being neglected in the daily distribution of food. The disciples revealed their values by their solution to the problem. They had the church select seven men to take over the responsibility of distributing food. In this way the disciples would not be distracted from what they felt really mattered—prayer and ministry of the Word.

Influencing Overall Behavior

Values affect behavior. They're ministry shaping. They beget attitudes that influence and drive behavior whether or not the church is even aware of them. They impact everything about the organization: its decisions made, goals set, priorities established, problems solved, conflicts resolved. They drive or move the ministry in a particular direction. In short, they're the basis for all the church's behavior, the bottom line that determines what they will and will not do.

Inspiring People to Action

Core values are a church's hidden motivators. Silently and sometimes not so silently they move people to take action. People know what they're doing but won't always know why they're doing it unless someone makes clear the particular value. Like the batteries that move the Energizer bunny in the television commercial, values energize people for ministry.

Shaping Ministry Character

Planted churches must live their values because their credibility rides on their doing so. Credibility rests on the shoulders of strong core values. A great example is Johnson and Johnson Pharmaceuticals. A number of years ago they were involved in a product-tampering fiasco. Someone mixed poison in with Tylenol capsules. One of the core values of the company is the customer's health. In fact, they believe this is their first responsibility. Consequently, rather than leave the product on the shelf and look the other way, they recalled Tylenol, thus losing major market share. However, there are many of us who still use Tylenol today because the company showed how much they value the customer's health.

Importance of Core Values

1. Determine ministry distinctives
2. Dictate personal ministry alignment
3. Determine what's important
4. Influence overall behavior
5. Inspire people to action
6. Shape ministry character

The Definition of *Core Values*

Now that we know the importance of a ministry's values, we need to be clear on what a value, and particularly a core value, is. I define a planted church's core values as its constant, passionate, biblical core beliefs that drive its ministry. This definition has five key elements.

Constant

First, values are constant, which means they are slow to change. This is true even in the early twenty-first century that is exploding with change that's without precedent. Everything seems to be changing. Some say knowledge doubles every two years. By the time a college student reaches his or her fourth year, the knowledge acquired in the first two years is already outdated.

The church must determine what should and shouldn't change. We saw in the last chapter that the church's functions must not change, whereas the forms those functions take must change if the church is to stay relevant to the culture. The church's functions, while not its only values, are its values. Thus, unless the church has some bad values or doesn't have certain vital values as a part of its DNA, its values won't change appreciably. This is also due to the nature of a value, which tends to resist change naturally.

Passionate

Passion is emotional. It's what we feel strongly or care deeply about. Our passions excite us and move us to take action. Values possess both an intellectual and an emotional component. They can appeal to and affect what we think, as well as how we feel. My experience is that, while you can win an argument intellectually through logic and reason, it's usually at the emotional level where someone is touched and finally persuaded.

It's the emotional or passion aspect of values that helps us discover them. I've discovered that a person's core values grab hold of the heart as well as the head. There is an emotional attachment with that which we truly value, and this helps us identify them. We may recognize the importance of values intellectually, but we really connect with them emotionally. Later in this chapter, I'll address how to discover your values and ask you to take a values audit, which lists a number of important values.

Biblical

In this book I'm mostly addressing organizational values, but they aren't just any values, they're biblical values. By this I mean they're organizational values that are either found in the Bible or align with it in some way. You may find values that align with biblical concepts reflected in other disciplines, such as the business world, the medical field, and engineering. In an earlier discussion I noted that all truth is God's truth, and God's truth may be found outside the Scriptures through natural revelation. Ultimately these values come from God.

Some values that are found in the Bible are the functions of the church: evangelism, biblical instruction, fellowship, service, worship, prayer, stewardship or generosity, communion, and others. Some that may not be in Scripture but align with it are such things as customer service, profit sharing, and product quality.

Some values that don't align with Scripture are the following: the status quo, complacency, prejudice, a critical spirit, complaining, self-centeredness, gossip, sacred cows, vested interests, as well as others.

Core Beliefs

First note that values are beliefs. They are rooted in the church planter's belief system. Every leader has some kind of belief system, good or bad, rational or irrational. A belief is a conviction or an opinion that you trust to be true and therefore have faith in. It's a conviction that others may share with you, especially those on your team.

Values are core beliefs. Not just any values will do. All of us hold or rate some values above others. We can discover these by narrowing down our list of values to four to six. Then we are getting to the core of our values or beliefs. We need to know the values that are at the very heart or core of our belief system.

Drive the Ministry

While the church is vision focused, it is values driven. Values are like the engine on a ship. Just as the engine drives the ship to its destination, so the values drive the church toward a particular destination or mission. Consequently, if the church isn't moving toward its preferred, articulated mission, it's a values issue, not a mission issue. Then it is necessary to check the values, as they will explain the reason the church is off course and ultimately where it will end up (mission). The values will take you to some mission, because that's what they do. Whether or not it's the desired and articulated mission of the church is the question.

The solution to the problem of a church whose values are driving it toward the wrong mission or a different mission is to change either the mission or the values. As I said above, values are constant and change very slowly if at all. I'll say more about this in the next chapter on mission.

The Theology of Core Values

My thinking on values in general and core values in particular has evolved over a period of time. At one point, I said little about ideal or good church values. However, when I helped churches and organizations discover their values, some asked if their values were good or bad.

As I pondered these questions, my first thoughts were to look at some current-day churches that God seemed to be blessing. Then God prompted me to look instead at the early churches in the New Testament. Unfortunately we don't have a lot of information on these churches or how they did church. We do, though, have more information on the Jerusalem Church because the earlier portion of Acts records the history and development of this church.

What I discovered to be most helpful was Luke's practice of stopping periodically and giving his readers an update on how the church was progressing. I call them summary progress reports, and they are found in Acts 2:41–47; 4:4; 6:7; 9:31; 12:24; 16:5; 19:20; 28:30–31. One other important point is that the Jerusalem Church was a spiritually healthy, biblically based church that was growing as the result of what God was doing among its people. Consequently, its core values should give us a good picture of the values of a spiritually healthy, biblically based church, which is exactly what I was looking for.

In particular I found the Acts 2:41–47 summary report to be most helpful in determining the church's organizational core values. There Luke identifies the following values in particular: evangelism (vv. 41, 47), instruction (v. 42), fellowship (vv. 42, 44–46), worship (vv. 42–43, 46–47), and service or ministry (v. 43). Therefore, a theology of core values consists of what the Scriptures say about core values. As I reviewed these, comparing them to the importance placed on them in other places in the New Testament, I concluded they were five essential core values of the church, and I would encourage both planted and established churches to consider them when evaluating their actual core values. They're not the only good core values but they are certainly at the top of the list. And my experience in using them to help churches evaluate the quality of their values has been exceptional because they are easy to understand and people quickly grasp what you're talking about.

I've observed that most evangelical churches list worship, fellowship, and biblical instruction as actual values, but not evangelism and service or ministry. Not only is this seen when evaluating a ministry's values, but it shows up as well when we examine the church's functions. We will return to this topic in chapter 10, which deals with disciple making.

The Jerusalem Church's Core Values
Acts 2:41–47

Evangelism (vv. 41, 47)
Instruction (v. 42)
Fellowship (vv. 42, 44–46)
Worship (vv. 42–43, 46–47)
Service or ministry (v. 43)

The Kinds of Values

Knowing the different kinds of values can be most helpful in understanding and discovering a church's values. I've observed five different kinds of values: conscious versus subconscious, shared versus unshared, personal versus organizational, actual versus aspirational, and single versus multiple values.

Conscious versus Subconscious Values

The new church's values exist at both a conscious and a subconscious level. Conscious values are those the people of the church are aware of, and unconscious values are those that they're not aware of. Most hold their values at a subconscious level. While there may be some awareness of what their values are, most people will have trouble articulating them. They simply don't take time to think about them. Thus it's the job of the church planter to raise the values from a subconscious to a conscience level so everyone knows and can articulate what the church's true or actual values are.

Shared versus Unshared Values

I can't say enough about the importance of shared values—holding values in common. When members of a church staff or congregation don't have the same values, it leads to disaster. Instead of pulling as a team, the people pull apart. There will be little common cause, little to hold them together. While they might believe they have the same mission, this mission won't be realized because they don't share common values.

Shared values benefit a ministry in a number of ways. James Kouzes and Barry Posner conducted research that involved more than 2,300 managers at all levels, representing public and private organizations located across the United States, regarding the importance of shared values.[2] Their studies revealed that shared values

- foster strong feelings of personal effectiveness
- promote high levels of company loyalty
- facilitate consensus about key organizational goals and stakeholders
- encourage ethical behavior
- promote strong norms about working hard and caring
- reduce levels of job stress and tension

Although these writers don't comment on the nature of these organizations, I believe we would all agree that these would be admirable accomplishments for a church as well as a business.

Other studies reveal that those workers in an organization who share values feel a deep sense of effectiveness, are intensely loyal, agree on key goals, behave ethically, work hard, care deeply, and experience less stress and tension on the job, whereas those who don't share values will experience few if any of these qualities that are vital to effective ministry, and that's why I say above that this will only lead to disaster in a planted or established church. To avoid this, it becomes the job of the church-planting team to communicate constantly and clarify the core values of the new work. I'll say more about how to accomplish this in the last section of this chapter.

Personal versus Organizational Values

Every ministry has a core set of organizational values, whether or not the members can articulate what they are. They are found in the persons in the group who share or hold many of the same values. Individuals that make up the organization also have a set of personal core values. Whether or not they're aware of it, they look for these in an organization they are joining. Often they will "church shop," looking for a church they like, which—in effect—is a church that shares their values.

When I help a church discover its values, I have its people take two values audits—a Personal Values Audit and a Church Values Audit, because I want each person to see if his or her personal values discovered on the Personal Values Audit align with those on the Church Values Audit. That way a congregant or potential congregant can know if he or she shares values with the church. And this, in turn, can save both the church and the individual from a lot of stress and disillusion on down the ministry road.

Actual versus Aspirational Values

Actual values are important to an organization. They are the beliefs that a person and ultimately the ministry own and act on daily. The people hold these values firmly. They exist in the present and are true about the ministry right now. You own and practice your actual values. They're deeply felt and affect much of what you do in the church much of the time, and there will be evidence of this. When working with a church to determine if a value is actual or not, I always ask, "Where's the evidence that this is truly an actual value?" Most of this chapter focuses on a ministry's actual, not its aspirational, values.

Aspirational values are beliefs that the individual or new church doesn't currently own. They deal with what should or ought to be, not what is. They are ones that every ministry should have, whether they aspire to them or not. No evidence can be found for aspirational values, even though most everyone wants these values to be actual. Until they are fully embraced, however, they remain aspirational. For example, two aspirational but not actual values that I find in far too many established churches are evangelism and ministry. Many church people simply aren't sharing their faith or getting involved in ministry.

The key to values discovery and understanding what really drives you isn't what you would like to value but what you truly do value. You simply can't fake actual values. You hold them passionately right now. Later when you take the values audits, I will ask you to identify not your aspirational but your actual values.

Concerning the Jerusalem Church, we know the values described are actual core values, because Acts 2:42 says, "They devoted themselves to the apostles' teaching . . . the fellowship . . . the breaking of bread . . . prayer." The phrase *they devoted themselves to* signals the church's actual values. If the text merely said that they discussed them or debated them or wanted to pursue them, they would be aspirational values. However, this isn't to say that a church's aspirational values are unimportant. In a sense we need to know our aspirational as well as our actual values. They're important if they're vital values that need to become actual values for the church to pursue its mission legitimately.

Single versus Multiple Values

Most if not all churches have multiple organizational values. Their core values are the ones that are highest in priority. In the values discovery process, they are the ones with the most votes. However, I've discovered that a number of churches have a single value that overrides all the rest. You'll find it at the top of the list with a significant gap between it and the rest. It's like an umbrella with the others appropriately arranged under it.

In a church context, such a single, robust value is very powerful. For example, it serves to unify the church, spell out the congregation's expectations of the pastor and his expectations of them, identify the church's key emphasis, the typical tool that is used, the desired result, as well as other important matters. The chart below presents several North American church paradigms and the unifying, dominating core value of each one. We'll look at one such value—biblical instruction—to get an idea of how powerful these values can be and to understand what the chart is communicating about them. Note that I've placed the values in the vertical column on the left, and the various matters they affect across the top of the chart.

Unifying Value	Role of Pastor	Role of People	Primary Purpose	Typical Tool	Desired Result
Biblical Instruction	Teacher	Students	To know	Sermon outline	Educated Christians
Evangelism	Evangelist	Inviters	To save	Altar call	Born-again persons
Worship	Worshiper	Worshipers	To exalt	Liturgy	Committed Christians
Fellowship	Chaplain	Siblings	To belong	Potluck	Secure Christians

Biblical instruction is found as a single dominating value in a number of churches, such as Baptist, Evangelical Free, and Bible churches, but it's most true of those churches that make up the Bible Church Movement. These are churches that are found all over North America but predominantly in the Dallas–Fort Worth Metroplex. I believe this is due to the ministry of Dallas Theological Seminary, because a number of its graduates become pastors of these churches.

Note that the role of the pastor in the Bible church is a teacher or expository preacher of the Bible. This is the expectation of those who make up these congregations. Should the pastor play a different role, such as an evangelist or leader of worship, the congregation would be disappointed and would likely look for another church. Note also that the pastor has expectations of the people. They are students whose responsibility is to take good notes in their sermon outlines found in the bulletin and to know and apply the Bible to their lives. If they don't conform to these expectations, the pastor will likely move on.

Unfortunately when there is one powerful, dominating value, the other vital biblical values tend to be ignored, which will eventually cause the church's demise. While such a church is strong on Bible teaching, they're weak in evangelism. And I've noted that a number of the more traditional Bible churches around Dallas are in steep decline in attendance. My prayer for them is that they will make the needed corrections before it's too late.

Kinds of Values

Conscious versus Subconscious
Shared versus Unshared
Personal versus Organizational
Actual versus Aspirational
Single versus Multiple

The Discovery of Core Values

So what are the core values that will drive your church? I've spent much time in introducing you to this topic; now it's time to wade in and find out what the actual values of your planted church are. In this section, we'll investigate who discovers the values and how.

In general there are two ways to start a church. One is a *hot start* and the other is a *cold start*. The hot start takes place when a church or existing group of Christians calls the church planter to come and plant a church with them. It's a hot start because the planter-leader is connecting with a group of believers who will likely be a vital part of the team from the beginning. The cold start takes place when the church planter moves to an area where he may not know anyone and starts the church from scratch.

In the cold start the church planter's core values will naturally become those of the church. Thus he needs to discover his own core values for doing church and share them with those whom he recruits to join him in the venture. In a hot start the church planter needs to take into consideration the values of the church or group that wants to start a church. He needs to know what his values are, and he needs to help the group discover their values. Once the values are uncovered, they need to determine if the values of the planter and the group align. This will dictate whether they can plant a church together or they'll go their separate ways. This is good because they can make this determination before they get very far along in the process.

How the Lead Planter Discovers His Core Values

Step 1: The Values Audit

Every church-plant leader needs to identify his actual core values. Thus the first step is to take a good values audit. I use the Church Core Values Audit that I've developed and validated over a number of years to help both established and new churches discover their core values. This tool is in appendix I. The advantage of this tool is that it includes most of the values one might have, a place to add any that aren't included in the audit, and a brief definition of each value for the purpose of clarity.

If you're a church planter involved in a cold start, then you need to take this audit now, remembering that you're looking for your actual core values. Be sure to read the directions and be very stingy with the 4s. Once you complete it, write down the values to which you assigned a 4. Finally, place these values in order of priority. Which would appear first on your list, second, third, and so on? Since you're discovering your *core* values, limit the number to a total of four to six, to identify what is truly at the core.

Step 2: Analysis

The second step in the process for the lead planter is to analyze his list of values. First, is there a single, dominating value? Is there one that seems so important that the others seem minor in comparison? It could be the one that is first on your list. If so, what is it, and how might you handle what could be a lack of needed balance?

Did you surface any unusual, unique values—values that few other churches possess? For example, Ed Young Jr. pastors Fellowship Church of Grapevine, Texas. One of his unique values that is found in few churches across America is creativity.

Are your values in-reach or outreach oriented? If all your values are in-reach oriented (e.g., worship, fellowship, Bible study), your new church won't survive. You must reach out to people, especially lost people.

Finally, and perhaps most important, how would your core values compare to the Jerusalem Church's core values of worship, fellowship, biblical instruction, evangelism, and service?

Values Analysis

---

1. Is there a dominating value?
2. Is there a unique value (or values)?
3. Are the values in-reach or outreach oriented?
4. How do your values compare to those of the Jerusalem Church?

Step 3: Aspirational Values

As you analyze your values, do you find that any essential values are missing, for example, the five core values of the Jerusalem Church? These may become your aspirational values because every ministry should have them. The third step in discovering your values is to determine if you have any aspirational values and—if so—what they are. In working with established churches, I find most often the two missing values that become their aspirational values are evangelism and ministry. This may not be the case for the lead church planter who may have a gift of or passion for evangelism. If he holds to the same core values as the Jerusalem Church, he may not have any aspirational values. If he doesn't, then he may have one or no more than two. I restrict the number of actual core values to six, but there would be a total of eight values if there are two aspirational values. Be sure to differentiate between your actual and your aspirational values when you talk about them. I'll give you some ideas on how to accomplish this in the next section on communication.

How to Discover Your Values

Step 1: Take a values audit.

Step 2: Analyze your values.

Step 3: Determine your aspirational values.

How Those in a Hot Start Discover Their Values

If you're part of a hot start, the first step for all involved is to take the Personal Core Values Audit in appendix K. You will use this later to discern if each person's personal values align with those of the church. The second step is to take together the Church Core Values Audit (appendix J), listing each person's top four to six actual values. To do this, use the storyboard process. Have each person call out his or her values, and have a couple of people write them down on four-by-six-inch Post-it notes. Place them on a whiteboard or a wall and see what you come up with. Eliminate any duplicates. Discuss whether you've really captured the core values of the ministry. Identify any that are aspirational. After this, give each person six small red dots and have them place them on what they believe are the church's six values. (Avery makes a quarter-inch red dot that is ideal for this process.)

Then the planter-leader and the group must discern if they have values alignment, whether they share the same core values. At this point, depending on the extent of alignment or sharing of values, all involved will know if there is a match between the planter-leader and the team.

The Communication of Core Values

Once you've discovered your core values and possibly those of a sponsoring church or interested group you might plant with, you're not finished. Next comes the communication of these values. It's imperative that the people who would be involved in initiating the church plant and those who would later join you know your values. If you don't tell others what the values are, the major purpose for uncovering them—values alignment—will be short-circuited, and you'll risk attracting those who don't share your values, which means problems on down the church-planting road. In this final section, I want to give you several ways to articulate your core values.

Here I will introduce you to a general communication plan that I'll use not only with your core values but later with the mission statement, the vision statement, and each of the five steps that make up the church's strategy.

The General Communication Plan

I do a lot of consulting with established churches, and one of the problems that shows up on the church analysis that I use with them is a failure to communicate well. This has been the case with every established church I've worked with over the past few years. And they consider it to be a most serious problem. Consequently I developed this communication plan to help the established church and church plants communicate better. This plan consists of asking and answering the following seven questions.

1. What should be communicated?
2. Who should communicate it?
3. When should it be communicated?
4. How should it be communicated?
5. Where should it be communicated?
6. How often should it be communicated?
7. Why should it be communicated?

Concerning core values, the answers to the above questions would be:

1. Core values should be communicated.
2. The lead church planter and any others who are a part of the church plant should communicate the values.
3. The core values should be communicated regularly or every time there is an opportunity.
4. They can be communicated in a credo, in sermons, on a website, in a brochure.
5. They should be communicated at any organizational meeting, worship service, new members class, and other meetings of the church.
6. They should be communicated regularly—weekly, monthly, annually.
7. Communicate values so that participants can determine if they share the same values—values alignment. Good communication also builds trust that is vital in leadership.

Since communication is such a problem for most churches, I would strongly encourage the church plant to form as soon as feasible a communication team who will take responsibility for seeing that the church communicates well. Its first project will be to communicate the church's core values.

Communication Specifics

There are several ways you can communicate your values formally and informally.

LIFESTYLE

The lives of those who will be part of the church plant communicate values. People live their values; thus, if evangelism is a core value, you'll find them sharing their faith.

SERMONS

It almost goes without saying that those who do the preaching, and I would suggest that church plants have at least two people who share the load and preach regularly, will communicate the values directly or indirectly in their sermons.

STORIES

You can tell a church's values by their stories. This is a vital part of its culture. When your people tell stories—and all do—what values are revealed? If the church values evangelism, the people will regularly share stories of people coming to faith. If the church values worship, the people will talk about experiences in worship.

MINISTRIES

Values are communicated by the church's ministries. The fact that a church has a good evangelism ministry says it values evangelism. If it has good Bible teaching, it values biblical instruction.

VISUAL IMAGES

Visual images express values. An audiovisual presentation, a well-designed logo, a button or pen with a fishhook or an *ichthus* (fish) image all convey the values of the church.

LANGUAGE AND METAPHOR

In a subtle way a church's language and metaphors communicate values. In the corporate realm Disney World provides a great example. Disney has no employees; its workers are referred to as the *cast*. A church can refer to its visitors as *guests* and it's people as *hosts* and *hostesses*. And it can refer to its people not as *members* but as *missionaries* or *ministers*.

NEW MEMBERS CLASS

An excellent place to address the church plant's core values is in a new members or even a new attenders class. People who attend such a class are expressing their commitment to or strong interest in the church and need to know its values for alignment purposes.

A BROCHURE

A well-designed brochure should be available for visitors at a welcome station in the church. Likely it would contain not only the core values but the church's mission and vision statements and possibly its strategy.

A WRITTEN CREDO

Churches and other organizations articulate their values in a written statement or credo, which they make available to any interested persons. If they can't articulate such a credo, their values are fuzzy and they need to rethink them. Using the values of the Malphurs Group, I wrote a values statement, which is in appendix L. You'll also find several churches' credos in appendix A of my book *Values-Driven Leadership.*[3]

If you wish to include your aspirational values in your credo along with your actual values, you could mark them with an asterisk. Another approach would be to introduce your actual values with the words, "We value the following . . ." Then you could introduce any aspirational values with the words, "We aspire to the following values . . ."

OTHER METHODS

With the above examples, I've touched only the tip of the values communication iceberg. Other ways to articulate your actual and aspirational values are through celebrations, skits and drama, cartoons, a performance appraisal, a state of the church message, and a series of frescos representing each value, mounted on the wall of the worship center or in some other location. The only limit is your creative ability to come up with new ways of communication.

**Formal and Informal
Values Communication**

Lifestyle
Sermons
Stories
Ministries
Visual images
Language and metaphor
New members class
Brochure
Written credo

Questions for Reflection and Discussion

1. Do you agree with the author's view that a church model that works in one part of the country may not work elsewhere? Why or why not? What's his solution?
2. Why does the author begin the church-planting process with values? Does this make sense? Do you agree?
3. Based on the reasons cited in this chapter, did the author convince you that core values are important? Why or why not?

4. What is your definition of a core value? Why is this important? Is it the same as or close to the author's definition?
5. The author listed a number of different kinds of values. Which do you think are most important to you as a church planter?
6. Would you describe your church-planting situation as a cold or hot start? What's the difference, and why does it matter?
7. What did you discover to be your values and those of a sponsoring church or interested group? Are any of your values dominating or unique? Are any completely inward focused? How do they compare with those listed for the Jerusalem Church in Acts 2:41–47?
8. Which of the ways to communicate core values most appeal to you in your situation? Any idea why?

6

What Are New Churches Supposed to Do?

Ministry Mission

The discovery of the church planter's core values will explain why the church does what it does. Churches are values driven. But ultimately what is the church supposed to be doing? What does God want the planted church or any church for that matter to do? Stephen Covey, author of *The 7 Habits of Highly Effective People*, said, "The main thing is to keep the main thing the main thing." So what is the main thing for God's church? The answer is *the planted church's mission*. While the church is values driven, it's mission directed. The purpose of this chapter is to present the importance, definition, theology, kinds, development, and communication of the new church's mission.

The Importance of the Mission

I've said on a number of occasions that you'll never do ministry that matters until you articulate what matters. Peter Drucker, the dean of America's business and management philosophies, says, "What matters is not the leader's charisma. What matters is the leader's mission. Therefore, the first job of the leader is to think through and define the mission of the institution."[1] Drucker is saying among other things that an organization's mission is what is most

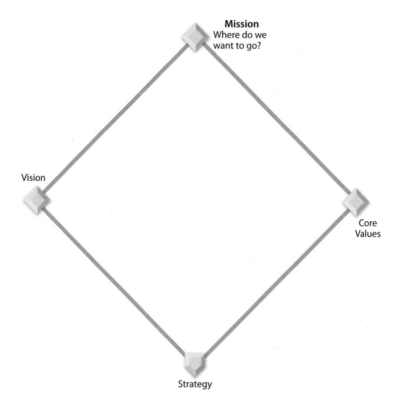

important. There are at least ten reasons a new church's mission is critically important to what God wants it to accomplish.

The Church's Direction

Mission dictates the new ministry's direction. The mission answers the question, Where are we going? I fly a lot because I work every weekend with a number of different churches sprinkled all across America. And it's most important that I have the right ticket and get on the right plane if I'm to get where I'm going. I recall boarding a plane at the Dallas–Fort Worth airport several years ago. I started down the jetway until I came to a point where it divided and led to two separate planes. This was most confusing, and several of us almost went in the wrong direction.

My experience in working with established churches over the years is that far too many don't know where they're going. They've lost sight of their mission. Drucker wisely observes, "The first task of the leader is to make sure that everybody sees the mission, hears it, lives it. If you lose sight of your mission, you begin to stumble and it shows very, very fast."[2] Some have a mission but it's the wrong mission; therefore they're headed in the wrong direction. Others have a mission and it's the right mission, but over the years it's become cloudy and unfocused. This must not be the case with the new church plant. It's imperative that it knows where it's going and that it articulates this repeatedly.

The Church's Function

Mission focuses on the new ministry's function or what it's supposed to be doing. An important question to ask is, What could you accomplish if everyone in the church knew and agreed with what you were attempting to do? This could prove difficult in an established church because of the different agendas of the congregation, but it can and should be the norm in the new church. It's the mission that nails your function or what it is you are trying to do. I've noted over the years that healthy, growing churches are clear about why they exist and what they're supposed to be doing. That's the reason the mission is so important to a spiritually healthy church.

The Church's Future

Mission predicts the church's future. The new church's mission as well as its vision have everything to do with what it will be. The mission spells out the congregation's preferred future, and the church's mission statement helps the congregation focus on it. We can't predict the future outside of a few biblical prophecies, but we can have a part in creating it.

The Boundaries for Decision Making

Every church faces numerous decisions along its journey, and it's the church's mission that helps it make the best decisions. How does it accomplish this decision-making function? It's the new church's mission statement that provides the boundaries or guidelines for what it will and will not do. An example from the business world is Southwest Airlines, which has the mission: "We are THE low-fare airline." The story is told that one of the marketing persons approached Herb Kelleher—Southwest's former president—about adding a chicken Caesar salad as a light entrée on its Houston to Las Vegas flight. Kelleher's response was to ask the person if adding the salad would make Southwest Airlines THE low-cost airline?

Just as Southwest's mission provided boundaries for Kelleher's decision making, so the new church's mission sets its boundaries. Churches can be tempted to start Christian schools, daycare programs, and other ministries that are potential distractions from their mission. The questions the church must ask are: How will this decision affect the mission of our church? Will it promote the mission or detract from it?

Ministry Unity

The mission is important to the new church because it inspires continued ministry unity. When consulting with the typical established church, one of the first areas I address is the church's unity. Most churches are struggling with a lack of unity, which means that they're pulling apart, not together, and this is a red flag—the formula for a slow death. The solution to this problem is to get all on the team to agree on the church's biblical mission, which is very clear according to Matthew 28:19–20 (more on this later in the chapter). To oppose this is to oppose Scripture in general and Christ's mandate for the church in particular. And most if not all realize this. Thus the mission serves well to get everyone on the same page.

Shaping Strategy

The mission shapes the strategy that will be used to implement the mission. The mission question is *what?* The strategy question is *how?* The mission always comes before and shapes the strategy. Strategy makes no sense without a clear mission statement. Nevertheless older churches often fall into the trap of following a strategy without a clear mission. In most cases the founding pastor communicated a clear mission and then developed a strategy to accomplish it, which consisted of the church's ministries or programs. Eventually that pastor left the church, and over time the mission was lost or forgotten, leaving the strategy or programs still in place. The congregation knows the *how*—the ministries—but has lost the *what*—the mission.

Ministry Effectiveness

Someone once said that all good performance starts with a clear direction. How can a new congregation in general and the staff in particular perform well if they don't know what they're supposed to be doing or where they as a ministry organization are headed? The mission statement provides and articulates the clear direction. Where there is no mission or an unclear mission, there will be general ministry ineffectiveness.

Providing a Cause

Everybody needs a cause. It brings meaning to people's lives. It coalesces and energizes people. Because it gives them something to live for other than acquiring material possessions, many people understand the value of a cause.

In Christ's church people need a cause. It gives them a sense of divine purpose; they know they're part of a "God thing," something that's much bigger than themselves. The church's mission provides the people with a cause, which ultimately is Christ's cause for his church.

Providing a Clear Focus

The church's mission is important because it provides the new church with a clear focus. It paints the bull's-eye on a target. Often I ask church leaders if they know the difference between a laser and a lightbulb. The answer is focused energy. The typical light that you find in most of our homes gives off or radiates energy in all directions and illuminates an entire room. However, the laser takes the same energy and focuses it on a specific area, making it useful in various ways.

People in our churches literally dispense energy as they serve. Without a clear focus, much of that energy is wasted. The mission serves to focus that energy so that the church can actually accomplish its goal.

Facilitating Evaluation

While I've not said much about it thus far, the church's mission is the Great Commission. I plan to cover this more in depth in the theology of the mission section. The Great Commission mandate from the Savior is to "make disciples!" Therefore success for any church is making disciples of Jesus. Key to the disciple-making process is evaluation. We must ask evaluation questions: How are we doing? Are we successful? Are we accomplishing our mission? Since the mission is to make disciples, the church can evaluate how it's doing by whether or not it's making disciples.

The Importance of the Church's Mission

The mission dictates the church's direction.
The mission focuses on the church's function.
The mission predicts the church's future.
The mission provides the boundaries for decision making.
The mission inspires ministry unity.
The mission shapes the ministry's strategy.
The mission enhances ministry effectiveness.
The mission provides the church with a cause.
The mission provides the church with a clear focus.
The mission facilitates evaluation.

The Definition of *Mission*

You'll never do ministry that matters until you clearly articulate what matters. Again, Peter Drucker writes, "What matters is not the leader's charisma. What matters is the leader's mission. Therefore, the first job of the leader is to think through and define the mission of the institution."[3] I have used this quote to emphasize the importance of the new church's mission. I repeat it here to emphasize the importance of defining that mission. How would we know if we're even talking about the same thing if we don't take time to define the mission? However, before articulating what the mission is, for further clarity, I'll begin by briefly stating what it isn't.

What the Mission Isn't

The mission of a new church isn't the same as its purpose. In the corporate world the two terms *mission* and *purpose* are used interchangeably as if they're synonyms. This is not the case in the world of the church. There is a theological distinction between the two. First, they differ in intent. The purpose of the church is to glorify God (Rom. 15:6; 1 Cor. 6:20; 10:31), whereas the mission of the church is to make disciples (Matt. 28:19–20).

Purpose and mission answer two different questions. The purpose is the reason the church exists—to glorify God. The mission is what the church is supposed to be doing—making disciples.

The two are different in scope. The purpose of glorifying God is very broad in scope, whereas the mission of making disciples is narrower. And their focus is different. The purpose focuses on God, but the mission focuses on man.

Finally, the terms are used for different contexts. The purpose of the church is seen out in the community. It's most important that the church glorify God in the world, which in the context of the church would be its neighboring community. The idea is that the church serves the community so well in the name of Christ that the community acknowledges God is among us and wants to know more about Christ. However, the mission of the church is seen by its members and any prospective church members. The church's community doesn't need to know that the church's mission is to make disciples, but the church does or it won't happen.

Differences between the Church's Purpose and Mission

	Purpose	Mission
Intent	To glorify God	To make disciples
Question	*Why* do we exist?	*What* are we supposed to be doing?
Scope	Broad	Narrow
Focus	God	Man
Context	External	Internal

What the Mission Is

With the distinction between purpose and mission, I define the church's mission as a broad, brief, biblical statement of what it's supposed to be doing. Let's look at the four components of this definition.

BROAD

First, the mission has breadth. Unlike a church's vision statement, the mission is broad. The vision statement is narrow, because it's a longer statement that contains more detail. For example, it can describe the church's focus group, programs, staff, and so forth, whereas a good mission statement doesn't contain much detail. There are several characteristics of a good mission statement. It is all-encompassing, overarching, and comprehensive. You'll see this when we look at a number of samples in the section on developing a mission statement.

BRIEF

It's important that the mission statement be brief. Peter Drucker would argue that a good mission statement will pass the T-shirt test—it must be short enough to fit on a T-shirt. The goal is that your people—young and old—remember the ministry's mission statement. It's much easier for the congregation to remember a short statement rather than a long one. For example, one of my favorite mission statements contains only seven words: "To know Christ and make him known."

BIBLICAL

The mission statement is to be biblical. We anchor our mission in the Scriptures, because they are our source of and basis for truth. Therefore we must know what the Bible says is the church's mission. Without a biblical standard, the mission could be anything, and all would be good.

Scripture contains a number of mission statements. For example, Adam and Eve's mission was to be fruitful, fill the earth, and subdue it (Gen. 1:28). Moses' mission was to lead Israel (God's children) out of Egypt (Exod. 3:10), and Joshua's mission was to lead them into the Promised Land (Josh. 1:1–2). And our mission as a church, according to the Bible, is to make disciples (Matt. 28:19–20).

WHAT THE CHURCH IS TO DO

Finally, from a business perspective, the mission of an organization articulates what business it's in or what it's supposed to be doing. While the church is an organization—a concept some struggle with— it's not a business. Still it must know what it's doing. And what it's supposed to be doing is what God wants it to do.

I've reiterated that the Bible teaches that the church's mission is the Great Commission. But what is that? If you just said Great Commission, most people wouldn't get it. I've defined it as making disciples. But again, I believe most wouldn't understand what making disciples means because our culture rarely uses the terminology outside the church. And my experience is that even churched people don't understand it. Part of the problem is that many don't know the meaning of the term *disciple*. I believe I must address the concept of the church's mission in more depth. What does the Bible say about the mission of the church or the theology of its mission?

The Theology of the Church's Mission

We can arrive at an understanding of the church's mission by examining the passages that present the Great Commission and then focusing on Matthew 28:19–20 in particular.

The Great Commission Passages

Most would agree that the Great Commission is found in four passages of Scripture. In the chart below, the passages are given, specifying the who, what, to whom, how, and where of each passage. We'll look here only at the who and what because they address our dilemma of trying to understand the commission.

Scripture	Who	What	To Whom	How	Where
Matt. 28:19–20	Disciples	"Go and make disciples."	All nations	Baptizing and teaching	
Mark 16:15	Disciples	"Go . . . preach the good news."	All creation		All the world
Luke 24:46–48	Disciples	"[Be] witnesses."	All nations	Preaching	Beginning at Jerusalem
Acts 1:8	Disciples	"Be my witnesses."		With power	Jerusalem, Judea, Samaria, ends of earth

WHO

The first question is who were the recipients of the commission? The clear, obvious answer is the disciples or apostles. They were to be the leaders of Christ's church as disclosed at Pentecost and revealed to us in the book of Acts.

According to the Gospel accounts, the Savior took much of his time to develop them for this upcoming role. Thus we're not surprised that he addressed the mission of the church to them. It was imperative that they know where Jesus wanted them to take the newly formed church. Eventually the mandate was passed on from the apostles to the leaders of the church, who were to preserve and pursue his mandate and pass it on to others. These leaders were the elders who were first-century house church pastors.

WHAT

The second question is what was the commission? What were its contents? The chart lists what the verses disclose. In Matthew 28:19–20 it was "Go and make disciples." In Mark 16:15 it was "Go . . . preach the good news." Luke 24:48 says, "[Be] witnesses." And Acts 1:8 says, "Be my witnesses."

We need to pause here and make several observations. First, note that both Matthew 28:19 and Mark 16:15 begin with commands to go. The point is the Savior didn't want the church to be passive. They weren't to wait for people to come to them; they were to be proactive and go after people.

In effect, they were to be out in the community rubbing shoulders with the people who lived there. This is what I refer to as the Great Commissional church. It views the church facility as a missions facility, the congregation not so much as congregants as missionaries, and the pastor as a trainer of missionaries.

Note that all of the passages, except possibly Matthew 28:19–20, have a strong emphasis on evangelism—preach Good News (the gospel) and be witnesses! Unlike what so many of our churches are doing today, Christ's mandate lays a heavy emphasis on reaching out to and winning lost people to him.

The Term Disciple

As we observe the Great Commission passages, our focus is drawn to Matthew 28:19–20 because it's different in some ways from the others. Note that Jesus tells us what he wants his church to do—"make disciples." Then he tells us how, using the terms *baptizing* and *obey*. (If you wish to dig more deeply into Matthew 28:19–20, see my treatment of the passage in appendix M.)

For us to obey Jesus's mandate, we need to understand what the term *disciple* means. My experience is that most today believe a disciple is a Christian who wants to grow and mature in his or her faith. And the best way to accomplish this is for mature disciples to take individuals aside and commit to helping them grow spiritually.

However, this isn't what Scripture teaches. In a broad sense in New Testament times, a disciple was a follower of someone such as Moses (John 9:28), John the Baptist (Matt. 9:14), or the Pharisees. Therefore the command to make disciples meant to make followers of Jesus. But we can do better than this. In a narrow sense, a disciple was simply a believer. Luke makes this very clear in the book of Acts: see 6:1–2, 7; 9:1, 26; 11:26; 14:21–22; 15:10; 18:23; and 19:9.

Note that the idea of a growing or mature believer fits none of these passages. For example, in Acts 14:21, Luke reports that Paul and Barnabas won a large number of disciples before they returned to Lystra. Obviously he's not speaking of mature believers but new believers. Therefore we can conclude that the command to make disciples refers to evangelism and edification. The new church is to make disciples or win people to Christ and then help them become growing disciples (see Matt. 28:20).

The Kinds of Church Missions

I've noted at least three kinds of missions as I've worked with churches. They are conscious versus subconscious, shared versus unshared, and correct versus incorrect missions.

Conscious versus Subconscious Missions

When I first began to address strategic planning, I believed that a church either had or didn't have a mission. If it knew what its mission was, it had one. If it didn't, it didn't have one. However, I've changed my mind. I believe that most if not all churches have a mission. They may know exactly what it is or they may not have a clue. It may be a biblical or an unbiblical mission. It may be poorly stated or well articulated. Regardless, most churches have one.

The way to discover a church's mission is to unearth its core values. You do this by raising them from a subconscious to a conscious level. As you'll recall, core values—no matter how good or bad—will drive the church toward a destination, which is its mission. Remember, churches are values driven and mission directed. Thus, if you discover the values, you'll get an idea of what the mission may be, especially if it's a dominating value. Several examples will help. If a church's dominating, overarching value is evangelism, the mission will be the salvation of lost souls. If the value is worship, the church's mission is worship. If the value is knowledge of the Bible, the mission will be biblical instruction.

Shared versus Unshared Mission

As we have seen, it is possible that people in a church do not share core values; this is also true for the ministry's mission. The first question is, Do the people of the congregation have the same mission? If not, they may attempt to move in a number of directions at the same time or pull apart. The second question is, Does the staff share the mission? Just as with the core values, staff alignment with the mission is critical to a staff person's future at the church. Failure to align here almost guarantees a short tenure for the staff person. Therefore mission alignment along with values alignment must be at the top of the qualifications for hiring staff. Another important question is, Do the pastor and board—if the church has a board—share the same mission? (I will say more about boards later, but I discourage a new church from putting a board in place too early in the life of the new church.) They must have the same mission because of the importance of the pastor and the board working together for the benefit of the church.

A shared mission is essential to the church's unity and ministry effectiveness. A mission that is not shared by all involved results in disunity and ministry ineffectiveness. Thus the new church must insist on mission unity on the part of the congregation, staff, lead pastor, and board.

Correct versus Incorrect Mission

As I said above, most churches will have a mission. The question is, Is it the correct mission? We discovered under the section on theology that the correct mission is the Great Commission that involves making disciples (Matt. 28:19–20). Any other mission is an incorrect mission, including these:

The mission is to teach the Bible.

The mission is to take care of people.

The mission is to worship God.

The mission is to serve.

The mission is to feed the hungry.

The mission is to visit people at home and in the hospital.

I'm sure you'll agree that all of these activities are good and found somewhere in the Scriptures, but they are not the church's mission. They fall somewhere under the functions of the church. We must consider whether intentionally pursuing the wrong mission is disobedience to the will of God. When he mandates that we make disciples, and we pursue taking care of people or one of the other missions above, should we expect him to bless our efforts?

Church Missions

Conscious versus Subconscious

Shared versus Unshared

Correct versus Incorrect

The Development of the Mission Statement

Now that we understand the importance of the mission, agree on its definition and theology, and recognize the different kinds of missions, we're ready to develop a mission statement that's unique to the new church. We must ask two important questions. Who develops the mission statement and how is it developed?

First, who develops the mission statement? In a church plant it is most often the lead planter who does this. He initiates and directs the process. Just as the new church's values are most likely his, the same is true of the church's mission, especially in a cold start. However, in a hot start others may and should be involved in the mission-developing process.

Mission development involves four steps plus some mission development options.

Step 1: Determine the Church's Mission

By now it is probably clear how to determine the church's mission. Here we are talking about the mission of all churches, and we know it is the Great Commission, as found in the four passages on the Great Commission (see the chart earlier in this chapter). The mission of the church is addressed specifically in Matthew 28:19–20. Regardless of how you articulate your mission statement, for it to be biblical, the Great Commission must be at its core.

Step 2: Clarify Your Mission

The mission statement must be clear. It's critical that you use biblical language or terms that your people can understand. The way you can determine this is by asking them questions about the statement: What does this mean? What does it mean to you?

Avoid abstract biblical terms, the meaning of which most people don't really understand, in spite of the fact that they've probably heard them used on numerous occasions in church. I'm referring to terms such as *disciple*, *glory*, *glorify*, *holy*, and so forth. Many of us refer to this as "Christianese" or "temple talk." This is insider language that I believe even the insiders (members and regular attenders) may not understand. Such language doesn't communicate to the person in the pews, unless you clarify what you mean. An example of this is Willow Creek Community Church's mission statement: "To turn irreligious people into fully devoted disciples." They could have said: "To turn irreligious people into disciples." And the advantage of such a statement is brevity that facilitates memory. However, they explain what a disciple is—"a fully devoted follower of Christ." This helps people better understand their mission.

Use terms that are not only clear but memorable. We want those who will be a part of our ministry to understand the mission and to remember it. When working with churches, I often ask about the people who attend the church on Sunday morning, "If asked, would they know the mission statement?"

There is a way to word mission statements that makes them most memorable. One that I mentioned earlier is "To know Christ and make him known." I've heard it only once and have never forgotten it. The genius of this statement is the use or repetition of similar words such as *know* to convey the concepts of coming to faith and spreading the faith.

Step 3: Articulate the Mission in Writing

Be sure to write down the mission because it will not have the authority of a leadership statement until it's clear enough to be committed to paper. If you don't quite have it, trying to write it will reveal this. Keep working on it, thinking about it, and rewriting it whenever you have the time. Don't be surprised if it suddenly pops into your head. That's often the way God gives his mission for the church.

Step 4: Make It Short and Simple

As I said earlier, the mission statement should be brief. The idea is to say more by saying less. Remember Peter Drucker's recommendation that it fit on a T-shirt. Perhaps a negative example will clarify this step. For several years my seminary and alma mater listed the following as our mission statement.

> The mission of Dallas Seminary as a professional, graduate-level school is to prepare men and women for ministry as godly servant leaders in the body of Christ worldwide. By blending instruction in the Scriptures from our doctrinal perspective with training in ministry skills, the Seminary seeks to produce graduates who do the work of evangelism, edify believers, and equip others by proclaiming and applying God's Word in the power of the Holy Spirit.

This statement gets an F because it doesn't pass the T-shirt test! In fact it communicates two mission statements: "The mission of Dallas Seminary as a professional, graduate-level school is to prepare men and women for ministry as godly servant leaders in the body of Christ worldwide" and "the Seminary seeks to produce graduates who do the work of evangelism, edify believers, and equip others." I'm glad to report that after recognizing the problem, the seminary changed this statement several years ago.

The Mission Development Steps

Step 1: Determine the church's mission.
Step 2: Clarify your mission.
Step 3: Write the mission statement.
Step 4: Make the mission statement short and simple.

Mission Development Options

Churches fall into one of two categories. Either they already have a mission statement or they don't have one.

If you've already developed a mission statement, use the four steps above to critique it. If it falls short but is close, the steps may help you improve it. If you're not even close, you may simply want to start over.

If you don't have a mission statement, you have three options: adopt an existing statement, tweak an existing statement, or create your own.

Adopt an Existing Statement

You may choose to adopt an existing statement. This assumes that you have a number of good statements to choose from or you've come across one you really like. I have included in appendix N some of the mission statements I've collected over the years. My thinking is that if you find a good one that matches well your idea of ministry, then feel free to use it.

Tweak an Existing Statement

You may have a statement that's very close to what you want but needs a slight tweak or two to make it work well for you. For example, several students that I trained at Tyndale Theological Seminary in the Netherlands came up with the following mission statement: "Our mission is to follow and make followers of Jesus Christ." Another church that I worked with in South Carolina liked this statement but made one change. They added the word *passionately* so that it read: "The mission of our church is to passionately follow and make followers of Christ."

Create Your Own Statement

You may be a creative person and prefer to develop your own statement. This is the option that I prefer because it will reflect the thinking and values of the church planter. Again, the mission statements in appendix N may help start the creative juices flowing. However, I must attach a word of caution or a disclaimer to this third option. When I have worked with established church leadership teams (usually around twenty-five to thirty people), I have found that some of the team members have not been satisfied with this creative option. It did not produce the statement they had hoped it would.

Mission Development Options

- Adopt an existing statement.
- Tweak an existing statement.
- Create your own statement.

The Communication of the Mission

As I said earlier, Stephen Covey is well known for saying, "The main thing is to keep the main thing the main thing." I couldn't agree with him more when it comes to the new church's mission statement. How do we keep the mission the main thing? The answer lies in communication. We can adopt the finest mission statement ever developed that follows my four steps perfectly, but if no one knows what it is, what good is it? The church's mission must be communicated. A church should follow the general communication plan and use formal and informal communication.

The General Communication Plan

In the last chapter I presented the general communication plan for communicating your core values. This same plan can be used to communicate the mission. Again, you would be wise to have in place a team that has the responsibility of communicating well such important concepts as values and mission.

Here are the seven questions, followed by answers that are specific to the mission. These make up the general communication plan.

1. What should be communicated?
2. Who should communicate it?
3. When should it be communicated?
4. How should it be communicated?
5. Where should it be communicated?
6. How often should it be communicated?
7. Why should it be communicated?

The following are answers to the questions concerning the mission.

1. The mission should be communicated.
2. The lead church planter and any others who are a part of the church plant should communicate the mission.
3. The mission should be communicated regularly or every time there is an opportunity.
4. The mission should be communicated in sermons, on a website, in a brochure, and other ways that I'll cover next.
5. It should be communicated at meetings, worship services, new members classes, and in church literature.
6. It should be communicated regularly—weekly, monthly, and annually.
7. The mission must be communicated so there will be mission alignment or to determine if the participants share the same mission. Good communication also builds trust that is vital in leadership.

Formal and Informal Communication

There are several ways you may communicate your mission formally and informally, many of which parallel the communication of your values. Consider each of the following: your lifestyle, word of mouth, preaching and teaching, church website, business cards, T-shirts, flyers, banners, a logo, a song, a skit, congregational recitation, in a visitors or new members class, a framed document mounted on a wall, brochures available at an information station, bulletins, and newsletters. As with communicating core values, the only limitation to articulating your mission well is your creative ability.

In working with a leadership team, I've asked them to take out a piece of paper, tear a small piece from it, write the mission statement on that piece, and then put it in their wallet in a place where they'll see it every time they open their wallet. This is a good way to be regularly reminded of the mission of the church.

Questions for Reflection and Discussion

1. What is the fundamental question of this chapter on mission?
2. Are you convinced that a church's mission is important? Why or why not?
3. Do you see a distinction between the church's mission and purpose? If so, what is it?
4. Do you agree with the author's definition of the church's mission? If not, what is your definition?
5. Did you find the chart that compared the various Great Commission passages helpful? Why or why not?
6. Do you agree with the author's view that making disciples must be the mission of the church? If not, what is your view?
7. How important is mission alignment among those involved in a new church?
8. Do you believe that a church that intentionally follows the wrong mission is out of the will of God? Why or why not?
9. Have you developed a mission statement? If not, why not? If so, did you critique it using the four steps in this chapter? Did it pass muster?
10. Which of the mission development options did you follow?
11. Do you have a communications team in place to help you communicate well? Why or why not?

7

What Kind of Church Will It Be?

Ministry Vision

The discovery of the church planter's core values and those of the church will explain why the church does what it does, and the development of the mission will explain that the church is to make disciples. The church is values driven and mission directed.

Now as we think about ministry vision, we must ask, What kind of church could we be if God has his way? Should you ask the church plant leader this question or what he sees when he dreams about the church five, ten, fifteen years from now, his answer is his vision for the planted church. The purpose of this chapter is to present the importance, definition, theology, development, and communication of the new church's vision.

The Importance of the Vision

The vision is of utmost importance to the new church because it provides energy, fosters risk taking, legitimizes leadership, empowers the church, sustains ministry, keeps the people looking forward, and motivates giving.

Provides Energy

Vision is important to the new church because it provides energy for those involved in the planting venture to see it through the difficult and good times.

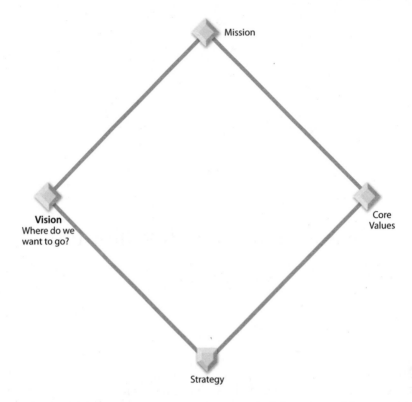

It's the fuel the new ministry runs on—not much happens without a vision. Visions are exciting. Bill Hybels writes, "That's the power of vision. It creates energy that moves people into action. It puts the match to the fuel that most people carry around in their hearts and yearn to have ignited."[1]

Fosters Risk Taking

Most established churches across America are risk aversive. Because so many are plateaued or in decline, they fear stepping out on the ministry limb for fear that it will break off, leaving them in dire straits. Some examples would be changing the worship style, the church's name, the church's location, and so forth. (I would argue that risk is necessary if churches are to accomplish their mission—no risk, no gain!) And doing nothing has put them in their current decline.

A church plant, by its very nature, invites risk, and risks must be taken to accomplish its vision. People are so weary of the status quo that they're willing to do whatever it takes to see their dream become reality. They understand and accept the truth that risk plays an important part in the adventure.

Legitimizes Leadership

People look to the church plant leader for vision. And the leader knows he received his vision from God and he's God's man to see it happen. Therefore, there's no such thing as a visionless leader in church planting. That would be a contradiction. It's the vision that legitimizes his leadership. Bill Hybels writes, "Vision is at the very core of leadership. Take vision away from the leader and you cut out his or her heart."[2]

Empowers the Church

Vision has an empowering effect on churches. Christ's church is the hope of the world, and Christ and his vision for the church empower his church (Matt. 16:18). This power enables the church to bring about Christ-honoring change in the community and the world. Again, Hybels writes, "Vision. It's the most potent weapon in the leader's arsenal. It's the weapon that unleashes the power of the church."[3]

Sustains Ministry

Church ministry in today's world has become a difficult profession. Along with the increasing number of declining churches, there's a high dropout rate that has diminished the tenure of pastors and their staff. I've heard that the current tenure for a senior pastor is around four to five years, and for youth pastors, one and a half years.

So what does a pastor do when he becomes discouraged in the midst of ministry? And keep in mind that it happens to all of us at some point. I would argue that it's the vision that keeps him going through the tough times when he and possibly some of his team are ready to throw in the ministry towel. If you'll let it, Christ's vision for his church will sustain you during these difficult times, because you know your picture for the future is his picture for your future.

Motivates Giving

It takes money to do ministry, and the church planter discovers this truth very soon in the planting process. When I share this with my pastoral students at seminary, it tends to prick the bubble of naïveté that surrounds their vision of the church they hope to pastor some day. Many of them simply want to teach the Bible and love people, not ask for money. Building a new church includes funding that church. Similar to going on the mission field, you have to raise up financial as well as prayer support if you want to start a church.

I've discovered while teaching at the seminary level that those who believe in your school aren't all that interested in paying the light bill or even your salary. They are most interested in what difference the seminary will make in the lives of its students and their impact on the world where they'll lead and minister. Hybels says that people who'll invest in your ministry "want some assurance that it's going to make a significant difference in the world. They want to know that their hard-earned money will be used to fund authentic ministry that impacts real people."[4]

I believe vision plays this role in ministry. Caught by the ministry's vision, people will be inspired to give. Hybels agrees and concludes, "People don't give to organizations or other people. They give to visions."[5]

Keeps the Church Looking Forward

The impact of the vision is felt when the church has a little age on it. Vision is the answer to a problem that eventually all church plants will have, the problem of becoming content with memories and ignoring what could be. Thus more energy is spent recalling the past than acknowledging the present and envisioning the future. If the church isn't careful here, it will wake up one day and discover that all it has are memories.

My point is that the leadership must continue to cast the vision throughout the life of the church. Vision casting doesn't stop when the church is first established. If the vision is continually cast, it helps people look ahead to what can be accomplished in the future. Then they will expect the future to be brighter than the past because they assume the church can have an even greater impact for Christ as time goes on.

The Importance of Vision

Vision provides energy.
Vision fosters risk taking.
Vision legitimizes leadership.
Vision empowers the church.
Vision sustains the ministry.
Vision motivates giving.
Vision keeps the church looking forward.

The Definition of *Vision*

We have seen how important a vision is, but what is it exactly? I define the vision as a clear, common, compelling picture of God's future for his church as the church planter believes it can and must be.

Clear

Vision clarity is essential to vision ministry if the vision is to bring the future into focus. The church is not only values driven and mission directed, it's vision focused.

People can't act on what isn't clear. Paul illustrates this in 1 Corinthians 14:8: "Again, if the trumpet does not sound a clear call, who will get ready for battle?" If your vision isn't clear, then—in effect—you don't have one. In addition, there's a fear factor involved where there's little if any vision clarity. If people are fuzzy about what the vision of the ministry is supposed to be, they are more likely to criticize what the leaders are trying to do. Rick Warren says that people are down on what they're not up on, and he's right.

Common

The term *common* can have several meanings. When I use the term to describe a vision, I don't mean that it's ordinary, familiar, natural, or wearisome, which are some of the definitions that you'll find in a dictionary. What I do mean is that a good vision is *shared*. Just as the new church's core values and core mission must be shared, so must its vision.

When the leader casts God's vision for the church plant, it's imperative that those who would move forward with the church share the vision, and those who don't should move elsewhere. In the past, those of us who teach church planting noticed that some of the first people to drop out of the church plant were those who made up its core constituency. Their response was, "We didn't know that the church would be like this." This is a vision casting faux pas. The vision caster can eliminate much of this by casting such a clear vision that those involved know precisely where the church is going and are committed to moving in that direction.

Compelling

A good vision is compelling. The right people want to be a part of it, and it serves to motivate these people. The ministry's vision inspires them to partner with what the ministry is convinced God wants it to do. A compelling vision moves people out of the pews and into the community and, most important, gives birth to ministry.

A Picture

If you want to get an idea of what God's future for the church will be like, look to the new church's vision. Vision is a "seeing" word. It paints a compelling picture of the church's future—God's snapshot of the future.

Whenever I cover this point with a group of leaders, I like to illustrate it by showing them a cartoon with the caption, "Frog Pioneers." It's a picture of three frogs, carrying shovels and wearing pioneer hats. Above the frogs is the statement, "We'll put the swamp here!" What's so ironic about this scene is that the frogs are in a desert, as signified by the cacti and parched ground around them.

I begin this vision exercise by asking what the group literally sees in the cartoon. The answers are the frogs, their hats, some rocks, the ground, the cacti, some hills in the background, and a scorpion. I follow up this question with what I refer to as the vision question—What do the frogs see? The answer of course is a swamp. The swamp is only in the frogs' minds, but in light of the power of a vision, it's only a matter of time before the desert will become a swamp.

Affects the Future

Vision and mission have several things in common, one of which is they both address God's future for the church—the church's ministry. Vision and mission hold exciting possibilities for the future—a picture of what you want the church to be, or what God has shown you it can be. The Savior's vision concerns disciple making, and the vision reflects what that will look like as it happens. And this is where the church's leadership is so important to the future of the church. Marcus Buckingham writes, "What defines a leader is his preoccupation with the future. In his head he carries a vivid image of what the future could be, and this image drives him on."[6] The vision is a driving force because it's God's vision for the ministry.

So are you the kind of leader who sees into the future and captures God's vision for your church? One way to find out is to take the Vision Audit in appendix O.

What Can Be

Vision has everything to do with what can be. Robert F. Kennedy, quoting George Bernard Shaw, said, "Some people see things as they are and say why? I dream things that never were and say why not?" A significant dream has great potential. It's not some wild-eyed, crazed image of the future. It's based on the bedrock of reality. Regarding what can be, John R. W. Stott writes, "It is an act of seeing—an imaginative perception of things, combining insight and foresight. . . . We see what is—but do we see what could be?"[7]

What Must Be

Not only does the church planter believe that the dream *can* be, he's convinced that it *must* be. This is the point in the definition when the passion element kicks in. I define *passion* as what you feel strongly about and care deeply for. It's an emotion, touching the heart. It grabs hold and won't let go. In fact an appropriate question here is, How far would you be willing to go to realize the dream? Would you be willing to die for your vision? Church history teaches us that many have died over the centuries for the cause of Christ's vision. And a modern-day example is Martin Luther King Jr., who died for his vision of equality for African Americans.

The Difference between a Mission and a Vision

In working with church leadership teams, I've discovered there is often confusion about the distinction between a mission and a vision. I've identified eleven differences between a mission and a vision.

1. *Definitions.* A *mission* is a broad, brief, biblical statement of what the ministry is supposed to be doing. The *vision*, however, is a clear, common, compelling picture of God's future for the ministry as the planter believes it can and must be.

2. *Applications or uses.* The *mission* is a planning tool. It helps the church plan for the future. The *vision* is a communication tool. It is used to help the church see the future.

3. The *length of the statements*. The *mission statement* is short, short enough to fit on a T-shirt. The *vision statement* is longer than the mission statement. The reason for a longer vision statement is that it allows the church planter to further clarify where he sees the church going. He can include much more information than he can in the mission statement. I have seen vision statements that range anywhere from one to twenty or thirty pages. I recommend that your vision be no longer than five pages and preferably one to two pages.

4. *Purpose.* The purpose of the *mission* is to inform people where the new church is going. The purpose of the *vision* is to inspire people to want to go there.

5. *Promotion.* The *mission* promotes knowing. When people understand the mission, they know where the new church is headed. The *vision* promotes seeing. When people hear and understand the vision, they see where the church is going.

6. *The source.* The source of the *mission* is the church planter's head. It's more intellectual. People who are good thinkers appreciate and value the mission. The source of the *vision* is the church planter's heart. It's more emotional. Consequently people who are in touch with their emotions appreciate and value the vision.

7. *The order.* This is somewhat like the question of which came first, the chicken or the egg? It probably doesn't matter whether the *mission* or *vision* comes first, but it seems easier to develop a vision after the mission has already been determined. When I teach leaders, I ask them to think about what the mission will look like when it's realized in the future. For example, what will making disciples look like five, ten, fifteen years from now? Their answer is their vision.

8. *Focus.* The focus of the *mission* is broad, while the focus of the *vision* is narrow. The church is vision focused. Because it's longer, it can focus on more than the shortened mission statement. For example, the vision

can focus on particular areas of ministry, while the mission is the broad aim of ministry in general.

9. *Impact.* The impact of the *mission* is to clarify where the church is going and what it will do to get there. The impact of the *vision* is to challenge people to go there. For example, the leader might say that the vision of the church is to present the gospel to every man, woman, and child who lives in the church community—its Jerusalem. And then he might challenge the people to sign on to accomplish this vision.

10. *Development.* The development of the *mission* is more like a science. It's logical and intellectual and can be taught. The development of the *vision* is an art. It doesn't always make sense and is more emotional. Thus it's more caught than taught. In a sense it's intuitive. It just happens and seems to come out of nowhere, though we know its source is God.

11. *Communication.* The vision and mission are communicated differently. The *mission statement* is communicated visually. You may see it printed in the bulletin, in a planning document, on the wall in the worship center, or on a business card. The *vision* is communicated through speaking it. You will hear it preached from the pulpit or presented in a state of the church message, or you may hear several people discussing it in the hallway between services.

The Differences between a Mission and a Vision

	Mission	Vision
1. *Definition*	Statement	Snapshot
2. *Application*	Planning tool	Communication tool
3. *Length*	Short statement	Longer statement
4. *Purpose*	Informs	Inspires
5. *Promotes*	Knowing	Seeing
6. *Source*	Head (intellect)	Heart (emotions)
7. *Order*	Comes first	Comes second
8. *Focus*	Broad	Narrow
9. *Impact*	Clarifies direction	Challenges commitment
10. *Development*	Science (taught)	Art (caught)
11. *Communication*	Visual	Spoken

The Theology of the Vision Statement

The theology of vision in essence is what the Bible teaches about vision. Unfortunately I can't create a chart of Scripture passages dealing with the church's vision as I did for its theology of mission. There simply isn't enough biblical information on vision. In light of this, some would question the emphasis and importance that I place on vision. Though I know of no biblical passage that teaches we have to have a vision statement, my experience in ministry has shown me the importance of vision to a ministry—the preceding section on the differences between mission and vision makes this clear. Wisdom says we would be wise to have a vision because of the powerful role it plays. And nowhere does Scripture prohibit or discourage the development of a vision.

One example of vision found in Scripture is in Deuteronomy 8:7–10, where Moses allows us to listen in as he casts God's vision for Israel. (I believe that we have only a small excerpt of what was originally said.)

> For the LORD your God is bringing you into a good land—a land with streams and pools of water, with springs flowing in the valleys and hills; a land with wheat and barley, vines and fig trees, pomegranates, olive oil and honey; a land where bread will not be scarce and you will lack nothing, a land where the rocks are iron and you can dig copper out of the hills. When you have eaten and are satisfied, praise the LORD your God for the good land he has given you.

I see this vision in the context of God's mission for Israel as revealed to Moses in Exodus 3:10: "So now, go. I am sending you to Pharaoh to bring my people out of Egypt." Note that many of the differences I emphasized in the last section characterize both this mission and vision. For example, Moses' mission is a statement of what God wants him to do, whereas the vision provides a snapshot of what it will be like when they arrive in the Promised Land. Theologically, God's mission for Moses was prescriptive for Moses, not us. And God's vision for Israel is descriptive, not prescriptive. It was for them, not us.

The Development of the Vision

We've finally arrived at a place where we're ready to develop a vision for the new church plant. We must answer two questions: Who develops the vision and how is it developed?

Who Develops the Church's Vision

Either the lead church planter or the church-planting core team develops the church's vision. The circumstances of the church plant will determine who should do it.

LEAD CHURCH PLANTER

If the church plant is a cold start, I would expect the lead church planter to seek God's heart and vision for the future church. Thus when he eventually recruits and connects with a church-planting team and eventually a congregation, he already has the vision. He simply needs to cast the vision regularly and use it as a recruiting tool to attract like-minded people to the ministry.

CHURCH-PLANTING CORE TEAM

If the church is a hot start and the planting pastor is called by a core team or group of people, then they may all be involved in the process of developing the vision. The planting pastor would work with the team to draft a vision they all share. One danger of this approach is that a common vision could be watered down and not have the impact of the planter's dream. This will depend on who makes up the team. Some lay leaders are key players with an uncanny ability to develop powerful visions with great impact. These people should be a part of the process.

Often the church planter arrives on-site with his vision already developed and encourages the team to embrace it.

Regardless of who develops the vision and the role they play, the lead pastor will be the "keeper of the vision." If everyone is responsible for the vision, then nobody is responsible for it. While you want the group to cast the vision, the primary responsibility lies with the planting pastor. If the vision isn't well cast, the blame lies with him.

How to Develop the Vision

FIRST BASE: PRAY

When I teach leaders how to develop their vision, I make use of the baseball diamond illustration again. I encourage visionaries and teams to touch four bases when developing their dream. First base is prayer. An example is Nehemiah's envisioning prayer found in Nehemiah 1. He simply asked God for his vision for the remnant in light of their physical and spiritual demise. They had fallen away from God spiritually (vv. 6–7) and were reaping the consequences physically (v. 3). The vision is found in verses 8 and 9 and involves God's gathering the remnant from where they had been scattered to Jerusalem—a place he had chosen as a dwelling for his name.

So when developing your dream, you must spend time seeking God's face for his vision for your church. I would challenge you to recruit a prayer team to pray specifically for the shaping of the dream. Right now people should be praying for you and the dream.

SECOND BASE: THINK BIG

I believe that one of the differences between church plants that grow and reach many people and those that have minimal impact is that those that have minimal impact both pray and think small. Earlier I mentioned J. B. Phillips's book *Your God Is Too Small*, reflecting the idea that far too many churches worship a small God. If you listened in on the prayers of these churches, you'd be disappointed in their vision for outreach. For some reason they think it's presumptuous to ask God for and envision reaching many unchurched, lost people. In Ephesians 3:20 Paul lightly slaps the church on the wrist because it doesn't ask or envision big enough: "Now to him who is able to do immeasurably more than all we ask or imagine, according to his power that is at work within us . . ."

As I said in chapter 3, if I were to plant a church where I live in Dallas, Texas, I would ask God for and envision reaching Dallas. The key is planting church-planting churches. First, I would plant several church-planting churches in the suburbs—possibly near the Lyndon Baines Johnson Freeway that circles Dallas. Next, I would plant churches in the inner city and eventually in some of the rural towns just outside the Dallas city limits. These don't have to be mega churches. They can be house churches or a combination thereof. By planting lots of church-planting churches rather than planting a single church, you launch a movement of new churches that can address the current church decline that plagues so many of our cities and towns across America.

THIRD BASE: EXAMINE THE SAMPLE STATEMENTS

In appendix P you will find some sample vision statements. As you study them, you will discover the kind of information that should be in a vision statement.

Most of the vision statements come from churches, but one is for the children's ministry at Clear Lake Community Church. We see that churches may want to cast vision for specific ministries of the church as well as the entire church. Three of the four church vision statements are for Boomer Generation churches. I view the Forest Meadow statement as more Next Generation. The statements vary in length from a page (Village View Community Church and Forest Meadow Baptist Church) to several pages (Saddleback, Irving Bible, and Clear Lake Community). One statement (Village View Community Church) appears to have patterned itself after that of Saddleback Valley Community Church.

As you thumb through the dream statements you'll observe the following specifics that are mentioned: core values, mission statements, land and facilities, attendance figures (numbers), unchurched people, community involvement, missionaries—career and short-term, global and local—personal life missions, church planting, evangelism and outreach, congregational mobilization and service, various ministries (worship, discipleship, prayer, Bible school, Christian school, youth and senior centers, assisted living, small groups, children, Bible studies, seminars, and others), various issues (marriage and family life, addictions, issues of our culture), themes (love, forgiveness, acceptance, hope, encouragement, unity, joy, courage, compassion, and others), multiple cultures, diversity, creativity and innovation, partnerships with other churches, leader development, and so on.

To attempt to include all these specifics in your statement would be a vision statement disaster. However, note or circle those that ignite your passions and address these in your dream statement.

HOME PLATE: EXPAND THE MISSION STATEMENT

If you've followed the order that I suggest in this book, then you will have already developed your mission statement. Developing your vision is accomplished by expanding your mission statement.

Assume that the following is your mission statement: "We exist to develop people into fully functioning followers of Christ." Then ask, What would such a vision look like five, ten, fifteen years from now? Kick back and describe what you see, or better, what God brings to mind—as ultimately it's his vision, not yours. Don't attempt to do this on one occasion, but allow yourself some time that may involve several sessions alone or with other key people. One other approach that some prefer is to develop a vision for each of the five strategy steps: community outreach, disciple making, team building (congregational mobilization and staff development), setting, and finances.

How to Develop Your Vision Statement

First Base: Pray
Second Base: Think big
Third Base: Examine sample statements
Home Plate: Expand the mission statement

Communication of the Vision

At this point in the envisioning process, you have birthed an initial vision. I use the term *initial* in the sense that the vision will and should change over time. Dreams are fluid, not static. It's a work in progress.

As important as the development of the dream is, the communication of the dream is critical. As with the values and mission, you can have a perfect vision statement, but if you don't communicate it to your church planting constituency, it won't happen. All is lost if you can't or don't communicate the vision! In this final section I'll address the who, what, and how of vision casting.

Who Communicates the Vision

Initially the lead church planter casts the vision, most likely during the conception stage and even before. However, as he drafts core leadership and a team, and they buy into the vision, then they become vision casters as well. It's important that just as you cast a fishing line out into the water and see what follows as you reel it in, so you do the same with the dream. As we cast the vision, who follows it or shows interest?

What to Communicate

We want to communicate the dream or vision that has been developed. Here I will focus on what I refer to as the vision aspects—the whole vision and the vision parts.

THE WHOLE VISION

The whole vision refers to the statement of the entire vision for the church. Most likely it will be cast several times a year, such as at the beginning of the New Year, during a state of the church message, and at other significant times.

THE VISION PARTS

The vision parts are the various portions that make up the entire dream. If you reexamine the sample vision statements in appendix P, you'll see that each statement contains vision parts, dealing with such topics as the facilities and grounds, congregational mobilization, missions, ministries, and family. The vision caster should opt to cast these parts more frequently as appropriate in the services. Thus, if he's preaching on the importance of a fully mobilized congregation or on family life, he would take the opportunity to cast the vision for those issues.

How to Cast the Vision

There are many ways to cast the vision. You should develop a plan to communicate it, which would include preaching the vision.

DEVELOP A PLAN

To develop a plan for communicating the vision, assemble a communication team. The team should use the general communication plan that I introduced in chapter 5 for communicating values and used in chapter 6 for communicating mission. The plan below has been adapted to the communication of vision.

1. What should be communicated?
2. Who should communicate it?
3. When should it be communicated?
4. How should it be communicated?
5. Where should it be communicated?
6. How often should it be communicated?
7. Why should it be communicated?

Concerning the vision or dream, the answers to the above questions would be:

1. The vision should be communicated.
2. The lead church planter and any others who are a part of the church plant should communicate the vision.
3. The vision should be communicated regularly or every time there is an opportunity.
4. The vision will be communicated primarily in sermons but also on a website, in a brochure, and other ways that I'll cover next.
5. It should be communicated at any organizational meeting, worship service, new members class, and other meetings of the church and in church literature.
6. It should be communicated regularly—weekly, monthly, annually.
7. Communicate the vision to create vision alignment among all involved in the church or to determine if participants share the same vision. Remember that good communication builds trust and this is vital in leadership.

PREACH THE DREAM

The primary, formal way to cast the vision is verbally, most likely through preaching. I have been misrepresented on this point, so I want to pause and make sure this is clear. I do encourage leaders to write down the dream so that it's clear, should someone later challenge what a group created as their vision. However, a written statement is only one way and not the best way to cast the vision.

OTHER WAYS

There are other ways to cast the vision that could supplement, not take the place of, the preaching of the vision. The ideas presented in chapters 5 and 6 can also be used for casting the vision. Here are a few by way of reminder: the church planter's lifestyle, informal conversation, stories and heroes, skits and drama, a new members class, a church brochure, a video presentation, and the church website.

Questions for Reflection and Discussion

1. What is the fundamental question that the vision addresses?
2. Are you convinced that your church needs a vision? Why or why not?
3. What is the author's definition of a vision? Do you agree?
4. Should the vision be yours or God's? What's the difference? Could your vision be God's vision?
5. What's the difference between a vision and a mission?
6. Is the fact that we're not commanded in the Bible to have a vision problematic? Why or why not?

7. Have you developed a vision for your church? Why or why not?
8. If you've developed a vision, how does it compare with the definition of a vision in this chapter? Does it pass muster? Does it contain all the elements mentioned in the definition? (Is it clear? Is it compelling? Is it God's vision? and so on.)

8

How Will You Accomplish the Mission and Vision?

Developing a Strategy

Once the church planter has discovered the ministry core values and plotted the new church's direction (mission and vision), he is ready to work on the fourth and final process component—the new church's strategy. The new church is values driven, mission directed, vision focused, and strategy accomplished. The fundamental, overarching question that summarizes the next seven chapters is the strategy question: How will we accomplish the mission and vision?

On the base path figure on page 114, we've circled the bases and reached home plate, which represents the strategy.

The strategy consists of five points that ask and answer five questions addressed in the following seven chapters. These are easy to remember because there's a logical flow—each relates to and builds on the prior point. Using the baseball diamond illustration, the five points of strategy can be represented by home plate, which is in the shape of a pentagon with five sides. Each side can represent one of the strategy elements. Our strategy goal is to work our way around the five sides, beginning at the top (community outreach) and finishing at the upper left side (finances).

This chapter is an introduction to developing your strategy. It addresses how to understand strategy, how to accomplish a strategy, and how to improve your strategy.

113

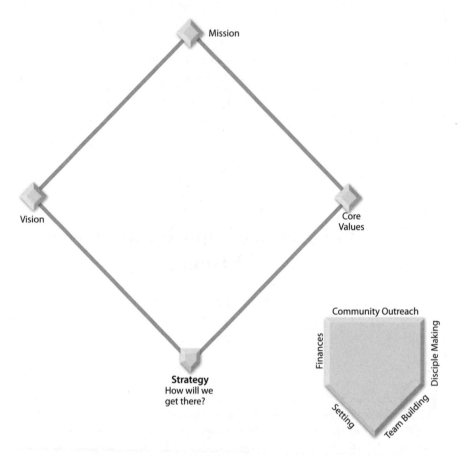

Orientation: How to Understand Strategy

The following is an orientation to strategy that will preview the five core elements that make up a strategy for church-planting work.

Community Outreach

The first element of the strategy is community outreach. We ask, How will we strategize to reach our community? The focus of chapter 9 is the community where the church will locate—the people who live around the church. I refer to this community as the church plant's Jerusalem, based on Acts 1:8, where Jesus commands the new church to be witnesses to its community in Jerusalem, Judea, and Samaria, and the ends of the world. The church's immediate community is its Jerusalem. We'll identify the boundaries of the community and ask who lives within its boundaries and how we might reach them for the Savior.

Disciple Making

The second element is disciple making. We ask, How will we strategize to make mature disciples? In chapter 10 we return to Christ's mission statement ("Make disciples!") and wrestle with how the new church will accomplish this mandate. The goal is to come up with a clear, simple pathway or process for disciple making that everyone knows and understands. We'll also discuss how to communicate and then evaluate the process.

Team Building

The third element is the dream team. We must ask, How will we strategize to build a special team who will make disciples of the community? The new church's dream team will be made up of the congregation, the staff, and later a governing board. In chapters 11 and 12 we'll explore how to mobilize the congregation for ministry and how to develop the staff for leadership. I'll also have a few things to say about board governance in chapter 12.

Setting

The fourth element is the setting (location and facilities) of the church plant. We must ask, How will we strategize to maximize our ministry setting? Where will we locate in the ministry community? From where will we launch out into the community and do ministry? And what kinds of facilities in the community are available for our gathering? In chapter 13 we'll focus on a potential church-plant campus, parking lot, worship facility, and educational spaces.

Finances

The fifth element is finances. We ask, How will we strategize to raise finances to fund the ministry? And how much will it cost? This is covered in chapter 14.

Church-Planting Process

1. Core Values
2. Mission
3. Vision
4. Strategy
   - Community Outreach
   - Disciple Making
   - Team Building
   - Setting (location and facilities)
   - Finances

Implementation: How to Accomplish Your Strategy

Now that you're familiar with the five core elements of your strategy, I'll address how to implement this strategy in your new church. Your church's ability to learn and rapidly translate that learning into action will give it a decided ministry edge in the community. Strategy is important because it closes the gap between your ideas about ministry and their execution. It translates your thoughts and ideas into action. You can design a most effective strategy for your church, but if you don't implement that strategy, it won't matter. Someone has said the proof of the pudding is in the tasting. How do you taste or implement your strategy?

Who Will Implement the Strategy?

The majority of established churches hire the pastor and staff to do the church's ministry. But according to Scripture, it should be the congregation (Eph. 4:11–13) who implement the strategy, for without their involvement, it won't happen and the church won't mature. Therefore the core leadership team *and* the people who make up the congregation should be involved in implementation. It is the responsibility of the lead pastor, working through the core leadership team and congregation, to see that this is done.

As the lead pastor works his way through the strategy, he will encounter problems. First, there will be an information overload. We have more knowledge or information today about church planting than ever before. For example, much of this information provides the planter with various options, such as what kind of church to plant. And once he decides on a model, other numerous options follow. He will know much that needs to be translated into ministry. Second, there are many tasks that need to be done. In both cases, church-plant lead persons will find themselves overwhelmed. This is the reason the new and growing congregation is so important to the new work as they play the primary role in implementing the strategy.

How Will You Work Together?

How will the congregation and the core leadership team work together to implement the strategy? From the church's beginning, implementation teams should be formed, made up of those who are committed to being a part of the new ministry. A team could consist of as few as two people and as many as nine, depending on the size of the church. I say no more than nine people, because that's the optimum size for groups that function well together. A group of more than nine people can become chaotic.

Each team will need a champion or leader. I advise church planters to ask people with leadership ability to be leaders of the teams. If you ask for volunteers, you may get people who are not equipped to lead. (This was how

Jesus's group of leaders was formed. He approached his disciples rather than make a general announcement to the crowd asking for volunteers.) Once you have a leader in place, let this person recruit his or her team.

Before the church works through each component or element of the strategy—community outreach, disciple making, and so on—it will form a strategic implementation team of two to nine people that will take responsibility to oversee that particular element of the strategy. The team is selected before work is done on the particular strategy element.

Team members will collect a lot of information from books on ministry and interviews with the church planter and other ministry leaders as they take responsibility for their component. They will set goals that will accomplish each element, have those on the team take responsibility for these goals based on interest and giftedness, make sure the teams have the necessary resources to realize the goals, and let the entire church know as they accomplish them. Finally, I encourage the church planter to meet monthly with the team leaders to encourage them, see where they might be struggling, hold them accountable for their goals, answer any questions, and celebrate their accomplishments with them.

Evaluation: How to Improve Your Strategy

As the church plant grows and as the teams implement their components of the strategy, the leadership needs to regularly evaluate their progress. That's how they'll get better and see that the ministry makes the necessary changes to function at its best as a new church. In several places in Scripture, I believe evaluation is encouraged. For example, the Savior evaluates seven churches in Revelation 2 and 3. Luke gives regular church progress reports in Acts (see, for example, Acts 2:41, 47; 4:4; 5:14; 6:1), which are evaluations. Finally, Paul lists the characteristics of a good pastor in 1 Timothy 3:1–7 and Titus 1:5–9, so we can evaluate those who desire pastoral positions.

From time to time a church must ask, How are you doing as a new church? I suggest you answer this question with the following formal evaluation process that you will need to put in place.

1. *Someone will need to be responsible* for seeing that evaluation takes place. Initially, this will be the lead church planter or someone on the leadership team.
2. *Determine who will be evaluated.* The lead church planter and any who make up the initial staff team must be evaluated. This group will expand as the church grows. For example, you may eventually evaluate Sunday school teachers, small group leaders, a board, and others.

3. *Determine which ministries will be evaluated.* For example, are the church's primary ministries (worship and preaching, Bible study, and small groups) making mature disciples?
4. *The people who do evaluations* will likely be the lead church planter, the staff, and possibly the entire congregation, while it's still small in number. (Later, as the church grows, it will become difficult for the entire congregation to do evaluations.)
5. *Determine what to evaluate.* The character, competence, and chemistry of staff and ministry teams should be evaluated. How well people perform their ministries, based on their ministry or job descriptions, should also be evaluated. As noted in point three, the church's primary disciple maturing ministries should be evaluated.
6. *Decide how to evaluate.* I encourage you to consider a performance-based approach, using the following scale. The level will be determined by comparing the performance with what is expected in the job description.

   • Exceptional performance
   • Commendable performance
   • Average performance
   • Below average performance
   • Unacceptable performance

   All would agree that exceptional and commendable performance are more than acceptable, whereas below average and unacceptable could cause the person being evaluated to be dismissed. What about average performance? Is average performance okay? Most ministries that I work with say average isn't good enough; they expect more. This makes sense. If a person's performance is only average or there is some other problem, he is obviously not ministering in an area for which God has designed him. Perhaps the person and the ministry would be better served if he found a position in which he could do exceptional or commendable work. There could be other problems as well, such as a failing marriage, control problems, financial issues, and others.
7. *Determine how often evaluation should be done.* It takes place informally every week, and I suggest an annual formal evaluation. If someone performs below the expected standard, then evaluate him or her every three to six months to monitor progress.
8. *Decide what to do with the evaluations.* The lead pastor or assigned evaluator should go over the evaluations with the person evaluated, and both should sign off on it, affirming that you have discussed the evaluation and both understand what has transpired.
   A positive evaluation should result in some kind of reward. Eventually, when the church is providing the salary for the person, then the reward

could be a pay increase or a bonus. Until then, you need to come up with some other creative way to reward the person who has done well. It could be a verbal thank-you, a written note of thanks, taking the person out for a meal, giving him or her some time off, or asking those who work with the person to record on a video what they've accomplished and give it to the person.

How to Evaluate Your Church

1. Recruit a leader of the evaluation process.
2. Determine who will be evaluated.
3. Determine which ministries will be evaluated.
4. Decide who will do the evaluation.
5. Determine what will be evaluated.
6. Determine how to do the evaluation.
7. Decide how often to evaluate.
8. Determine what you'll do with the results.

Introduction to Strategy

Orientation: How to understand strategy

Implementation: How to accomplish your strategy

Evaluation: How to improve your strategy

Questions for Reflection and Discussion

1. Do you feel that the strategy orientation or preview is helpful in preparing you for what is to come? If so, how?
2. Do you believe the author has covered the major components of a good strategy for the church plant? If not, what's missing?
3. The chapter underscores the importance of implementation. Do you agree that implementation is important to your new church? Why or why not?
4. Do you have enough people at this point in your development that you can form strategic implementation teams?
5. How many implementation teams will you recruit, and what is each team expected to contribute to the church?
6. How important is evaluation to the ministry? Do you plan to implement an evaluation process? Why or why not? Will you follow the evaluation plan outlined in this chapter or go with another plan?

9

Who Will Be Reached?

Engaging the Community

This chapter on strategy focuses the church plant-er's attention on the church's community. The strategy question asks, How will the church strategize to reach its community? Here we will look at the importance, definition, and theology of community, followed by a section on the development of the strategy to reach the new church's community. I will close the chapter with a few comments on the communication of that strategy.

The Importance of Community

Vital to the Life of the Church

Community is vital to the life of the church. Joel Hunter is the senior pastor of Northland Church in Longwood, Florida. In *Christianity Today* he is quoted as saying, "As the traditional church has a rougher and rougher time, our challenge will become a motivational factor: either we build relationships with people in our communities or we will die."[1] Far too many of our established evangelical churches are inward focused and unacquainted with their communities, and their communities are unaware of them. As

Hunter warns, a significant number of these churches are in numerical decline and dying.

Place of Ministry

In the early twentieth century, the evangelical church (who were labeled *fundamentalists*) made an important decision. Theological liberalism was having an impact on people, especially those living in the community. This impact was felt because those considered theologically liberal were addressing social concerns, such as caring for the sick, providing food for the hungry, assisting the poor, treating alcoholism, helping with education, and many other concerns. The fundamentalists labeled this the "social gospel" and declared it out of bounds for their churches. "We'll have nothing to do with it!" they declared. "We'll let them preach their social gospel and we'll preach Christ's gospel." Unfortunately, this meant abandoning communities, leaving them in the hands of the mainline churches. The result was an inward-focused church that didn't address the needs of those around them.

Recently, however, evangelicals, such as Rick Warren, Bill Hybels, and Next Generation pastors are calling evangelicals back out into their respective communities not only to preach Christ's gospel, but to address and minister to people with AIDS, the poor, the disenfranchised, and those with other needs.

As we'll see in the theology section, the church's ministry must extend beyond the church's walls to include those in the community. We've learned that social issues are merely an outward sign of deeper spiritual issues. But as the Savior demonstrates in the Gospels, we won't get people to consider their spiritual needs unless we address their social needs. Community is important because our communities are where ministry takes place.

Location of a Great Church

Community is important because it can make the plant a great church. How would you know a great church if you saw one? Jim Collins, who wrote *Good to Great*, suggests an answer. He writes, "How do you define greatness in a church? A great church has a distinctive impact on a community. If it disappeared, it would leave a serious hole in the community."[2] The planted church must ask, Will the people in the community even know we're in the community? Community is important because involvement in and ministry to that community are marks of a great church—at least the community thinks so.

The Importance of Community

- Vital to the life of the church
- Place of ministry
- Location of a great church

The Definition of *Community*

I use the term *community* in two ways. One involves geography and the other involves people.

Geography

First, community is geography—the area or land where the new ministry locates. Community is the church's geographical sphere of spiritual influence. People live in a community, and strategic-minded churches seek to exert a spiritual influence on them, to reach people for Christ in their unique community.

To understand how to reach people, you'll need to understand where they are located and why. There's a reason people locate where they do. This quest will involve us in a study of demographics and psychographics that we'll explore in the section of this chapter on developing a strategy to reach your community.

In that same section we'll also see that community is limited geographically. For example, people will drive only so far and so long to go to a church. Also in some locations there are geographical barriers, such as mountains or bodies of water, that prohibit travel. I encourage you to stake out your community and establish a geographical area for which you'll take responsibility.

People

Community is also people, those who populate the geographical area. The new church's community is made up of people. As you'll recall from chapter 6 on mission, there's a theological distinction between the purpose and the mission of the church. Christ left the church here on earth to glorify himself (see, for example, Rom. 15:6; 1 Cor. 6:20; 10:31). Thus the object of the church's purpose is God. The mission, however, is to make disciples. Consequently the object of Christ's mission for his church is people—who will become disciples. The church is in the people business, or better, the people-reaching business. Its mission is all about people. Therefore, to be true to Christ's mandate, it is imperative that the church reach its community because its community is people.

Since geography and people make up community, the definition of community can be the people who populate a church's geographical sphere of spiritual influence.

The Theology of Community

There are two core passages that spell out the theology of community. The first is Matthew 28:19 and the second is Acts 1:8. We'll begin with Matthew 28:19.

Matthew 28:19

Repeatedly in this book I've said that, according to Matthew 28:19, Jesus's mission for his church is to make disciples. However, if we're not careful, we can miss the command that precedes the mandate. Matthew 28:19 reads, "Therefore go and make disciples of all nations." And we can make the same mistake in Mark 16:15, where Jesus says, "Go into all the world and preach the good news to all creation." I'm referring, of course, to the word *go* in both passages. It's important to this discussion to note that the word is used in the Greek as a participle in both passages, and participles aren't usually translated as imperatives or commands. However, whenever they appear in constructions such as those found in these verses where they precede the main verb or command, they take on the characteristics of the command itself. So in essence what we have in each verse are two important consecutive commands.[3]

Part of Christ's mandate for his church in Matthew 28:19 is that it *go*. Matthew says to go to "all nations." Mark says to go into all the world. In either case the point is that the church's mandate isn't to stay—or in some cases hide away—inside the four walls of the church. It's to move out, reach out, and connect or "rub shoulders" with people where they are in their communities.

Throughout much of the twentieth century churches have been somewhat invitational. A part of their strategy has been to encourage their people to invite and bring their friends, both lost and saved, to church where they can hear the gospel. This strategy has reached a lot of people, and there's nothing wrong with it, but the biblical emphasis is more incarnational than invitational We are to give bodily form to the message by taking it into the community. We are to invite, and we are to go. Thus we have all the more reason to develop an incarnational strategy for going out into and reaching out to our communities. We're to be Great Commissional churches.

Acts 1:8

While in Matthew 28:19 and the other Great Commission passages we find Jesus's mandate for his church, in Acts 1:8 we discover his last words for his church. And Jesus's last words are lasting words. He's about to leave the earth and ascend into heaven. Certainly his last words have import.

So what are his last words? In Acts 1:8 he says: "But you will receive power when the Holy Spirit comes on you; and you will be my witnesses in Jerusalem, and in all Judea and Samaria, and to the ends of the earth." I'm convinced that in Acts 1:8 Jesus's last words are teaching us that the Great Commission has both geographical and ethnological implications. He instructs his church where and to whom it is to be a witness.

GEOGRAPHICAL IMPLICATIONS

Jesus instructs his church *where* to be a witness. They were to witness in Jerusalem (where they were located), Judea, Samaria, and the ends of the earth. I picture what you would see if you dropped a rock in the middle of a pond and watched the waves ripple across it until they reached the shore. This is simply a further amplification of Mark 16:15 where he said to go to "all the world."

When reading the verse in Mark, the first thing that comes to mind is international missions. No doubt about it, the passage is teaching that we have a responsibility to take the gospel to other countries beyond our own. So often, however, we miss the fact that in Acts 1:8 we are told to be witnesses in Jerusalem and Judea, or where we are currently located. It's been my experience that many churches have involved themselves heavily in foreign missions (the "ends of the earth") but have done little if anything in their Jerusalem and Judea. I praise these churches for their involvement internationally but not for their lack of outreach at home.

ETHNOLOGICAL IMPLICATIONS

Jesus also instructs his church *to whom* it is to be a witness. Reread Acts 1:8 and note they were to go to Samaria. Remember that the Samaritans were different ethnologically from the Jews. They were a mixed race with a heathen core. Consequently the Jews hated the Samaritans. They wouldn't even walk through their territory; when traveling from Galilee to Judea, they would go out of their way to walk around it. Jesus was asking the disciples to do what no self-respecting Jew would do—go to the hated Samaritans. Thus when he spoke these words, the disciples must have been aghast. (This same truth is key to understanding the parable of the Good Samaritan in Luke 10:30–35.)

What's the point? The church is to be Christ's witness to the community regardless of its ethnicity, or maybe I should say *in light of its* ethnicity. The church is to reach out to all peoples.

I've observed a growing heterogeneous blend of the races in a number of larger urban and suburban communities in America and around the world. An example would be the large number of Asians in California, Mexicans in Texas, Central Americans in southern Louisiana, and Cubans in Miami, just to name a few. Thus when the new church discovers who lives in its community, then it will need to plan strategically how it will reach all who live there, especially those of a different ethnicity from the church. I'll say more about this later in the chapter when I address church planting.

Strategizing to Reach the Community

Developing a strategy to reach the church's community is a three-step process that determines where the church's community is, who the community is, and how to reach the community.

Step 1: Where Is Your Community?

Mark 16:15 commands that we go into all the world. Therefore, in a sense, the whole world is our community. In Acts 1:8 Jesus breaks this down into somewhat smaller, "bite-size" communities. In that verse Jerusalem is the immediate community, Judea and Samaria the intermediate communities, and the ends of the earth is the international community. Thus if the church planter and his team believe this could prove helpful in their outreach, they could divide Mark's "world" into three kinds of communities.

IMMEDIATE COMMUNITY

The location of the planted church is its immediate or local community, and this is most important to its outreach strategy, which I'll return to and focus on shortly. I'll use my church—Lake Pointe Church located in Rockwall, Texas, a community near Dallas—as an example of how this might help. Our immediate community could be primarily the city of Rockwall. It could, but not necessarily, include several nearby cities and towns such as Heath, Mesquite, Garland, and Rowlett. The church would determine this based on their distance from Rockwall.

INTERMEDIATE COMMUNITY

A church's intermediate community could be nearby towns, cities, or counties, depending on their location and distance from the church. Lake Pointe has planted churches in several nearby towns and cities, which would make up our intermediate community.

INTERNATIONAL COMMUNITY

The rest of the world could be a church's international community. This community is furthest from the church. Lake Pointe's international community is the rest of the world where we've either planted or supported churches in China, Europe, Australia, Cuba, Russia, and several other countries.

The planted church will begin by discovering its immediate or local community and then eventually move out from there.

Kinds of Community

Immediate community (Jerusalem)
Intermediate community (Judea and Samaria)
International community (the ends of the earth)

DETERMINING YOUR CHURCH'S IMMEDIATE COMMUNITY

A church planter must determine where to locate the church in the immediate community. In the process, he should answer two questions: How long a distance will people drive to attend the new church, and how long are people willing to spend getting to the church? While the answer to either question could help determine the boundaries of your immediate community, I prefer to ask both and weigh the answers carefully.

We have some good research involving driving times that can help us determine the boundary of our local community. Dr. Win Arn conducted a national study in which he discovered that 20 percent of the people surveyed drove less than 5 minutes to get to church. Forty percent drove 5 to 15 minutes. Twenty-three percent drove 15 to 25 minutes, and 17 percent drove 25 minutes or more to get to church.[4] Thus 83 percent drove 25 minutes or less to church. The bulk—60 percent—drove from 5 to 15 minutes. You would think that these times would vary across America. However, in researching churches I've worked with, these figures prove amazingly accurate. Where I've seen a difference is in rural versus urban contexts. Those in urban and suburban settings have greater access to freeways and turnpikes. People in rural areas tend to want to drive a shorter distance because of the roads. Thus the church planter should drive out—using the times allotted above—and see how far you get.

Travel Time to Church

20 percent drove less than 5 minutes.
40 percent drove 5 to 15 minutes.
23 percent drove 15 to 25 minutes.
17 percent drove 25 minutes or more.

83 percent drove 25 minutes or less.
60 percent drove 15 minutes or less.

When I consult with churches, I always ask about their driving time and distance to the church. One reason is that the information is requested on the Church Analysis that I give them. The other is that they're reasonable indicators of the church's community boundaries. However, in some situations, I've used other methods to complement time and distance studies. On occasion I've used a church's zip code or zip codes, and found that they may set reasonable boundaries for the immediate community. And sometimes I'll use city limits or county lines to stake out the community.

Step 2: Who Is Your Community?

Step 1 precedes step 2 for a simple reason. You have to determine where your boundaries are before you can discover who lives there. Once you establish your local or immediate community, you're ready to "meet" them.

To accomplish this, you must realize the importance of knowing who the people are, discovering who they are, understanding who they are, and comparing who they are to who you are, the people who either make up or will likely make up the church plant.

THE IMPORTANCE OF KNOWING WHO THEY ARE

The reason you need to know the people in your community is because knowing them will help you to reach them for Christ. Several biblical passages are good examples of this. In 1 Corinthians 9:19–23 Paul expresses how he used his knowledge of people to win as many of them as possible. He says that to the Jews he became like a Jew, to those under the law he became like one under the law, to those not under law, he responded accordingly, and to the weak he became weak. He couldn't have done this had he not known something about them.

In Acts 2 Peter delivers a sermon to the Jews assembled in Jerusalem to celebrate Pentecost. Note that in this sermon he made a number of references to the Old Testament Scriptures. He knew his audience and that these references would be meaningful to them. In Acts 17:18–34 Paul preached to some pagan philosophers, reasoning with them about their own worship practices, rather than appealing to the Old Testament, which would have meant little to them. Again, he knew his audience.

DISCOVERING WHO THEY ARE

The way to discover who makes up your community involves collecting and analyzing demographic information concerning age, education, marital status, number of persons per household, number of owners and renters, number of women and men, race, household income, drive time to work, and lots of other information.

Demographics

Age
Average levels of education
Percentage of married people and singles
Number of persons per household
Percentage of owners and renters
Number of men and women
Predominant racial groups
Median household income
Drive time to work

Some sources for demographic information are the census (if you are doing your study at the beginning of a decade when the census has recently been done), denominational agencies (such as the Southern Baptists), professional groups (Buy Demographics.com and others), Thearda.com (church demographics), local government (city and county), utilities companies, and real estate agencies. You could also Google this information.

UNDERSTANDING WHO THEY ARE

Gathering psychographic information will help you understand the people in your Jerusalem. Whereas demographics looks at people from the outside, psychographics addresses the inside. This information reveals the hearts and minds of the people in your community. It helps you understand their values, what motivates them, and their perceptions of the church in general.

The problem with psychographics is obtaining information. Percept is the only organization I know of that provides such information (www.perceptnet .com). Otherwise, you collect it on your own by reading, asking questions, and getting involved. For example, while vacationing in San Francisco I heard this: "The church is a parasite. It owns the best property, pays no taxes, and helps no one." In an interview in Plano, Texas, someone said, "The church doesn't contribute anything to the community." Such comments, along with others you will hear concerning the church and other issues, give you an idea of what the people in the community are thinking.

COMPARING WHO THEY ARE WITH WHO YOU ARE

As you discover who the people are in your community, it's natural to compare them with those who are already part of your church. You'll discover that the church will attract those who have more in common with your people and may not attract those who have little in common. The more people feel you understand them, the more attracted they are to the group. They really believe that you can help them in their struggles, because you're like them demographically and are going through or have been through the same struggles. This is the reason it's important to do your research before settling on a location for your church. Consider who is already in your church plant and the kind of community they will attract. If you as the church planter feel led to reach a community that is different from you—ethnically, racially, social-economically, linguistically, or in some other obvious way—you should first recruit people to your church-planting team who are like those in the community and let them take the lead in reaching out to the community. It's also true that sometimes God calls people to win a community that is different from them.

Step 3: How Will You Reach Your Community?

When thinking about reaching your community, you need to answer three questions: How many people can we reach? What kind of church will it take? What kind of ministries will it take?

HOW MANY CAN YOU REACH?

The question of how many your church could reach is what I call a "vision size" question—what is the size of your vision? It also involves a "stretch goal." Here's an example of what I mean: What would happen if you challenged your people to win one person to Christ each year? You could call it Goal 1:1:1—each one reach one each year. Assume you start with one hundred people, how many would there be in five years? If each one reached one each year, then in year two you would be up to two hundred people, year three you would double to four hundred people, year four you would reach eight hundred, and in year five your total would be sixteen hundred people. Do the math and you can understand why some churches seem to explode with growth. This is the question I like to ask: Is this doable? I've never gotten a no answer yet.

WHAT KIND OF CHURCH WOULD IT TAKE?

What kind of church would it take to reach all these people? Rick Warren has said that it takes all kinds of churches to reach all kinds of people. What kind of church would it take to reach *your* community? Work your way through the following eight questions to find what kind of church it would take.

1. What kind of pastor would it take?
   - young, middle-aged, elderly?
   - educated, a gifted leader, someone with a passion for lost people?
   - a good preacher, creative and innovative?
   - married with a family?
2. What kind of staff would it take?
   - young, middle-aged, elderly?
   - educated?
   - with a gift for leadership?
   - of a specific ethnicity?
   - married with families?
   - with values, mission, and vision alignment?
   - supportive of the pastor?
3. What kind of people would it take?
   - welcoming, friendly, kind, accepting, warm?
   - multiethnic?
   - professional?
   - blue-collar?
   - easy to talk to?
4. What kind of worship?
   - traditional?
   - classical?
   - blended?
   - contemporary?
5. What kind of facilities?
   - clean, well kept?
   - with ample seating, ample parking, lots of education space?
6. What kind of ministries?
   - preschool, children?
   - youth, college?

- singles?
- adults?
7. What kind of technology?
   - high tech?
   - low tech?
8. What kind of response to seekers?
   - seeker driven?
   - seeker sensitive?
   - seeker tolerant?

Most important, how willing are you and your core leadership to change and become the kind of church it would take to reach your community? For saved people, most of these questions involve preference. For lost people, however, they involve eternal damnation (Rev. 20:10–15). Your answers to these questions have eternal consequences for the unchurched lost in your community.

What Kind of Ministries?

What kind of ministries will it take to reach your community? This question is different from the last question, which dealt more with inward-focused ministries. This one asks about outward-focused ministries, the kind that reach out and minister to your community. I'll cover five of them: prayer, community specific, evangelism, church planting, and multisite ministries.

Prayer Ministries

Prayer is the foundation for any and all ministries, so a prayer ministry for lost and dying communities is essential. Here are some prayer suggestions:

1. Take prayer walks through your community.
2. As you conduct demographics studies of the community, draw up a prayer map and pray for specific needy areas.
3. Draft a prayer team that prays specifically for reaching out and ministering to the community.

Community-Specific Ministries

Both Matthew 28:19 and Mark 16:15 challenge Christ's church to go! At the very least this would include involvement in the church's community. But what kind of ministries to the community could the church launch? Here are a few ideas:

1. Rent a theme park and invite police, firemen, soldiers, or teachers, and their families.
2. Allow the community to use your facilities for meetings.
3. Open an on-campus coffee shop, especially if you're located in an area where there are many businesses.

4. Start a sports league. (Upward Bound has been very popular among churches I've worked with.)
5. Offer marriage and family counseling.
6. Provide youth mentoring programs.
7. Offer after-school programs.
8. Volunteer as mentors in the public schools.
9. Offer life skills classes: managing money, raising children, time management, and others.
10. Offer common cause programs dealing with such issues as education, housing, mentoring, parenting.
11. Send inner-city kids to camp.
12. Serve at a soup kitchen.

Pastor Steve Sjogren provides numerous ways to serve the community in his seminal work *Conspiracy of Kindness* and on his website (www.servant evangelism.com).

PERSONAL EVANGELISM

The problem with the community-specific ministries is that while doing them we don't always use the opportunities that arise to share our faith with the community. I call it "pulling the trigger." There comes a point when in our service to the community we "pull the trigger" or share our faith. But some of our people don't know how to present the gospel to a lost person. We need to train people in evangelism. I suggest the following:

1. Help people discover their evangelism style. Is it confrontational, relational, invitational, intellectual, testimonial, or some other style?
2. Ask them to write the names of three lost people on a card and to begin praying for them daily.
3. Encourage them to memorize a plan to present the gospel. There are several good ones. I recommend "Roman's Road" or "Bad News–Good News."

Roman's Road
- All have sinned (Rom. 3:23)
- The wages of sin is death (Rom. 6:23)
- Christ died for our sins (Rom. 5:8)
- Accept Christ and be saved (Rom. 10:9–10)

Bad News–Good News
Bad News
- We're all sinners (Rom. 3:23)
- The punishment for sin is death (Rom. 6:23)

Good News
- Christ died for you (Rom. 5:8)
- You can be saved by faith in Christ (John 3:16)

4. Sometimes Christians spend time or fellowship only with other Christians. They call it separation from the world. Encourage your people to spend time with both Christians and non-Christians. Challenge them with this: if someone took a picture of their friends, would there be any lost faces in the picture? Suggest that they find a common interest (fishing, hunting, jogging, going to a museum, walking in the park) and invite the lost person to do it with them.
5. People should target their natural relationships. Who in the following groups are not Christians: family members, neighbors, co-workers? They should decide to spend time with these people and look for opportunities to share their faith.

Personal Evangelism

- Discover your evangelism style
- Pray for three lost people
- Memorize a plan to present the gospel
- Spend time with non-Christians
- Target your natural relationships

CHURCH PLANTING

One of the most effective means of reaching the community is church planting. Unless something is terribly wrong, planted churches are very evangelistic, far more so than the typical established church.

When you study demographic maps of your community, note those areas that are heavily populated with Anglos, Asians, Hispanics, African Americans, and other ethnic groups. Should you find that they show little interest in visiting your church, don't let this bother you. Remember that people feel most comfortable with others who are like them. We can't expect non-Christians to have Christian attitudes. If they won't come to you, then eventually you go to them. Come up with a strategic plan for establishing churches in the areas of your community that are populated by specific ethnic groups. Your goal is to plant churches that, in turn, plant churches, and you'll want to include ethnic churches in the mix.

MULTISITE CHURCHES

A recent development among churches is the multisite movement. This is another effective way to reach your community for Christ. Whereas church planting involves starting a new and likely different church from the sponsoring church, multisite churches are those that provide ministry in several places that is much the same as that of the initiating church. Simply stated, it's the same church in many locations. The advantage is that the primary church is no longer limited by its location or geography and this approach to doing church allows it to use fully all the features of the primary church. Thus the multisite approach will help your new church address lack-of-space issues and help you reach more people in your ministry community. A disadvantage is that it can be expensive because it may involve the purchase and remodeling of other church facilities.

I encourage a young church plant to consider and be open to becoming a multisite church in the future. You will find that this strategy is more doable later in the life of your church. Again, finances may be the deciding factor as to when you embrace a multisite outreach. But it is a great strategy for impacting a community, and perhaps God will do something to make it possible for you to pursue multisite campuses early in the planting stage. By all means keep it on your strategy back burner and be looking for opportunities that God may bring your way to pursue this approach to reaching your Jerusalem.

Ministries to Reach Your Community

Prayer ministries
Community-specific ministries
Personal evangelism
Church planting
Multisite churches

Communicating the Strategy for Reaching the Community

Again, as with the topics in the previous chapters, you need to have a plan to communicate your strategy for reaching the community. This will be the job of your church-planting communication team, who will use the following general communication plan as its primary tool.

1. What should be communicated?
2. Who should communicate it?
3. When should it be communicated?
4. How should it be communicated?
5. Where should it be communicated?
6. How often should it be communicated?
7. Why should it be communicated?

Concerning the strategy for reaching the community, the answers to the above questions would be:

1. The strategy for reaching your community should be communicated.
2. The lead church planter and any others involved in the leadership should communicate it.

3. The strategy for reaching your community should be communicated regularly or every time there is an opportunity.
4. It should be communicated in sermons, on a website, in a brochure, and other ways covered in previous chapters.
5. It should be communicated at any organizational meetings, worship services, new members classes, and in church literature.
6. It should be communicated regularly—weekly, monthly, and annually.
7. If your church is to accomplish your strategy for reaching the community, people need to know and understand what it is. Remember that good communication builds trust, and this is vital in leadership.

How to Strategize to Reach Your Community

Answer the following strategic questions:
Step 1: Where is your community?
Step 2: Who is your community?
Step 3: How will you reach your community?

Questions for Reflection and Discussion

1. Do you believe that community as explained by the author is important? Why or why not?
2. Do you agree with the author's definition of community? If not, how would you define it? What are some of the elements that make up community?
3. The author pointed to two passages that address the church's responsibility to its community—Matthew 28:19 and Mark 16:15. What do they contribute to this discussion?
4. What are the geographical and ethnological implications of Acts 1:8?
5. Do you find the author's use of *immediate, intermediate,* and *international community* helpful? Why or why not?
6. How far or how long do you think people will drive to get to your church? Based on this information, what might be the soft boundaries of your community?
7. Who lives in your community? Have you driven through your community? What do demographics tell you about your community? Are they accurate based on personal contact?
8. Concerning the author's suggestions, which ministries would help you reach out and minister to your community?

10

What Is the Goal?

Making Disciples

This strategy chapter focuses on the church planter's goal for reaching the community. We found earlier in this book that the goal or mission of the church is to make disciples. However, this goal raises at least three important questions for church planters. First, does or will your new church have a clear, simple, memorable pathway for making disciples? My experience is that most churches don't. And this is most surprising in light of Jesus's clear command to make disciples.

The second question is, How is the church doing at making disciples? In an attempt to answer this question, church consultant Bob Gilliam developed a "Spiritual Journey Evaluation" that he gave to four thousand attendees in thirty-five churches in several denominations scattered from Florida to Washington.[1] He learned that most people in these churches aren't growing spiritually. Of those taking the survey, 24 percent said that their behavior was sliding backwards and 41 percent said they were static in their spiritual growth. Gilliam believes this is because most churches aren't intentional about making disciples and that the churches on his survey are normative.[2] I believe the most important reason is they don't know how.

Gilliam offers six reasons for the failure of churches to make disciples, the first four of which are key to my strategy for making mature disciples. (The last two reasons that I'll not address here are: leaders aren't model disciples and

137

reproduce after their kind, and leaders don't know how to become intentional without splitting their churches.)[3] Here are the four key reasons:

1. Their leaders don't know what a disciple looks like.
2. They don't know how to make a disciple even if they can define one.
3. They don't know how church programs work together to make disciples.
4. They have no way to measure progress.

The third question concerning the goal of making disciples is, Are churches that aren't making disciples healthy? If not, are they doing more harm than good? Could they be more of a threat to people's spiritual health than a help? In short, are these toxic churches? If the answers are yes, then we now have a better understanding of why the church is in decline in North America and Europe.

Therefore the focus of this chapter is how to strategize to make mature disciples. This is a most important question for church planters if they want to develop a clear, simple pathway for making disciples; avoid the errors of the churches that took Gilliam's survey; and not become toxic churches.

The process that I will present in this chapter is a five-step strategy.

Step 1: Articulate Christ's Mission for the Church

As I've already stated, the mission of the church is to make disciples (evangelism) and mature them (edification). In the last chapter I gave some information about evangelizing the community. In this chapter I want to emphasize the goal of spiritual maturity. Thus your church will need to set up a process whereby it assists people in moving along a continuum from prebirth (preconversion) to the new birth (conversion) and on to growth and maturity. The ultimate goal is the spiritual maturing of the saints (Col. 1:28–29; Heb. 5:11–6:1).

Prebirth	New Birth	Maturity
Lost	∧	Saved and growing

At this point I hope you have already developed a mission statement for your new church. I've provided a number of them for your scrutiny in appendix N. If you have not developed your mission, I would suggest that you put this book aside and craft your statement before reading any further. Your mission statement will be key to your understanding of the rest of this chapter.

Step 2: Identify the Characteristics of a Mature Disciple

This step involves asking and answering two vital questions: What are the characteristics of a mature disciple? and How will you communicate them to your people so they will remember them?

Characteristics of a Mature Disciple

I believe that there are at least five core characteristics of a mature Christian. Actually there are numerous characteristics, but for memory and communication purposes, I've reduced them to the following: mature Christians are involved in worship, fellowship, Bible study, evangelism, and service or ministry. I would argue that a believer who is authentically involved in these has arrived at some stage of maturity in the sanctification process.

These should look familiar, because I have already identified them as the five functions and the essential core values of the church. I believe that most if not all the characteristics of maturity fit under one of these five basic characteristics. For example, I've not listed prayer and giving, but I would place both under worship. And I would place the ordinance of baptism under evangelism and that of the Lord's Supper under worship. This should give you an idea of how this works. If you differ with my list, then I would encourage you to study the Scriptures and arrive at your own list of characteristics. However, for the sake of clarity, I will use my list in this chapter.

Communicating the Characteristics

How do we communicate these characteristics so people won't forget them? There are several good ways. Here are a few:

1. My experience has been that most people can remember the characteristics as I've stated them above: worship, fellowship, Bible study, evangelism, and ministry. (Or if people need an aid to jog their memory, use the terms *worship, instruction, fellowship, evangelism, service,* with their acronym WIFES.)
2. Some churches—especially Boomer churches—seem to like alliteration. For example, you could use the five Cs (or other letters) that represent these same characteristics: celebration (worship), community (fellow-

ship), cultivation (Bible study), conversion (evangelism), and contribution (service).

3. A word could be chosen to represent spiritual maturity, with each letter
   of the word standing for one characteristic. One church I worked with
   has the word *grace* in their name, so they built their maturity characteristics using the letters in the word *grace*. The G stood for grow (Bible
   study), the R for reach out (evangelism), the A for act (ministry), the C
   for connect (fellowship), and the E for exalt (worship).

Step 3: Determine the Discipleship Pathway

Now that we've identified the characteristics of a mature disciple, the next step
is to craft a clear, simple pathway for helping people develop those characteristics. This pathway consists of the new church's primary or most important
ministries that you expect your people to attend each week if they are to
mature as disciples.

To accomplish this step you need to address each of the following:

1. Understanding the church's proper role in maturing disciples.
2. Determining which of the church's ministries are most important to
   making mature disciples. These are its primary ministries.
3. Understanding how to use the church's primary ministries to develop
   the characteristics of maturity in disciples.

Understanding the Church's Role

As we look at the development of mature disciples, we must not overlook
the important role that God plays. It is the task of God the Holy Spirit to
transform us into the likeness of Christ (2 Cor. 3:18).

If the Christian is to become a mature disciple, he or she must be fully
committed to the process. This is personal and individual, as each Christian
takes responsibility for his or her individual spiritual growth and maturation.
This means that the believer can never legitimately blame the church for his or
her lack of growth. While the church may not help appreciably, the primary
one to blame for lack of maturity is the believer.

The role of the church in helping Christians mature is public and corporate.
To mature as disciples, Christians need others in the body (1 Cor. 12:12–31),
because we mature in community. I count at least fifty-nine verses in the Bible
that tell us we need one another. Thus the role of the church is to come alongside
and help the Christian accomplish spiritual maturation. This is so important
that I will focus on it in the rest of this chapter.

The church must determine which ministries best enable its people to internalize the characteristics of maturity. These are both primary and secondary ministries.

PRIMARY MINISTRIES

There are seven reasons that the church's primary ministries are critical to making mature believers:

1. They are the core ingredients that make up the church's pathway for developing mature disciples.
2. They mark the essentials for disciple making, and, therefore, the people are expected not just to attend but to participate in them.
3. They are limited in number, because you can do only a few ministries well—and less really is more!
4. They reflect spiritual momentum or progress toward maturity as indicated by the believer's authentic participation in each of the primary ministries.
5. They focus ministry energy on what's really important—the ministries that are essential to disciple making.
6. They focus ministry resources, such as time and money, on what's most important.
7. They reflect how people are assimilated into the life of the church. For example, people may attend the worship service first, next a small group, and so on.

What might these primary ministries look like in a church context? The following church models and their primary ministries will serve to further clarify and illustrate the primary ministries. As a church planter you need to be aware of various church models and the primary ministries they've embraced. I encourage you to study these ministries and see if there are any you might include in your church. Perhaps you'll adopt the primary ministries of one of them. Or you might combine the ministries of several models and come up with a unique blend of your own that fits your culture, who you are, and where you're located.

TRADITIONAL CHURCHES

First is the traditional church model, which has been around for at least a century, maybe longer, depending on how you define it. And most contemporary churches have modeled themselves after it in one way or another. Some of us refer to its primary ministries as the "three-to-thrive" model. Believers are expected to come to the church's worship service and Sunday school on Sunday morning. Then they are to return Sunday evening for what may be another preaching and worship event. And finally, they are to return on Wednesday night for a prayer meeting or similar gathering. This is very common in Baptist churches. Of course there are traditional churches that function differently that are mainline churches and liturgical churches. They tend to have one primary service that involves the liturgy and a homily.

SEEKER CHURCHES

Seeker churches, such as Willow Creek Community Church, usually have four primary ministries. On Sunday morning they have a seeker service where members bring their lost, unchurched friends to hear the gospel in a clear, understandable format. There is often what is called a new community service that's primarily for the benefit of believers. For example, once a person accepts Christ, he or she attends the midweek new community service to become grounded in the truths of Scripture. Also Willow Creek expects its believers to become intimately involved in its small-groups program. And they help people discover their divine design (gifts, passions, and temperaments) and expect them to become actively involved in ministry.

PURPOSE-DRIVEN CHURCHES

Saddleback Community Church represents the purpose-driven church model. It has four primary ministries. The first is what they refer to as bridge events with the purpose of connecting the church to the community. Some examples are Christmas Eve services, Easter services, and concerts. Their seeker service is much like Willow Creek's and takes place on the weekends. Their small groups meet for fellowship, personal care, and to gain a sense of belonging to the church. And their Life Development Institute offers a wide variety of ways to grow spiritually, such as its classes 101, 201, 301, and 401. They also include a midweek service for believers that they place under life development. Perhaps the midweek service is a fifth primary ministry, depending on whether they expect their people to attend this service.

FELLOWSHIP BIBLE CHURCHES

God has wonderfully used Gene Getz to plant and raise up the Fellowship Bible Church movement. While some of these churches are located around the country, they're concentrated in Dallas, Texas, and Little Rock, Arkansas. The Fellowship Bible Church model consists of two primary ministries—the Sunday morning preaching-worship event, when the pastor teaches the Bible and people worship; and the small-group ministry that provides for fellowship, sharing, and personal spiritual intimacy.

BIBLE FELLOWSHIP CHURCHES

I like to include the Bible Fellowship model because it has spread across America and has been embraced by my church. Usually these churches have three primary ministries. There is a Sunday morning worship and preaching session. And the Adult Bible Fellowship (ABF) ministry, which ranges in size from five to fifteen or twenty people, functions basically like a small church.

The teachers teach, visit their members in the hospital, and follow up on those with needs in their fellowship, among other things. Another ministry is the gathering of those in the ABF (often a few men with men, and a few women with women) for fellowship and other purposes.

OPTIONAL CHURCH MODELS

Optional church models are churches that may have several primary ministries. They all seem to have the preaching-worship event in common. However, they allow some options for the other primary ministries. For example, their second primary ministry may be a Sunday school class or a small-group ministry. They expect their people to opt for one or the other but allow them to choose. This model has worked well for churches with both older and younger people in attendance. Generally the older people prefer Sunday school and the younger prefer the small group.

Pastor Jeff Gilmore, my friend and former classmate at Dallas Seminary, has embraced this model at Parkview Evangelical Free Church in Iowa City, Iowa. The reason is that the University of Iowa is located there, and he has a sizable contingency not only of older people but of younger people as well, many of whom are students.

Now that you are familiar with a number of church models and their primary ministries, pray about and determine what your primary ministries will be. They will form your disciple-making pathway.

SECONDARY MINISTRIES

The primary ministries of the church, and not the secondary ministries, are most critical to maturing disciples. It is these ministries in which the church expects its people to participate. The church's secondary ministries are electives. If properly designed, they can address particular problems that believers may be facing during certain seasons of their lives. Sometimes we need a temporary shot in the arm that secondary ministries can supply.

In most churches there are numerous secondary ministries, especially in larger churches, because people believe that if you offer more options, you'll attract more people. A few examples of secondary ministries are men's and women's Bible studies, emotional and spiritual counseling, marital counseling, a child-raising seminar, courses on financial management, the annual Easter and Christmas programs, twelve-step programs, divorce recovery, Mother's Day Out, a Christian school, choir, vacation Bible school, sports programs, Awana, blood drives, health fairs, and food pantry.

The purpose of secondary ministries is to support in some way the primary ministries but not replace them. If you find that your people prefer being involved in a secondary ministry, it may say something about the quality of that ministry. Perhaps you need to evaluate and improve a primary ministry or two.

For example, if men or women prefer to attend a Bible study over a worship service with preaching, the preaching may not be deep enough.

DISADVANTAGES

The secondary ministries have several disadvantages. One is that they can detract from the primary ministries. Like the barnacles on a ship, they can impede the progress of the primary ministries by distracting people from them. When people prefer to attend one of the secondary ministries, they may get sidetracked in their quest for maturity.

Also secondary ministries can increase the complexity of the church program. A new believer or other visitor may be confused when he or she sees all the ministries that the church offers. The person may not know what to attend and what is okay to miss. Churches should strive to be simple and not confusing and this calls for fewer secondary ministries.

Another disadvantage is that these ministries diffuse ministry energy, often sapping energy from the primary ministries. And the church can get stuck, trying to do too many things for God rather than the few things it needs to do well.

SUGGESTIONS

The planted church has a real advantage over established ones because it doesn't yet have secondary ministries that have become sacred cows for some in the church. My suggestion is that you be slow to start such ministries. Put in place certain requirements, such as not to expect staff involvement in secondary ministries or fund-raising, and the leaders of any proposed new ministry needs to be involved in the church's leadership development ministry.

Using the Primary Ministries to Make Mature Disciples

Now that we've identified the church's primary or best ministries for making its disciples, we need to know how it can use these ministries to develop the characteristics of maturity in growing disciples. Earlier in this chapter I listed the five characteristics of a mature disciple—being involved in worship, fellowship, Bible study, evangelism, and service. Then we looked at various primary ministries that make up the church's clear, simple pathway of discipleship. In this section I want to return to the characteristics and show you how they work together with the primary ministries to lead a believer and ultimately the church to maturity. To accomplish this I will introduce you to the maturity matrix. It's a tool I've developed to help churches see and make the connection between their primary ministries and their characteristics of maturity. It should prove invaluable in crafting your new church's strategy or process for forming mature disciples.

THE MATURITY MATRIX

The maturity matrix consists of a horizontal and a vertical axis. You can create your own matrix by drawing a horizontal line, as in the first figure below, across a piece of paper or even a napkin if you happen to be in Starbucks; then write your characteristics on that line. Draw a vertical line, connecting at the left side of the horizontal line. Write your primary ministries along the vertical line. Draw lines, forming columns and rows of boxes that correspond to the various characteristics and ministries you listed. What you should see is a matrix much like that in the second figure below.

Maturity Matrix

Characteristics of Maturity

Primary Ministries

Characteristics of Maturity

	Worship	Fellowship	Bible Study	Evangelism	Ministry
Worship/ Preaching Service					
Sunday School					
Small Group					

Primary Ministries

THE DIAGNOSIS

Now you want to determine if your proposed disciple-maturing process is sound. Does it do a good job in connecting the ministries with the characteristics of maturity? To do this, work your way down through your primary ministries. Look at the list of characteristics and determine which one each ministry should foster, then place a check mark in the corresponding box. For example, ask which characteristic(s) the worship-preaching ministry is designed to incorporate into the life of the disciple. Obviously the answer is worship and likely biblical instruction. If your next ministry is a small group, determine which characteristic(s) you want it to help foster and place a check mark under it. Most likely the answer is fellowship. The goal is that after you've worked through all the primary ministries, all the characteristics are checked.

What happens when you complete this exercise and a characteristic or two is not checked? (Typically *evangelism* and *service* are the ones that aren't checked.) Then you must either add a ministry that encourages the development of the characteristic or assign it to one of your existing ministries. Let's assume that your matrix is similar to the second figure above and has three primary ministries—worship, Sunday school, and small groups. Suppose that after you check off the characteristics, you note that *evangelism* and *service* aren't checked. A good option is to build into either your Sunday school or small groups, or both, some ways for these characteristics to be developed. For example, the Sunday school class and/or small group could adapt ongoing evangelistic and ministry projects as a group. They might share their faith at a local community center and minister in the children's ministry once or twice a month. The advantage of doing these as a group is that they can encourage and hold one another accountable.

Step 4: Communicate Your Disciple-Making Ministries

Once you've developed your disciple-making strategy and evaluated it using the maturity matrix, you're ready to communicate it to those who'll become part of the church plant. This is the responsibility of the church planter and his communication team.

Develop a Communication Plan

First, as with the core values, mission, and vision, you should develop a plan to communicate your disciple-maturing strategy by using the general communication plan. Here are the questions to ask:

1. What should be communicated?
2. Who should communicate it?
3. When should it be communicated?
4. How should it be communicated?
5. Where should it be communicated?
6. How often should it be communicated?
7. Why should it be communicated?

The answers, as they relate to the disciple-making strategy are:

1. The disciple-making strategy should be communicated.
2. The lead church planter and any others involved in the leadership should communicate it.

3. It should be communicated regularly or every time there is an opportunity.

4. The disciple-making strategy should be communicated in sermons, on a website, in a brochure, in classes, and so on.

5. It should be communicated in any organizational meetings, worship services, new members classes, church literature, and so forth.

6. It should be communicated regularly—weekly, monthly, and at least annually.

7. If you want your people to become mature disciples, you need to communicate the role the church will play in seeing that this happens. Remember that good communication builds trust and this is vital in leadership.

Use Visuals

Some churches have used visual objects effectively to communicate their strategies and their primary ministries.

For instance, Andy Stanley, who pastors North Pointe Church near Atlanta, Georgia, uses the rooms of a house to illustrate and explain his ministries that lead one to maturity. They actually build on stage a house that contains three rooms. Each room represents a vital ministry of the church. For example, the foyer corresponds to the worship service, the living room corresponds with Bible study events, and the kitchen corresponds with the church's small-groups ministry. Each room elicits an emotion that is felt in the various ministries.

Other visuals that you could design to illustrate your ministries are an apple (the skin, flesh, and core), some base paths (the four bases in baseball), a stool

(its legs), and a tree (the leaves, branches, and roots). Again, the only limit is your ability to come up with some new, creative images.

Step 5: Measure Progress in Making Disciples

At this point in the process, you've developed your church's disciple-making strategy, but how will you know if it's making disciples? The answer is to measure your congregation's progress. Remember, what you measure is what you get! Or another way to say it is, what gets measured, gets done. I suggest two ways to measure your progress. One is to count heads and the other is to conduct a spiritual inventory.

Count Heads Regularly

You may be uncomfortable with counting heads. You've attended or heard stories about churches that did this to excess. All you heard about were the numbers. However, you shouldn't allow the abuse of numbers to detract you from gathering such information. As we've seen in the book of Acts, Luke counted heads (Acts 2:41; 4:4) to discern how the Jerusalem Church was progressing in crafting its disciples. Let's face it, the old adage "People vote with their feet" is true. If your ministries aren't reaching and transforming people, they'll stop attending and look elsewhere.

I would literally count heads and track the number of people at each primary ministry. And I would do this weekly. You could set up the following chart for the three vital ministries.

Attendance Chart

Primary Ministry	Date	Date	Date	Date	Date	Date	Date
Worship/Preaching							
Sunday School							
Small Groups							

Conduct a Spiritual Inventory Annually

A problem with counting heads is that it may not accurately reflect how your people are progressing spiritually. Do numbers alone validate our strategy for making disciples? The honest answer has to be, not always. In facing this problem, Willow Creek Community Church developed the Spiritual Life Survey found on page 149. They gave the survey to those attending their church. They asked people to identify where they were in their spiritual life, using four stages: exploring Christ, growing in Christ, feeling close to Christ, and being Christ-centered. (I explain these briefly below.) They believe that while no tool is perfect, this survey has served them well in reading where their people are spiritually.[4]

I challenge you to look this tool over, make any corrections you feel are necessary, and plan to use it with your people. Annually you could survey your congregation during a worship service or you could do it online. Continue to tweak the survey if necessary until you and your leaders feel that it really measures the congregation's spiritual development.

Spiritual Life Survey

Which of the following statements best describes you?

1. **Exploring Christ**
   "I believe in God, but I'm not sure about Jesus. My faith isn't a significant part of my life."
2. **Growing in Christ**
   "I believe in Jesus and am working on what it means to get to know him."
3. **Feeling close to Christ**
   "I feel really close to Jesus and depend on him daily for guidance."
4. **Being Christ-centered**
   "My relationship with Jesus is the most important relationship in my life. It influences everything I do."

Developing a Strategy to Make Disciples

Step 1: Articulate Christ's mission for the church.
Step 2: Identify the characteristics of a mature disciple.
Step 3: Determine the discipleship pathway.
Step 4: Communicate your disciple-making ministries.
Step 5: Measure progress in making disciples.

Questions for Reflection and Discussion

1. Do you agree with the author's view that few churches are making disciples? Why or why not?
2. Do you find Bob Gilliam's findings helpful in understanding why churches aren't making disciples?
3. Are churches that aren't making disciples causing more harm than good? Explain your answer.
4. Do you sense the need for churches to craft clear, simple, memorable strategies for making disciples? Why?
5. Do you agree with the author's characteristics of a mature disciple? If not, what are your characteristics?
6. The author argues that the individual Christian, not the church, is responsible for his or her spiritual growth. Do you agree? If not, why not? Who then is responsible?

7. Is breaking down the church's ministries into two categories—primary and secondary—helpful? Does it make sense? Why or why not?

8. Why is it important that you use your ministries to develop characteristics of maturity? Would the maturity matrix help you accomplish this? Have you tried it yet? If so, what was the result?

11

Who Will Implement the Goal?

Mobilizing a Congregational Team

The new church's strategy consists of five components that address five strategic issues. As we've looked at strategy so far, we have seen that the first component is community outreach, which identifies who the new church will reach. The second is disciple making, which identifies how it will reach or what it will do for that community. The third strategy component—the team who will make disciples of the community—will be explored in this chapter and the next. The team consists potentially of three groups that comprise the entire new church. They are the congregation, the staff, and possibly a governing board. I will give information to help you develop a strategy for building these teams, specifically the congregation and staff teams.

The purpose of this chapter is to help you create a strategy for mobilizing your congregation for ministry. Your congregation consists of people. And Peter Drucker observes, "People determine the performance capacity of an organization. No organization can do better than the people it has."[1]

How do you strategize to mobilize the people you have? The answer is to take the following six steps.

Step 1: Grasp the Importance of Mobilizing Your Congregation

If a new church doesn't value mobilizing its people, it simply won't happen. Therefore it's imperative that I address *nine* reasons mobilization is so important to the new ministry.

1. *Mobilization clarifies who in the body of Christ is in the ministry* and is responsible for accomplishing the church's ministry. Many established churches believe that the pastor and any staff are responsible for accomplishing ministry. As we will discover in this chapter, Scripture teaches that everyone in the church is involved.
2. *Mobilization moves the congregation from sitting to serving.* It involves people in the church's ministry. The story is told of how someone once asked former Oklahoma football coach Bud Wilkenson how he would describe the game of football. His answer was that football is a game that involves eighty thousand fans, sitting in a stadium, who desperately need exercise, while there are twenty-two players out on the field who desperately need rest. What an accurate description of ministry in far too many of today's churches—most of the people in the church are just watching ministry take place. The goal of mobilization is to get the fans out of the stands and onto the ministry playing field.
3. *Mobilization increases giving.* Several years ago I came across some research on congregational mobilization that indicated that people who are involved in ministry tend to support the church more than those who aren't. A reason for this is that they value and believe in what the church is doing with the result that they're willing to get behind and support it financially.
4. *Mobilization increases ministry.* There are two reasons for this. First, people discover their divine design or how God has gifted them to do ministry. And second, people discover their direction in life—God's will or what he wants them to do with their life—and this results in their getting more involved in their ministry.
5. *Mobilization provides lay leadership.* It cultivates needed leadership for the church. I've never come across a church that would dare put the message "No leaders needed" on its sign. Leadership is the hope of the church, and it's the church's ministries that bring these leaders to light. Their involvement in ministry clarifies who they are and brings them to the surface.
6. *Mobilization raises up future staff.* Ministry encourages and surfaces leaders who will become future staff. I believe that the dream of every church in general and pastors in particular should be to raise up ministry staff from the congregation. And it's in the context of

such ministry that a person senses and experiences God's leading to full-time ministry.

7. *Mobilization lightens the staff's load*, making ministry easier for the staff. Most churches tend to be understaffed. Consequently, when people are properly involved in ministry, it frees staff up to lead and equip them rather than having to do most of the ministry themselves.

8. *Mobilization brings God's blessing.* We have a great God who enjoys blessing his children as much as a father or mother does. Good things happen to those who serve God. These blessings may be protection from danger, a good marriage and family life, a fulfilling job, finances, and even fertility, according to the Old Testament. While some who minister may not experience any of these blessings, all will experience a closer walk with God and his peace and joy.

9. *Mobilization promotes spiritual maturity.* A properly mobilized church is a spiritually mature church. In fact this may be the most important reason biblically. According to Ephesians 4:11–13, God has gifted those in the body of Christ to do his ministry. And the result is the building up or maturing of the church. The reverse of this is that those churches that have few people involved in ministry are not and will not mature. And this indicates they've missed God's ultimate purpose or goal for the church.

Why Mobilization Is Important

Clarifies who's in the ministry
Moves the congregation from sitting to serving
Increases giving
Increases ministry
Provides lay leadership
Raises up future staff
Lightens the staff's load
Brings God's blessing
Promotes spiritual maturity

Step 2: Understand the Problem

The primary problem in mobilizing a congregation is what I refer to as the *church's unemployment problem*. The majority of people aren't involved or aren't properly involved in the life and ministries of their church.

The Pareto principle addresses this. It's also known as the 80-20 rule. When applied to the church, it says that only 20 percent are involved in 80 percent of the church's ministries. I have observed that this has been the case with most of the established churches I've worked with.

I know of at least six reasons why people aren't involved.

1. A faulty recruitment process is used that is based on emotion and coercion.
2. The leadership has a lack of knowledge as to how to mobilize the congregation for ministry.
3. Some people are waiting for a personal invitation for involvement.
4. Some pastors feel threatened when laypersons are involved in ministry.
5. Many people are simply too busy doing things outside the church.
6. Most congregations are convinced that ministry is the pastor's job.

While all of these reasons are important, I would like to focus on the last reason, because I believe it has the deepest ramifications for Christ's church. There are several reasons congregations believe that ministry is the responsibility of the pastor and his staff. Here are six of them:

1. *The staff is trained to do ministry.* Many on church staffs have been to seminary or have experienced other training to prepare them for ministry.
2. *The staff is ordained to do ministry.* Many churches recognize their full-time staff by ordaining them to the ministry, which allows them to do ministries that laypersons think they can't, such as weddings and funerals.
3. *The staff has been called to the ministry.* Many believe that for one to pursue ministry, he or she must experience a special God-given call to that ministry and that God doesn't call those who are content with being laypersons.
4. *The staff is paid to do ministry.* As one old-timer said to his pastor, "That's what we pay *you* for!"
5. *God doesn't use laypersons in the way he uses staff.* When people feel this way, it's not unusual for them to call on the pastor to pray at a potluck meal or to bless their endeavors at the church. They really believe that God hears the prayers of the pastor and values them more than the prayers of the congregation.
6. *The final reason is the most important one.* How many times have we heard: "We've always done it that way"?

You may ask, "So what?" The *so what* is that Satan has used what amounts to a lie to cripple the church around the world and especially in North America. If businesses operated this way, they would quickly go out of business. And according to the latest statistics, the church *is* going out of business. It has been brought to its knees—not in prayer but in overwhelming ministry ineffectiveness.

Step 3: Embrace the Biblical Solution

The good news in the midst of all this bad news is that there's a solution to the unemployment problem, and it's a biblical solution. So what does the Bible teach about who's to do the ministry? Scripture teaches that God has called all believers—congregants as well as staff—to the ministry. I use the term *call* here not in the sense of a special, subjective call from God to the ministry. Perhaps I should use the term *will*. Scripture teaches that it is *God's will* that all be involved in ministry.

1. The call to salvation is a call to service (Rom. 8:28–30; Eph. 2:8–10).
2. In a sense every member is a minister or, better, a priest. This is the biblical teaching of the priesthood of the believer (1 Peter 2:5; Rev. 1:6; 5:10). All are believer priests who serve God.
3. God has given each of us a unique divine design with which to do ministry (Job 10:9–10; Ps. 139:15). This design consists of spiritual gifts (Rom. 12:6–8; 1 Cor. 12:27–31; Eph. 4:11–13; 1 Peter 4:10–11), as well as our natural gifts (1 Cor. 12:4), our passions, and our temperaments.
4. God has given all of us the indwelling Holy Spirit to empower us to do the ministry (Eph. 3:16, 20).
5. God has blessed the body with various gifts to equip all in the body for ministry (Eph. 4:11–13).

This leaves us with a question. If we're all called to do the ministry, what is the role of the church's pastor and staff? Does Scripture address this? I believe that the Bible teaches that there's the office of pastor. I'm convinced that the elders mentioned in the Bible were the first-century pastors of house churches, who taught (1 Tim. 3:2; 5:17), protected (Acts 20:28), and led their churches (1 Tim. 3:4–5; 5:17).

I don't see any biblical references to a church staff, at least as we know them today. However, that doesn't prohibit us from forming staff teams. Absence of proof isn't proof of absence. And Scripture gives us freedom in these areas. I suspect that the only biblical requirement for staff persons is that they not take the privilege of doing the ministry away from their congregation. I'll say more about the role staff could play in the next chapter on building the staff team.

Step 4: Envision a Fully Mobilized Congregation

In light of all that the Bible teaches about ministry and the biblical role of the congregation, what would a church look like if it obeyed Scripture and mobilized its people to do the ministry? That's a vision question. Remember that vision is what you see, the ministry snapshot you get when you picture your new church five, ten, fifteen years from now.

Envision what your new church would look like if people with leadership gifts were leading, people with teaching gifts were teaching, people with shepherding gifts were shepherding, people with helping gifts were helping, people with the gift of encouragement were encouraging, people with evangelism gifts were evangelizing, and people with administration gifts were doing administration. What you would see is a biblically based, spiritually healthy, mature church.

When I work with established churches on congregational mobilization, I like to show two videos from my church that help them grasp such a vision. The first is a video of an older lady who not only exudes tremendous enthusiasm as she does ministry, but can't understand why people aren't more excited about and involved in their church's ministries. The second is a video of an attorney who has so invested his life in doing ministry among our Hispanic church population that he's learned Spanish to be more effective.

Step 5: Design a Process

You can teach what the Bible says about mobilizing the congregation and you can envision it all you want. However, if you don't have a process in place to mobilize your people, it can't and won't happen. And if you don't prepare for putting a good process in place, you will never get to the point of mobilization. You'll need to recruit someone to take the lead in this process. If you prefer a staff person, then it would be the staff person responsible for ministry or service. However, as a new church, if you don't yet have any staff persons, you could use a layperson. This person would need to recruit some volunteers to form a mobilization team.

Then you need to determine who will go through the mobilization process. The answer is everyone. Why would a person not want to be involved? My church has made involvement a requirement for membership. We set high expectations for our members, and ministry involvement is one of them. We've learned that what you expect is what you get.

Finally, determine the length of the process. How much time will the mobilization process take? For each individual it will probably take four or five hours of training. And it should be an ongoing part of the new church's life.

I suggest that you develop a mobilization process that consists of three phases: a discovery phase, a consulting phase, and a placement phase.

Phase 1: Discovery

The discovery phase involves explaining the divine design concept, explaining the 3Ds (divine design, direction, and development—described in chapter

2), and asking people to take assessment tools, such as a spiritual gifts inventory, a passion audit, and a temperament indicator. It should take around two hours to accomplish this phase and could be done in a group context.

Phase 2: Consulting

In the consulting phase the mobilization leader reviews with the individual the results of the tools, confirming or validating the findings, and answering any questions. Based on the person's gifts and aptitudes, the leader helps the individual discover his or her ministry direction or how he or she might best serve God in the church. For example, if the person has gifts of leadership and teaching, God wants the person to lead and teach, and the person should be connected with a church-related ministry. This phase would take from two to three hours and could be accomplished one-on-one.

Phase 3: Placement

In phase 3 the mobilization leader encourages the individual to select a potential ministry from those discussed in phase 2. It would be a ministry that complements the believer's divine design, something the person is wired for. If there are two or three ministry positions in the new church that fit the person's design, he or she might want to follow up all of them.

After the person has chosen a particular ministry, he or she will need training. This would likely involve a brief internship with someone who is experienced in the same ministry and is good at it. This could be someone in the church that is sponsoring the church plant or someone at another church in the community. Then encourage the person to embrace and assume the ministry.

Mobilization

Phase 1: Discovery	*Phase* 2: Consulting	*Phase* 3: Placement

Step 6: Communicate the Vision for Mobilizing Your Congregation

You can thoroughly understand the biblical teaching on congregational mobilization and you can have an outstanding plan in place; however, if people don't know about it, they won't be a part of it. As we've seen in previous chapters, this is a matter of communication. The communication team must cast the vision of mobilization using the communication plan.

How to Mobilize Your Congregation for Ministry

Step 1: Grasp the importance of mobilizing your congregation.

Step 2: Understand the problem of mobilizing your congregation.

Step 3: Embrace the biblical solution for mobilizing your congregation.

Step 4: Envision a congregation fully mobilized for ministry.

Step 5: Design a process for mobilizing your congregation.

Step 6: Communicate your vision for mobilizing your congregation.

Questions for Reflection and Discussion

1. Are you convinced that mobilizing your congregation is important? Why or why not? What do you believe is the most important reason for doing it?
2. Why are some congregants not involved in ministry?
3. What does the Bible teach about who's to do ministry? What are the roles of the pastor and the staff?
4. Envision what it would look like if most of your future congregants were mobilized for ministry. What do you see?
5. What kind of process will you put together to mobilize your congregation for the ministry?

12

Who Will Equip the Implementers?

Building a Staff Team

The previous chapter and this one deal with the third component of the strategy—the team that will make disciples in the community. This team consists of two groups that comprise the new church. They are the congregation and staff. (I recommend that later you add a governing board to the team.) The purpose of chapter 11 was to develop the team by helping you create a strategy to mobilize your congregation for ministry. The purpose of this chapter is to create a strategy that will help you build your staff team. There are twelve steps to take when building your staff team.

Step 1: Recognize the Importance of the Staff

Initially you as lead pastor or church planter may be the only staff the new church has. However, you would be wise to recruit a church-planting staff team. Valerie Calderon writes, "Ninety percent of struggling plants started with only one person. Eighty-eight percent of fast-growing church plants have teams."[1] They will be important to your future growth and success as a new church and can make or break your ministry. A characteristic of many if not all the churches that God seems to be blessing across America is an excellent staff.

We're all privy to stories of staff meltdowns that have devastated churches and left multiple scars. Gary McIntosh stresses the importance of the staff when he writes, "Research in the field of business suggests that the cost of a bad hire—in lost time, money, and customers—can be three to five times the employee's salary."[2] Though your staff will most likely raise their own support, still the impact they have on the ministry is substantial. In the last chapter I quoted Peter Drucker, who said, "People determine the performance capacity of an organization. No organization can do better than the people it has."[3] Not only is this true of the congregation, it's true of the staff.

Step 2: Understand the Definition of *Staff Team*

When you address building a staff team, it's important that you know who are staff. I define the staff team as two or more gifted, competent, spiritual leaders who have committed to serve together to accomplish the church's disciple-making mission. There are several things to note about a staff team.

1. *The staff team consists of two or more people*, otherwise the term *team* wouldn't make sense. It's important to note that New Testament ministry was team ministry. Both Jesus and Paul ministered through teams (Mark 3:13–19; Acts 11:25–26).
2. *The staff are gifted.* They have a combination of gifts that complement, not compete, with one another.
3. *They are competent.* They're good at what they do.
4. *They are spiritually motivated* and are a part of the team for the right reasons.
5. *They commit to work together.* This involves staff chemistry. They work hard at getting along and have put aside any petty differences for the sake of the team.

Step 3: Understand the Ministry of the Staff

Develop Lay Leaders

As the new church grows and you recruit and bring on more staff, what will you expect them to do? Most churches, including planted ones, hire staff to do ministry. For example, the worship pastor does worship, and the youth pastor does youth ministry. But what does the Bible say about the functions of the staff and what they should do?

Since the Bible doesn't address staff or their ministries, at least as we know them today, I would argue that God gives us the freedom to use staff in a way that best promotes the church and its ministries. The staff will need to do or lead ministry, but I believe their greatest contribution is to develop leaders from the congregation. This is a new paradigm for church staff. We saw in chapter 11 that the congregation is to be mobilized to do the church's ministries. And it's the staff's primary role to develop these leaders.

Bill Hybels has wisely observed that the church is the hope of the world, and leaders are the hope of the church. Thus the church rises or falls based on its leadership. Calderon reports that when a planted church develops its leaders, the odds of survivability increase by 178 percent.[4] One of the primary reasons the church is doing so poorly in Europe and North America is a lack of leadership. Note that I didn't say it lacks leaders. Churches do have leaders; the problem is that they're not intentionally developing those leaders, who thus lack leadership ability. This is where I believe that staff should enter the picture. The greatest contribution they can make to the church in Europe and North America is to train its lay leaders to lead its congregations as they do the ministry. Therefore, I would task the staff with leadership development.

Critical Leader Development Questions

This raises several questions that the church planter must consider. Does or will the staff know how to develop leaders intentionally? Are they developing leaders now? Will staff be recruited based on their ability to develop leaders? Will they be or have they been trained in how to develop leaders? And does or will the church have a clear process for training leaders?

Step 4: Decide on the Number of Staff

The church planter needs to determine how many staff the new church should have. What is the best size when staffing for growth? Following Gary McIntosh's lead, I encourage the following congregation-staff ratio:

Good Staffing for Growth

Average Worship Attendance	Full-time Staff	Support Staff
1–150	1	1
151–300	2	1.5
301–450	3	2
451–600	4	2.5
601–750	5	3
751–900	6	3.5
901–1050	7	4
1051–1200	8	4.5
1201–1350	9	5

From this chart we see that good staffing for growth is one full-time staff person for every 150 people attending the worship service.[5] Lyle Schaller recommends one full-time staff person for every 100 active members.[6] The thinking behind these figures is that an effective staff person could build and lead a ministry that involves 150 people. Unfortunately, the deciding factor for the number of staff in most established churches is cost. The church planter, however, has the advantage of recruiting staff who are highly motivated to be on the team and have raised their own funds.

Step 5: Determine the Roles of the Staff

I place all potential staff into three big categories: ministry, administrative or operational, and specialist staff. In this section, I'll focus primarily on the ministry staff. As I said in step 3, the expectation and overall ministry of the staff is to develop leaders. The new church should expect all its ministry staff to be involved in leadership development. However, the ministry staff will function in certain specific areas of ministry within the church that vary from staff to staff. I refer to these as their staff roles.

Two Basic Staff Roles: Age-Specific and Functional

There are two basic staff roles: age-specific and functional. (Some churches have a life-stage staff instead of an age-specific staff role.) The difference is that age-specific staff focus primarily on a particular age group and thus have limited involvement with the rest of the congregation. Some examples are the youth pastor, the children's pastor, the pastor of adults, and others.

Most churches focus primarily on and recruit age-specific staff to minister under the direction of the senior pastor. However, I propose that churches also have what I refer to as functional staff. As we saw earlier, there are five functions of the church: worship, fellowship, Bible teaching, evangelism, and ministry, and the functional staff focus on these vital functions rather than on a specific age group. For example, a worship pastor, a pastor of community (small groups), biblical instruction (Christian education), evangelism (missions and outreach), and ministry (congregational mobilization) would be functional staff. Unlike the age-specific staff, they serve all of the congregation.

I encourage the church planter, as the church grows and he adds staff, to strive to maintain a balance between the age-specific and functional staff. You don't want all of one or the other, as we commonly see in churches today, but a balance of both. A church planter would most likely begin with a worship pastor (functional staff) and quickly add a youth pastor (age-specific staff) for balance and overall effectiveness. And as the church grows, he would maintain that balance by staffing back and forth between age-specific and functional positions.

The Executive Pastor

Though the focus of this section has been on the ministry staff, I do want to call your attention to a relatively new staff position that falls under the administrative staff category. It's the executive pastor. While the responsibilities of these pastors vary, most are involved in planning, administration, working with the staff, and ministering that assists the lead pastor in some way, such as pastoral visitation and even preaching. Most established churches bring on an executive pastor when they get to around seven hundred people in attendance. However, a growing number of church plants see the value of the executive position and have an administrative pastor on board at the beginning.

Step 6: Recruit the Staff

A never ending problem that has plagued Christ's church over the centuries is finding good staff.

What to Look For

The key to recruiting great staff is knowing what to look for. I believe we should look for the four Cs: character, competence, chemistry, and cause. *Character* speaks for itself. You almost assume that character would be one of the qualifications if not the leading qualification for staff. I would look for staff who meet the character qualifications in 1 Timothy 3:2–7 and Titus 1:6–9. (See appendixes F and G for my character audit.)

The second qualification is *competence*. You want to recruit staff who are good at what they do. Not only do they get the job done, but they do it well.

Chemistry is the third qualification. It addresses how well the staff gets along with the church and how well it works together. The issue here is what I refer to as alignment. I believe a staff member should align with the church's ministry, which includes values, mission, vision, and strategy. He or she should also align with the church's doctrine and theology, and the staff should align with one another emotionally, creating a healthy emotional climate.

The final C is *cause*. My pastor strongly believes in this fourth qualification. This means the staff are cause-oriented people who are so motivated that some would work for free. They have a will to win and refuse to take no for an answer. They get the job done—no excuses. And the good news is that they're attracted to church planting. Thus, I would certainly look for this in potential staff.

The Four Cs
of Staff Recruitment

Character

Competence

Chemistry

Cause

Where to Look

Where might you find these potential staff people? If the church planter is a seminary student, he could recruit other students who share the vision. Potential staff could also be those who are a part of a church that sponsors church plants. As the new church grows, the church planter will be able to raise up staff from within the church. This would likely mean that the new church has a leadership development process in place to identify and train these future staff persons.

Step 7: Deploy the Staff

Some established churches face a problem with staff deployment. This involves getting the right staff person in the right place at the right time. If he's not careful, the church planter can make major mistakes in staff deployment that have the potential of adversely affecting the entire staff and congregation.

The table below illustrates the importance of deploying the right people in the right positions at the right time.

Four Rs	People	Place	Time
1. Recruit	Right people	Right place	Right time
2. Reaffirm	Right people	Right place	Right time
3. Redeploy	Right people	Wrong place	Right time
4. Replace	Wrong people	Wrong place	Wrong time

The first row presents the goal of staff deployment—getting the right person in the right place at the right time. Thus staff deployment is affected by three major factors: the person, the position, and the timing. The second row assumes that you've deployed staff well—you have the right people in the right place at the right time. The third row indicates that you may have the right staff in the wrong position but at the right time. When this is the case, you need to redeploy the staff person to the right place on the staff. However, if you don't have a right place for him or her, you may have to direct the person to another church, and this always proves difficult.

Finally, row four represents a deployment disaster. You have the wrong person in the wrong place at the wrong time. You must encourage this person to find another ministry more suitable to who he or she is. To keep the wrong person in the wrong place at the wrong time is unfair to the person, and it keeps the right person from ministry in that position. Both people are affected adversely. The wrong person must be freed up to find the right place—most likely in another ministry.

Step 8: Evaluate the Staff

Most people don't look forward to being evaluated. They feel threatened by it. Yet they are evaluated constantly on an informal basis. Because formal evaluation provides a way for staff to get better at what they do, I encourage lead church planters to make informal evaluation formal. That way their staff can benefit from it.

Ken Blanchard has said that evaluation is the breakfast food of champions. I say it's the breakfast food of leaders. Strangely most people don't realize that staff evaluation is a key component of leadership development. Evaluation tells the staff person where his or her strengths and weaknesses lie. Then the staff know where they're excelling and where they need to do some work. When we fail to do evaluation for whatever reason, we leave out a key component of our leadership development process.

How to Evaluate Staff

To evaluate staff I would adopt the KISS principle (Keep It Simple Simon). This means your process should be as simple and straightforward as possible. The leader could evaluate the staff, and the staff as a team could evaluate him. Eventually, if the church has a governing board, this board could evaluate the lead pastor and he would, in turn, evaluate the staff. What is evaluated? I would evaluate both the person and his or her ministry performance.

What Is Success?

What constitutes successful ministry performance should be clear early in the leadership development process. Is the leader looking for exceptional performance, commendable performance, average performance, below aver-age performance, or unacceptable performance? You may wish to refresh your memory by reviewing these in chapter 8. Most would agree that exceptional and commendable performance represents success and below-average or unac-ceptable performance doesn't represent success and is unacceptable. So what about average performance? The staffs and church leaders I've worked with feel that average doesn't represent success. If the person is accomplishing only average leadership and ministry, then something is wrong. More than likely it's a placement or deployment problem. The wrong person is in the wrong place, possibly at the wrong time. He or she may need more training, or perhaps the individual is not wired to do the job. Do this person and your church a favor by getting him or her some help or—if need be—direct the person to another ministry.

Step 9: Spell Out Job Expectations

It's imperative that every staff person on your planting team have a job or ministry description. This description is important because it spells out what your expectations are for this person, and this tool will serve you well in recruiting and evaluating staff. The staff person should have input into this description along with the lead planter and possibly other staff, especially an executive pastor. Over time you can adjust this description to the staff person's speed (some work faster than others) and ministry goals.

I must add a warning. At the end of the ministry description, some pastors add the statement, "And anything else the pastor wants them to do!" I would counsel you not to do this, because it's unfair to the staff person and usually involves a work overload. If you insist on adding such a statement, then either remove some current task from the description or increase the salary—if the person is receiving a salary.

Recently columnist and church observer Todd Rhoades asked eighty-five church staff people if they knew what was expected of them at work. Here are the results:

- 26 percent (one in four) responded that they have very clearly defined expectations that are measured regularly.
- 38 percent said the expectations of their job were "kind of fuzzy" and that the follow-up by their supervisors sometimes happens and sometimes does not.
- 22 percent said they felt that the expectations of their job change constantly, and they're never quite sure what to concentrate on.
- 14 percent (12 out of 85) said they don't have a clue what's expected of them.[7]

In which category would your staff fit?

I would include the following in a ministry description:

1. Job title
2. Job profile
3. Job summary

4. Job expectations
5. Reports to
6. Works with

The job profile lists the characteristics of the person in this position (spiritual gifts, passion, temperament, and so forth). The job summary is a general, overall statement of what the staff person will be doing. The job expectations spell out all the key tasks and responsibilities of the person.

Step 10: Organize the Staff

To know where staff fit into the organizational structure of the church-plant organization, we must look at the ministry's organizational chart. It plays three critical roles in the organization of the ministry team: clarifies the organizational hierarchy, is key to the staffing blueprint, and manages the span of control.

Clarifies Organizational Hierarchy

The organizational chart establishes a needed hierarchy that is most important to the organization. It tells staff to whom they're responsible, for whom they're responsible, and with whom they share responsibility. Drucker wisely says, "In any institution there has to be a final authority . . . someone who can make the final decisions and who can expect them to be obeyed. In a situation of common peril—and every institution is likely to encounter it sooner or later—survival of all depends on clear command. . . . It's the only hope in a crisis."[8]

Key to Staffing Blueprint

The organizational chart enables the design of a staffing blueprint that the church can use as a guide for recruiting and hiring future staff. As I said earlier, good people are hard to find. And if you begin to look for them now before you need them, your chances of finding them improve dramatically. The staffing blueprint helps you know what positions you will need to fill in the future.

Below you will see a sample staffing blueprint that you can follow. As you look at the sample, think about where Christ figures into your new ministry. It's vital, of course, that he be at the head of the church. Next, decide where the pastor fits in and how he relates to Christ. All would agree that he is under Christ. Then where do staff fit? And what's their relationship to the leader and to one another? On the organizational chart below, there are both functional and age-specific staff to show where they might be on the blueprint. Also note that most of the staff report to an executive pastor. Finally, you will need to determine where the congregation fits in the big picture of the church.

While it will take some time before you will have enough staff to complete the blueprint, it's important to have a plan in place at the beginning. Remember, to fail to plan is to plan to fail. Also keep in mind that you could begin to implement some of your blueprint now by filling some of the positions with your talented, gifted lay leaders.

A Staffing Blueprint

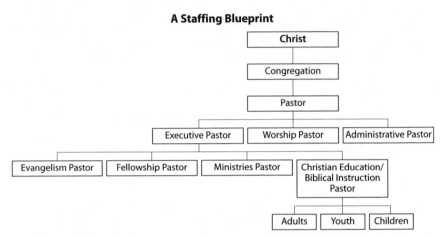

Manages the Span of Control

The organizational chart helps those in leadership know if they're trying to manage too many people, an issue that will become important later in the life of the ministry. The staff whom one person manages are called that person's "span of control." There should be a limited number of direct reports to the pastor. The rule of thumb is that no more than three to six staff should report to a single leader. In the early stages of the church, the church planter may be the leader to whom all the staff report. If it's more than six, he will need to make adjustments, such as recruiting another staff person to manage or delegate the responsibilities to someone who's already on the team.

Step 11: Develop the Staff

Earlier I encouraged you to recruit staff persons who would be able to develop lay leaders who, in turn, would lead the congregation in ministry. But the staff members themselves need to be developed as leaders. How might you accomplish this?

Why Develop the Staff?

One reason for developing staff is that people cannot train and lead leaders if they are not leaders themselves. Therefore the leadership skills of the staff must be developed. Then they can pour into others what's been poured into them. They train and develop as they've been trained and developed.

Leaders are learners, and if they stop learning, they stop leading. The leadership development of staff insures that they won't stop learning. There is a lot of good information available on leadership and the training of leaders. One of the books I recommend is *Building Leaders*, which I wrote with Will Mancini (Baker Books). Hopefully the training will create within the staff a powerful thirst to keep exploring this vast field of leadership in general and Christian leadership in particular.

When Will Staff Be Trained?

In general, staff development is a never-ending process and should be ongoing. And at the staff person's annual evaluation his leadership development plan, described below, is carefully reviewed and updated based on the results of the evaluation.

Who Will Train Staff?

There are several options for who will train staff. The church-planting or senior pastor is one possibility. However, I've not found many senior pastors who are good at mentoring staff. Perhaps they don't have the time it would take to do it well. And I suspect that most staff would be reluctant to share with the lead pastor information that could lead to a poor evaluation and possibly termination.

The executive pastor or other staff members could be trainers of staff, but again this may be problematic for those being trained. Training can be done through asking that certain good books be read and seminars be attended. The problem here, however, is accountability. How can you be sure the staff actually received the training that was intended?

I think the best route to go is to use an outside person, such as a consultant, who is a specialist in staff leadership development. Not only would he know his stuff and provide objectivity, but he would bring both confidentiality and accountability to the process.

What Should Be Included in the Staff Development Plan?

Regardless of who does the training, a unique professional leadership development plan must be crafted for each staff person, which would be structured around the 3Ds: design, direction, and development.

First, you would assess the staff person to discover his or her *divine design*. How has God wired him or her? What are this person's natural and spiritual gifts, passions, and temperaments?

Then determine what the design tells you about the second D—the person's *direction*. For example, if the staff person has a leadership gift, God wants him or her to lead. Finally, once staff know their design and direction, what should they do to grow and *develop*?

I believe that good development addresses five areas of competence: character, knowledge, skills, emotions, and the physical body. *Character* addresses who the person needs to be to lead in his or her position. *Knowledge* is what he or she needs to know to lead. *Skills* are what leaders need to be able to do to lead and minister at their position. *Emotions* address where the leader needs to be emotionally to lead, and the *physical body* refers to exercise, diet, and other physical needs.

Five Staff Developmental Competencies

- Character competence
- Knowledge competence
- Skills competence
- Emotional competence
- Physical competence

A Governing Board

Finally, I want to take some space to address the need for a governing board as part of the ministry team. Some churches, such as Presbyterian churches, have governing boards in place. Others that are congregational, such as Baptists, don't. The primary issue has to do with polity, how the church is organized, which determines where the power rests. Depending on the structure, power may rest with the congregation, a board, or the pastor.

My experience ministering with a board has been positive, but I have pastor friends who have had bad experiences. It is my recommendation that the planted church not put a board in place early in the life of the new church, giving the church time to make some decisions. The planted church needs to determine its polity or where the power will rest. Then if it decides to go with a church governance board, such as an elder board, it should hold off until the leadership has had time to determine who is qualified to be on that board and who isn't. One of the mistakes that the church can make early in the planting process is putting spiritually immature people in a position of power on the board. Scripture warns us about this (see 1 Tim. 5:22). Thus the church would be wise to wait—one to two years—until it's had time to discern who are its spiritually mature people.

Step 12: Communicate Your Vision for Staff Building

As with the other elements that make up the church-planting process, I encourage leaders to communicate their vision for staffing and staff building.

Again, communicating the vision could be the job of the church-planting communication team, who would use the communication plan to disseminate this information.

How to Build Your Staff for Leadership

Step 1: Recognize the importance of your staff.
Step 2: Understand the definition of *staff team*.
Step 3: Understand the ministry of the staff.
Step 4: Decide on the number of staff.
Step 5: Determine the roles of the staff.
Step 6: Recruit the staff.
Step 7: Deploy the staff.
Step 8: Evaluate the staff.
Step 9: Spell out job expectations.
Step 10: Organize the staff.
Step 11: Develop the staff.
Step 12: Communicate your vision for staff building.

Questions for Reflection and Discussion

1. Do you believe that the new church's staff are important to its ministry? What does the research show?
2. Do you agree with the author's definition of the staff? Why or why not? If not, what is your definition?
3. The author calls for an entirely new paradigm of ministry for the staff. What is it? Do you agree or disagree, and why?
4. Does the idea of dividing ministry staff into age-specific staff and functional staff and then balancing the two make sense? Why or why not?
5. Would you benefit by bringing on staff an executive pastor early in the planting process? Why or why not?
6. For your church, whom might you recruit as staff and where would you find them?
7. How do you feel about staff evaluation? Do you believe that it's important to effective ministry? Why or why not?
8. What are your expectations for your staff? Will you have a ministry description for each one for the sake of clarity, ministry effectiveness, and evaluation?
9. Do you have or do you plan to have an organizational chart for the staff? Why or why not? Does making a staffing blueprint make sense?
10. Do you plan to pursue staff development in the new church? Why or why not?

13

Where Will the New Church Locate?

Establishing a Ministry Beachhead

W e've addressed the first three components of the five that make up the strategy: community outreach, disciple making, and team building. The team consists of a mobilized congregation, the staff, and possibly at some future point a governing board, all of whom will work together to make disciples of the community.

This chapter presents the fourth strategy component—choosing the setting for the new church, the place where it will locate and from which it will launch its ministries out into the surrounding community. It's important to maximize the ministry setting, and this is where strategy comes in. First, I'll address the reason setting is important to the church plant. Next, I'll define setting. Third, I'll present the theology of setting, and finally, I'll walk you through a process to maximize your setting so that you can strategize to reach your community.

The Importance of Setting

The setting is important to the church plant for several reasons: it affects who will and who will not attend the church, it determines the church's visual presence in the community, it determines the effectiveness of ministry to the community, it can provide strategic advantage, and it provides the church with a way to accomplish its goals.

Church Attendance

Setting is important because it determines who will and won't visit and attend your church. Actually, the moment you decide where the new church will locate, you eliminate some people and include others. This sounds awful, so I need to explain further. In chapter 9 I discussed drive time and church attendance. There we learned from a national survey that people will drive only so long to attend a church—83 percent of people will drive twenty-five minutes or less to get to church. My experience is that this figure is generally accurate, but may vary, depending on whether a person lives in a suburban, urban, or rural setting. For example, those in suburban settings will have greater access to freeways and turnpikes than those in a rural setting that may have to navigate back roads to get to church. Thus, they may not be willing to drive as long to travel to church.

Visual Presence

Churches serve as a visual reminder to the community that spiritual things are important. And when people have a special need they believe a church can address, they remember where their neighboring churches are. The church's physical presence sends this message: "When you need us, you know where to find us, but we hope you'll pay us a visit before then." Where the planted church chooses to locate will affect its visual presence. If the church targets urban people, that presence will be felt in an urban community, and the same is true of a suburban or rural community.

A Place of Ministry to the Community

Earlier, in chapter 9, I addressed the difference between the new church's incarnational and invitational approaches to ministry. There we found that Matthew 28:19 commands the church to go and make disciples. Most established churches are invitational—that is—they invite the community to come to them to be ministered to within the facility itself. But what if they won't come? The "go" in the verses makes it clear that churches are to embrace an incarnational approach to ministry. They're to move beyond their four walls and go out into community to serve people and encourage them to accept Christ. If the community won't come to them, they'll go to the community.

Either way, the church's facility is a part of the new church's ministry. It's a place that facilitates ministry in some way. Either it's the place where we gather to worship together or it's the place from which we launch out into the community to do ministry, and the people in the community will connect us with the facility. It's their way of identifying us and knowing who we are and where we're from.

Strategic Advantage

When I was a seminary student, a requirement to graduate from Dallas Seminary was to write a master's thesis. One of my classmates wrote his thesis on the strategy behind Paul's missionary journeys. He pointed out that all of Paul's travels to various cities around the Mediterranean weren't simply aimless wandering. Instead, he chose each location strategically, based on how its geographical locale would impact the spread of the gospel. For example, we read in Acts 19:1 that Paul set up shop in the city of Ephesus. Since Ephesus was the gateway to Asia Minor, everything and everybody who traveled to Asia Minor went through Ephesus. Thus Paul put himself in a position to see the spread of the gospel to Asia Minor and beyond. Luke reports, "This went on for two years, so that all the Jews and Greeks who lived in the province of Asia heard the word of the Lord" (Acts 19:10). This model suggests that we would be wise to locate the new church plant not just where we can afford the land or rent, but in a locale that is strategic to reaching the community.

Providing a Means to an End

An important question for any church is whether its setting is an end or a means to an end. Ultimately, which is more important, the end or the means to that end? The obvious answer is that the end is much more important than the way we get there. When it comes to setting, the goal is for the facility to provide a place to gather for worship and from which to launch out into the community. The facility could be a mud hut in Africa, an igloo in the Arctic, a house in suburbia, or a building downtown. It doesn't matter as long as it serves as a means to facilitate worship and outreach.

The problem is that over time the means become the end, especially in some of the historic downtown first churches. People become enamored with what may be ornate facilities and forget about the purpose they serve. It's all about their memories. Their son or daughter was baptized or married in the church's facility, and that makes it special. And these memories of the church's past become stronger than its vision for the future.

To be more strategic and to pursue its vision, there could come a time when the church needs to relocate to another facility in another community. If the facility that is the means has become the end, then chances are the people will reject a strategic relocation because they're not thinking in terms of ministry but of memories. Therefore it becomes important early on that the new church make the end-means distinction crystal clear concerning its facilities. It's imperative that the emphasis be on the end, not the means to that end.

Five Reasons Setting Is Important

Setting affects who will and won't attend the church.

Setting provides the church with a visual presence in the community.

Setting provides a place from which the church can minister to the community.

Setting provides the church with strategic advantage.

Setting provides the church with a means to an end.

The Definition of *Setting*

So what exactly is the church's setting, and how am I using this term in the context of church planting? *Setting* is anywhere the church's ministry takes place. This is affected by several factors.

Physical Presence

Setting is the new church's geographical location, its physical presence in its ministry community. So we're not surprised when Paul writes to "the church of God in Corinth" (1 Cor. 1:2; 2 Cor. 1:1). In simple terms it's a piece of land, an address, a campus, or a ministry site. It could be just a thin slice of land or several acres, depending on what God has provided. Because its mission is to reach its community, the church locates there so as to have impact on the community.

Facilities

The new church needs more than geography or an address or land. It needs facilities on the site where it will meet. The physical setting includes a place where people will gather for public worship. It could be in someone's home, a rented facility, another church's facility, or a number of other places. In addition, the physical setting will include educational facilities where Christian education or biblical instruction takes place, such as a Sunday school ministry, small groups, an Adult Bible Fellowship (ABF), or some other similar kind of meeting. Thus the new church should consider its need for a facility in the community that can accommodate both worship and Christian education.

Parking Area

The setting also includes parking area, whether on or off campus. Unfortunately, public transportation in much of North America is at a premium. Thus most Americans depend on their cars to get them to and from church. Having a place to park those cars is part of the church's setting. Though parking isn't the best use of a church's campus, it's necessary to the church's ministry. You will need to think through the best way to provide for parking needs and how to accommodate guest and handicapped parking. Most church planters fail to take parking into consideration when they are looking for the best campus and facilities for their church. The urban church plant may find that off-campus parking is a good alternative.

Not Just Geography

Most churches' ministries are limited to a campus or piece of land that tends to restrict or limit ministry. However, this does not have to be the case. The church's setting can also be an electronic presence in the community. Churches must realize that they can minister to their communities and beyond through the internet, using their websites and in other creative ways, such as some social networking, chat rooms, and even texting. The clear advantage here is that, unlike their physical presence, electronic presence isn't limited to geography.

While some churches are using this medium for ministry, I'm surprised that more established churches in general and planted churches in particular haven't taken advantage of the airways to extend their ministries. And I suspect that eventually, as land becomes scarce and more expensive, especially in states like California and New York as well as major metropolitan areas around the country, and as megachurches continue to grow and experience landlock, churches will look for new ways to deliver ministry electronically.

The church's setting can also be extended through using a multisite approach to its ministry. In chapter 9, I explained that a multisite church is one that has a number of different campuses rather than just one campus. These campuses may be in the same town, city, or state but could also be somewhere outside the continental United States. Any of the campuses would provide the same ministries, including the same preacher's message, delivered by videotape or simulcast.

A multisite setting is a great opportunity for a planted church and should be considered early in the planting process, because opportunities may come along to pursue this less geographically restricted approach to ministry. For example, there may be a church in the area that has a campus and facilities but is dying. The new plant could extend its ministry to include this campus and other church campuses in similar situations.

The Theology of Setting

The church setting is primarily geography—it's where the new church locates and meets, but setting is not the church. It's not uncommon for us to speak of going to church on Sunday morning or Saturday evening or running up to the church for a meeting. But even though we call the facilities the church, it's really the people who are the church—born-again people. Note again that in

1 Corinthians 1:1, Paul writes to "the church of God in Corinth," distinguishing between the church (the people) and where it is located (in Corinth).

The term *church* is never used in the Bible for a building or geographical location. It is used predominantly to refer to the local and universal church or body of Christ. The local church is the believers that gather at a particular geographical location for ministry. It may be a city church such as that of Corinth (1 Cor. 1:1) or one of the house churches that make up a city church (16:19). The universal church is simply all who make up the body of Christ, whether assembled or not (Acts 8:1–3; 9:31).

In the Old Testament the tabernacle and later the temple were places where God was present (Hab. 2:20) and because of this they were considered holy ground. You would go there to meet with God. What about today? Is there something about the church's setting that makes it sacred? Do we purposefully go to the church's facility to meet God there? Is he present there as he was in the Old Testament?

The New Testament teaches that the temple in the Old Testament has been replaced by a new temple, which is the church or all believers in Christ (1 Cor. 3:16–17; Eph. 2:19–22). It's not the physical dwelling where God now resides, but the church is people, born-again people. Paul teaches that their bodies are the temple of the Holy Spirit (1 Cor. 3:16; 6:19–20). And they, in turn, dwell in or at a physical location, the church's facility. Thus it's the people and not the site that's sacred. When the new church moves into a specific church location, it may want to dedicate it to the Lord's use, but that doesn't necessarily make it sacred.

The Process of Choosing a Setting

Thus far we've addressed why setting is important to the planted church, we've clarified what setting is, and we have a theology of setting. It's time now to examine a process for choosing a setting. We need to craft a strategy for locating a campus, facilities, and parking area that are best for our church.

Locating a Church Campus

Locating the church campus is the most important decision, because when you locate a strategic campus for your ministry community, you have made the decision for the location of the facilities and parking as well. They will be part of the whole package. At this point you need to keep all three in mind—campus, facilities, and parking area. And you actually begin with the campus—the geographical site.

You may want to purchase a site, and this might be possible if there's a sponsoring church that can provide the funding, or an established church that has closed its doors and makes its campus available to a new church. (This would be an excellent post-ministry strategy for dying churches—death gives birth to new life.) Should you be able to purchase a site, keep in mind that neighborhoods change over the years, and this will challenge your strategy for your community. Ask if you'll be willing to change your ministry target should ethnic people who are different from the church move into the community. While the church starter may be fully open to a new, different ethnicity, will the congregation be as open? Most church starts either rent or lease their site, and usually available finances determine possible locations.

When making decisions about a setting and facilities, consider the following: the community, the appearance of the location, its visibility, its accessibility, its size, and its reputation.

COMMUNITY

First, and most important, determine where the people you plan to reach (pre-Christians) are located in the community. Most likely you accomplished this during the community outreach step (see chapter 8). If you were an established church, you would ask this of your current congregation. However, as a church plant, you may not have a congregation, only a core team that's in place. You want your location to be convenient to the community you wish to reach, so the needs of the future congregation are what must be considered, not what the church planter or core team might prefer. For your unsaved, unchurched community, the church's location—in a sense—is a life-and-death issue (Rev. 20:11–15).

APPEARANCE

When looking at potential property and facilities, consider how they and the immediate neighborhood look. Try to view the campus through "lost" eyes. How would the people you believe God is leading you to reach view the location? Some may not care, but others will have high expectations. Think about inviting a lost friend to this location. Would you be embarrassed by the campus? If so, this would probably keep you from inviting people to your church.

VISIBILITY

If you are considering a building that is already standing, think about its visibility. When pre-Christians drive by, will they notice it? Does it stand out? Does it blend in with the other buildings or houses along the street? What can you do to gain good visibility? Ask similar questions about land on which you might establish your campus.

The best way to achieve visibility is to locate along a major thoroughfare or busy street. And an expressway location would be fantastic because of its visibility from the road. Regardless of where you locate, you will need a sign identifying who you are.

ACCESSIBILITY

Whereas visibility concerns seeing the campus, accessibility addresses finding the campus. How easy will it be for people to find the church at this location? Keep in mind that unchurched, lost people are anxious about attending the new church and are looking for any excuse to turn around and return home. Having difficulty finding the church is a great excuse. I've heard lots of horror stories of churches that made it difficult for lost, unchurched people to find them.

SIZE

The size of the campus is always an issue as God grows the new ministry. How can you know what is the right size? To begin with, what is your vision for growth? Do you want to become a large church that reaches lots of people or do you want to remain a smaller church that meets in houses? If the latter, then a campus isn't a factor. The rule of thumb is that you'll need one acre for every one hundred people on campus at one time. This figure refers to usable acreage. Only parts of a piece of property may be usable due to drainage areas, irregular property shape, utility easements, retention ponds, steep slopes, zoning issues, and so on.

REPUTATION

One final consideration in locating a campus for the new church is the site's reputation in the community. When I came to faith while attending the University of Florida, I joined a small country church located on the outskirts of Gainesville, Florida. It was a recent church plant that struggled mightily to grow. The people in the surrounding community simply wouldn't attend. Many of us were concerned and couldn't figure out what the problem was. Then one day a neighbor volunteered that over the years, just about every bizarre religious group that came to town had rented the campus. And as far as the neighborhood was concerned, we were just another in a long succession of religious groups that would be there today and gone tomorrow. It was a graveyard for failed visions.

How would you know the reputation of the campus? Simply ask a few of the people in the neighborhood about the property. Most would be glad to "clue you in."

**Factors to Consider
in Selecting
a Church Campus**

Community

Appearance

Visibility

Accessibility

Size

Reputation

Providing Church Facilities

The preceding information on selecting a church campus applies to the facilities as well. Here are some additional considerations for the facilities.

Space Issues

When evaluating a facility for the church plant, consider each of the following space-related concerns: the worship area, education space, fellowship areas, offices, bathrooms, and storage. Evaluating these areas will help you decide if a facility is best for you. If the facility you're considering doesn't provide some of these features, can you think of ways of making up in some way for their absence?

The church's facilities will determine the ultimate size of the church at its campus. The worship center, for example, should be only around 80 percent full. Americans in general like their space, and if they don't know one another, then they prefer to sit with space between them.

Potential Facilities

At the beginning, new church plants often rent a facility. Two types that are most popular and commonly used are a school and a movie theater. Should you opt for a school, consider public schools and private schools. (The latter could be an option if the public school system is resistant to churches using their facilities.) There are also community colleges and universities that may have space available. They're usually found in easy-to-locate places, and most everyone knows where they are.

A movie theater would provide an auditorium with a stage, a sound system, and bathrooms. A church plant in the college town of Denton, Texas, opted for a theater in a fine arts center. The church has some people who were very good at marketing who took advantage of the facility. For example, they designed a mailer that looked like a piece of film with this headline: "If life has you feeling like a rebel without a cause, check out the new feature at the Fine Arts Theater."

Other possible options for the church plant are: existing church facility, storefront, public or community center, hotel or motel, private business, home, parachurch facility, bank building, coffee shop, restaurant or cafeteria or pub, the YMCA or YWCA, a park, amphitheater, country club, warehouse, and even a funeral home. Almost any facility that has four walls and a door could qualify, as long as it's clean and well maintained. Each of these options has its strengths and weaknesses, so consider carefully.

Providing Church Parking

For some churches parking is a real headache, so be sure to look for adequate parking when you select a church campus. The following are several rules of thumb that will assist you in determining what adequate parking will mean for you.

1. Provide one parking space for every two seats in the worship area.
2. Provide five handicapped parking spaces for every one hundred spaces.
3. Provide four visitor spaces for every one hundred parking spaces.
4. One acre will accommodate one hundred cars.

What if the church grows to the point that you run out of parking space? Here are several possible solutions:

1. Opt for multiple worship services.
2. Ask volunteers to drive one car.
3. Ask volunteers to park close by and walk to the services.
4. Offer a valet service to a remote parking lot.
5. Purchase or rent adjacent or nearby properties for parking.
6. Use property that is normally used for other purposes (for example, a soccer field).

Making Good Decisions

This chapter has dealt with finding the best, most strategic setting for the ministry community to locate its new church. We've seen that a location strategy is needed that will identify the best campus, facilities, and parking area for the planted church so that it can carry out its five functions.

Even with the information in this chapter, you may struggle when attempting to make the right decisions. I suggest the following regarding good decision making.

1. Ask God for his wisdom in making your decision (James 1:5).
2. What parameters do available finances, needed space, and other requirements prescribe?
3. Seek godly counsel.
4. Ask what your heart tells you.

Questions for Reflection and Discussion

1. Did the author convince you that your new church's setting is important to the ministry? Why or why not?
2. Do you believe that your church's setting affects who will and won't come to church? Why or why not?
3. How might the new church's setting affect the community?
4. Have you given much thought to a church's electronic presence? How might you have such a presence in your community?
5. If the church—according to the New Testament—isn't a building or setting, then what is the church?
6. Do you believe there's anything sacred about the church's setting? Why or why not?
7. Do you plan to purchase a facility or will you need to rent or lease one?
8. What are some options as to where the church might meet? Have you considered a school or theater? Why or why not?
9. Do you have a potential church campus in mind? Where is it located? Does it pass the test on each of the following: community, appearance, visibility, accessibility, size, and reputation?
10. Do you anticipate any parking issues? If so, what are they?

14

What Will It Cost?

Raising the Finances

You've learned that the new church's strategy consists of five core components. We've addressed the first four: community outreach, disciple making, team building, and ministry setting. This chapter addresses the fifth and final strategy component— stewardship or finances. The purpose of this chapter is to help you address the strategy for financing the new church and its ministries. I'll address the importance of stewardship, its definition, a brief theology of stewardship, and a process for raising the finances necessary to accomplish the church's ministries in and to its community.

The Importance of Stewardship

Like businesses and other organizations in this world, churches need money to do ministry. Because of the evil that's associated with the abuse of money in all civilizations throughout history, to connect it in some way with the church and its ministry causes raised eyebrows. Many of us naively assumed that the church would be different, that for some reason it was exempt from a need for "filthy lucre," but nothing could be further from reality. God in his wisdom hasn't seen fit to excuse the church from its dependence on money or the need to raise and manage funding for its ministries. Thus God wants the church to be reasonably and biblically involved in financial matters.

Holding Churches Accountable for Their Finances

We discovered earlier in this book that the church's mission is to make disciples (Matt. 28:19–20; Mark 16:15). However, to fund its ministries, the church has to raise finances. As a part of discipleship, it's imperative that established and new churches hold themselves accountable for their stewardship of God's resources. We have seen what can happen when they don't. Early in the twenty-first century, it has not been uncommon to hear of senior pastors, staff, and employees who have embezzled their churches' funds. It seems as though every time you open the newspaper or go online, you read of such a situation. And far too many other churches are guilty of squandering finances, though this may not be as serious and is more difficult to prove. Obviously it's imperative that churches have in place a process for handling their money that keeps everyone accountable.

Addressing a Matter of the Heart

A church's attitude toward stewardship reveals where it is spiritually. In Matthew 6:21 Jesus says, "For where your treasure is, there your heart will be also." His point is that what you truly value will occupy your attention much of the time. It's a matter of the heart. Most pastors don't like to preach and teach on money, because they know that a certain church contingency will complain that all they ever preach on is money. I encourage pastors not to neglect preaching on money, because the people who complain the most are the ones who give little to the church. When they hear such a message, they come under conviction and thus complain. That's not to say that a church can't go overboard in stressing finances. But this is signaled not by an occasional message on biblical giving but when everything is couched in terms of the church's financial needs.

Encouraging People to Give

Each church is responsible for teaching its people what the Bible says about stewardship. It informs people of what God expects from them in the area of their finances, their financial responsibilities to God.

The problem is that too many of our pastors don't know what the Bible teaches about stewardship and money and a few don't want to know for fear of the consequences. Regardless, I encourage pastors to teach more about this important topic. For example, later in the section on raising funds, I'll suggest that pastors set aside no less than a month each year to inform their congregation about biblical stewardship. Note that I didn't say they should spend one month each year on fund-raising. This topic must be covered, but Scripture says much about stewardship that people need to understand, such as how to be on the receiving end of God's financial blessings, how to manage one's finances, and how to invest money. We need to seek a reasonable balance between the biblical teaching on stewardship and on giving and generosity. My experience is that most congregations want to hear such messages.

The Definition of Stewardship

Stewardship is our management of God's temporary, earthly resources in general and finances in particular to accomplish his eternal, heavenly purposes (see 1 Chron. 29:10–20).

The Theology of Stewardship

Scripture has much to say about money and stewardship. One person writes that there are more than twenty-three hundred verses in the Bible that address these topics.[1] Of course it's well beyond the scope of this chapter to present all this material. Therefore, I will briefly summarize what the Old and New Testaments teach us about stewardship.

A Summary of Old Testament Teaching on Stewardship

Stewardship begins with God. He owns everything in heaven and earth (1 Chron. 29:11, 16; Ps. 24:1–2). This includes such things as wealth and honor (1 Chron. 29:12), people (Ps. 24:1–2), animals, birds, and creatures of the field (50:10–11), and much more. Because he owns all things, he is sovereign over them, especially the affairs of men. Daniel writes of God, "He does as he pleases with the powers of heaven and the peoples of the earth. No one can hold back his hand" (Dan. 4:35). And again he says, "The Most High is sovereign over the kingdoms of men and gives them to anyone he wishes" (v. 32).

Furthermore, God has entrusted this world as a stewardship to mankind, who is responsible for managing it (Gen. 1:28; Ps. 8:3–9). This began with Adam in the garden. "The LORD God took the man and put him in the Garden of Eden to work it and take care of it" (Gen. 2:15). And in spite of the fall, the stewardship of God's resources still extends to us today (Ps. 8:3–9).

A Summary of New Testament Teaching on Stewardship

The New Testament Greek word for steward is *oikonomos,* which is rendered *manager* in the NIV translation of this term. In the classical Greek it was used of a person, usually a slave, who was responsible for and ran the affairs of a household for a master. Much the same holds true of its use in the New Testament, especially in Luke 12:42 and 16:1–13. In these two passages Jesus uses two parables to illustrate stewardship truths, that is, that we as his disciples are in charge of and are to manage his household while he is away, and we need to prove ourselves faithful to this call on our lives. Today God's household is his church.

Included under the biblical teaching on stewardship is giving, which involves our honoring God by returning to him a portion of all that he's provided for us. Much of the biblical teaching on finances concerns giving (see Matt. 6:1–4, 19–24; Mark 12:41–44; Acts 20:35; Rom. 12:6–8; 2 Cor. 8–9).

Handling the New Church's Finances

Now that we understand why stewardship is important to the new church, we have a definition of stewardship, and we have a broad, general understanding of what the Bible teaches about stewardship, we're ready to address a process or plan for stewardship in the new church. Calderon notes, "Church survivability is increased by 178 percent when there's a proactive stewardship development plan within the church plant."[2] I'll break this stewardship process into three manageable steps.

Step 1: Decide Who Will Be Responsible

The new ministry's pastor must accept responsibility for directing or managing the church's finances, because pastors must be able to lead their churches in this vital area of church ministry. There are several texts that I believe indirectly imply this responsibility.

1 TIMOTHY 3:4–5

In 1 Timothy 3:4–5 Paul provides Timothy and ultimately the church with the necessary qualifications for a pastor. While the term *overseer* is used here and not *pastor*, the overseers or elders were the first-century house church pastors who were the approximate equivalent of today's pastor. It's likely that the churches used these qualifications to determine if a man or candidate was qualified to be a pastor, and potential pastors used them to see if they were qualified before seeking such a position.

In these verses Paul writes that a pastor "must manage his own family well and see that his children obey him with proper respect. (If anyone does not know how to manage his own family, how can he take care of God's church?)" While the passage says nothing about finances, I would argue that management of one's family and the church would include the proper handling of finances, among other responsibilities that also aren't mentioned. The proper management of finances is critical to the well-being of any family, and the same would apply to Christ's church.

1 Timothy 5:17

A second passage is 1 Timothy 5:17, where Paul writes, "The elders who direct the affairs of the church well are worthy of double honor." This passage mentions finances by implication and also refers to the pastor's salary. On the subject of managing the church's finances, I'm referring to the portion of the text that addresses the pastor's function—directing the affairs of the church. As above, my argument is that directing the affairs of a church would seem to include its finances, whether in the first or the twenty-first century.

Acts 11:29–30

A third passage is Acts 11:29–30. We discover in this passage that the church in Jerusalem needed financial help due to a severe famine (v. 28). In response, the disciples in Antioch sent financial relief ("their gift") to the Jerusalem church, specifically to the elders or pastors. And thus this passage connects finances with the pastors. It would appear to indicate that pastors were involved in the church's financial affairs. If nothing else, they were involved in the distribution of funds to those in need.

A Question

At this point, I need to ask a key question. If the new pastor doesn't assume leadership and direct the church's finances, who will? Perhaps the new church could assign a board person or even a member of the staff to take on this responsibility. However, the church may have no board or even staff at this early stage in its life. And most congregations look to the pastor, not some other person, for the vision and leadership of the church. This is as true of the church's financial affairs as it is for other areas of leadership.

The first church I pastored was a church plant. I look back on that experience and I'm amazed at my naïveté, especially in the area of church finances. I was the pastor and I assumed the responsibility for counting and depositing the offering every Sunday. I also wrote the checks. And this went on until one day a person noted all this and challenged me to turn this responsibility over to a team of accountable people. I use this illustration as a negative example to stress that the new church would be wise to have some kind of accountability process in place to protect both the church and the pastor. While the pastor is ultimately responsible for the use of finances, there should be a financial review team in place and a yearly independent audit, using a CPA if possible.

A Second Question

I need to ask a second question. Why do most pastors shy away from leading in the area of church finances? I think there are several reasons for this. Some pastors don't realize how important finances are to a church, particularly a new one. Finances can mean it sinks or swims. Some pastors don't understand that directing the church's finances is a leadership matter. And most likely, many simply don't know how to lead in this area. I hope to correct this in the rest of this chapter.

Step 2: Determine How Much Funding Is Needed

You may or may not like budgets. I don't like budgets that are complex and hard to follow but I do like those that are simple and easy to follow. It's really not that hard to build a simple budget, and now is the time very early in the life of the church to build such a budget.

A budget is necessary for accomplishing the new church's ministry and should be a simple, strategic, financial leadership tool in the hands of the financially savvy ministry leader. It's my view that pastors should be able to lead their church in financial matters. I consider the budget a key player in directing the funding of the church's ministries.

Determining the funding needs for the church's ministries is a twofold exercise that focuses on the new church's budget. It involves building a budget that serves the new ministry and then regularly monitoring and analyzing the budget to see how the church's finances are progressing.

BUILDING THE NEW CHURCH'S BUDGET

Building your budget involves using a blueprint to plan and construct a simple budget for your ministry. This blueprint addresses where you allocate the funds that God provides you. Before we look at the allocation of funds, let's take a moment to review briefly the sources of funding.

We learned in chapter 3 that funds can come from a number of and combination of sources: a sponsoring church, a home church, the core church-planting team, a prayer team, the leadership core, a denomination or other similar organization, family, friends, acquaintances, and others. Most likely it is the church-planting pastor who will be responsible for raising much of this funding.

Now we're ready to examine the allocation of these funds. Steve Stroope is the pastor of Lake Pointe Church in Rockwall, Texas, a suburb of Dallas. He is my pastor, with whom I wrote *Money Matters in Church*.[3] When it comes to leading and working with church finances, Steve is the best I've ever seen. We believe and teach that churches should allocate funds to four specific areas: missions and evangelism, personnel, ministries, and facilities. This is the blueprint for a church budget.

The Blueprint for Building a Church Budget

- Missions and Evangelism
- Personnel

- Ministries
- Facilities

Spiritually strong, growing churches allocate around 10 percent to missions and evangelism, 50 percent to personnel (this ranges from 40 percent in large churches to 60 percent in smaller churches), 20 percent to the church's ministries, and 20 percent to the church facilities. Let's briefly examine each of these areas.

Allocation of Church Funding

- Missions and Evangelism—10 percent
- Personnel—50 percent (40–60 percent)
- Ministries—20 percent
- Facilities—20 percent

MISSIONS AND EVANGELISM

A vital missing component in the ministry of the majority of established churches all across America is evangelism. That's because evangelism isn't a core value in most of these churches. However, most established churches do give to missions. It doesn't make sense, but people in these churches will write checks for missions but they don't do evangelism.

I encourage newly planted churches to set aside 10 percent of their budgets for evangelism and missions. Calderon writes, "80 percent of fast-growing churches allot a full 10 percent of their budget to outreach and evangelism. Only 42 percent of slow-growing church plants allot this much."[4] This is money that will come primarily from the initial congregation and the fund-raising efforts of the lead pastor.

A new church should begin with funding evangelism and outreach efforts in the community (local missions). This could include funds for evangelistic training, community mailers, and actual hands-on outreach events. Then the church could gradually add support of foreign missionaries over time as the new church grows, balancing commitment to local and foreign mission efforts and encouraging a world perspective among the congregation.

PERSONNEL

I recommend that a church allocate 50 percent of the budget to ministry personnel. At the beginning of the church plant, most of these people should raise their own support. However, as the new church begins to grow and support itself financially, monies will become available to hire and support its ministry staff. If the church grows and becomes a large church, 30 to 40 percent of its funds may be allocated to staff, depending on how involved a church's lay people are in its ministries. The rule here is that the more laypeople do the ministry, the less staff you need. If the church stays small, as much as 60 percent may be allocated for staffing.

MINISTRIES

In chapter 10 I addressed the kinds of ministries through which churches could accomplish their disciple-making missions. I divided them into primary and secondary ministries. The primary ministries are the essential ministries for making mature disciples. The secondary ministries are electives and may help the maturing process. I advise a church to allocate 20 percent of its funds to the primary ministries, which include age-specific and functional ministries. Initially, most of the funding for the church's ministries would be raised by the church planter and his leadership core and then would gradually come from growing congregational support.

FACILITIES

Over time, growing church plants have to make decisions affecting their facilities. If they begin by meeting in a rented facility, they often opt to build or purchase facilities before long because they grow weary of setting up church every week and wrestling with the various issues that can plague a rented facility, such as poor maintenance, missing equipment, and dirty facilities.

The new church should allocate 20 percent of its budget to facilities. This includes monies for maintenance, utilities, a mortgage payment, and so forth. Initially, the church-plant team will raise these funds. However, in time they should ask their growing congregation to give to meet the facility needs, and this could include a special building fund dedicated solely to the facilities. Later in the church's life, it should have capital campaigns for special building projects.

MONITORING THE NEW CHURCH'S BUDGET

Once a budget that serves the new ministry has been developed, it must be regularly analyzed or monitored to see how God is providing and blessing and to track how the church is progressing financially. This will also help the church maintain a lean budget at a time in its early life when finances are likely thin to begin with.

Analyzing and monitoring the church-plant budget includes asking the following ten questions.

1. What percentage of the church's funds is allocated to evangelism, personnel, ministries, and facilities? Are we holding to the recommended percentages?
2. Is the budget outreach or in-reach oriented? Outreach oriented churches are heavily involved in evangelism and may budget funds for ministries in and to their communities. Plateaued and dying churches are in-reach oriented. Thus the new church wants to be and usually is outreach

oriented. You would think that the budget of an outreach-oriented church would be balanced with half its funding going toward outreach and half to in-reach. However, what we've observed is that outreach-oriented churches spend around 10 percent of their budget on outreach and 90 percent on in-reach activities, which is okay. Thus, a church doesn't have to set aside much of its budget to be outreach oriented.

3. In its early phases, is the church's monthly and annual giving growing, plateaued, or declining?

4. Are most of the people supporting the church financially or is it only a few faithful givers? The Pareto principle seems to hold true for too many of our established churches—20 percent of the people are providing 80 percent of the funding. Is this true of the planted church in its early life? I would encourage church planters to address what the Bible teaches about finances at least once a year, as well as in the early stages of the launch.

5. What is the church's per capita giving? This is similar to the prior question, because both look at individual support of the ministry. Begin to track this early in the life of the church. This question raises a second question: What is average and good giving for an individual in the church? According to one study, the answer to the first question for most churches is $200 a year.[5] The answer to the second question, according to another study, is $52.75 per week, or $2,743 annually.[6]

6. Are funds set aside in the budget for any ministries that would better be supported outside the budget by a special fund-raiser, such as a capital campaign or other method? These ministries could be missions in general or a special missions project that's over and above what is in the budget, benevolence fund, and other fund.

7. As the church grows and ages, it can embrace some bad habits in how it budgets. The way to address this is to work your way through each line item in the budget (there shouldn't be too many of them), asking, why is the church paying for this? Some examples of questionable spending would be for men's and women's ministries, church retreats, curriculum, use of buses for trips. The specific people who benefit from these activities or resources should cover the cost of them.

8. What is the cost for operating each of the church's ministries (youth, worship, children, adults, and the others)? Which are the high-cost and low-cost ministries? And are any of these ministries bringing in funds that cover their expenses?

9. Does the church hold high giving expectations of its people?

10. If the church supports a denomination, is it a wise use of its funds? Is it getting its money's worth?

Step 3: Discover How to Raise the Needed Funds

We saw earlier in this chapter that a vital aspect of a pastor's leadership of the church is directing or managing its finances. This is especially true when raising finances for the ministry. But how can pastors raise funding for the new church and its ministries? I believe that if they adopt the following ten points, they will see a significant increase in their congregation's giving to the church.

1. *Articulate a theology of stewardship.* It would address what the Bible teaches about money in general and giving in particular. The pastor needs to know and understand what the Bible teaches about this important area, because he will be expected to teach this truth. We've included such a theology in appendix A of *Money Matters in Church*.

2. *Regularly cast the church's vision.* Many of us who work with churches have discovered that vision and finances go hand in hand. Churches that are good at vision casting are good at raising funds for their ministries. People aren't interested in paying the light bill; they're interested in supporting ministries that will have impact and make a difference in the community. And it's the church's vision that articulates this impact. Regularly casting the vision means you will do it at least monthly, but it's best if done at every natural opportunity.

3. *Provide opportunities for giving.* Steve Stroope (my pastor) accomplishes this with what he refers to as the "five pockets of giving." They are the general fund, the missions fund, the building fund, the benevolence fund, and designated giving. All of these are valid giving areas for a church plant. Some people don't like to give to the church's general fund. However, they will give to specific areas, such as the missions or benevolence funds. By providing alternative opportunities, the church increases the likelihood that people will contribute in some way to what God is accomplishing through the church.

4. *Implement a churchwide stewardship ministry.* This ministry should consist of the following: an annual one-month series of sermons on what the Bible teaches about stewardship and giving; an annual series at the Sunday school level on what the Bible teaches, allowing for discussion and interaction on finances; an annual series at the small-groups level on finances, allowing for discussion and the holding of one another in the group accountable for each person's giving commitments; a session on giving as a part of the church's new members class; financial counseling for those who are struggling with handling their finances; an occasional seminar or workshop for those who have interest in learning how to budget, invest funds, and so forth; and a ministry of deferred giving that helps retirees or those near retirement to know how they can

continue to invest in the church's ministry, through wills, trusts, estates, and annuities, long after they've departed to be with Christ.

5. *Constantly communicate the church's financial circumstances and needs to the congregation.* As Rick Warren has said on numerous occasions, "People are down on what they're not up on." Also people will trust leaders who make a point of communicating with them. They feel that these leaders aren't trying to hide anything from them. And this trust is vital when it comes to money and the giving of money. It's imperative that the congregation trust the leadership. Constant communication can take place through an online newsletter, snail mail, email, a website, announcements from the pulpit, podcasts, and other means.

6. *Conduct capital campaigns.* I believe that an exciting as well as an effective way to raise funds, especially for special projects, is the capital campaign. My pastor is adept at leading capital campaigns. His expertise on conducting them can be found in chapters 13 to 15 of our book *Money Matters in Church.*

7. *Make it easy for people to give to the church.* At my church we use an envelope system to accomplish easy giving. The envelope serves as a visual reminder to give, it facilitates giving, it serves as a record of one's giving, and it allows people to designate their giving. Another easy way for people to give can be online.

8. *Cultivate giving champions.* Scripture makes it clear that some in the church have a spiritual gift of giving (Rom. 12:8). And just as we cultivate the gifts that others have, such as leaders, so we should cultivate givers. This means thanking them for their giving, counseling them in their giving, and letting them know of special needs when they can exercise their gift.

9. *Recruit a pastor of stewardship or generosity.* Several innovative established churches are creating a new, full-time pastor or staff position that ministers to the church body in the area of giving in general and generosity in particular. The desire is to integrate a culture of generosity into every area of congregational life. I would challenge the church planter to recruit such a pastor of generosity for the planted church. This could easily be an older, retired person, who has worked in the area of finances in the business world or simply a gifted leader who has a passion for congregational generosity.

10. *Challenge people to give.* In commenting on a major study conducted on church finances, Rob Moll says, "Meanwhile, the study found that a major reason Christians do not give is because they are not asked to." A pastor could challenge the entire congregation to increase their giving over the next year by 1 or 2 percent. This isn't much to many congregants but would make a difference in the new church's budget.[7]

How to Raise Funds for Ministry

Articulate a theology of stewardship.

Regularly cast the church's vision.

Provide opportunities for giving ("five pockets of giving").

Implement a churchwide stewardship ministry.

Constantly communicate the church's financial circumstances.

Conduct capital campaigns.

Make it easy for people to give to the church.

Cultivate giving champions.

Recruit a pastor of stewardship or generosity.

Challenge people to give.

Questions for Reflection and Discussion

1. Did you already understand the importance of finances to the new church or did the author have to convince you? Why or why not?
2. Should you stop preaching on money and finances when a few people complain about your emphasis on money? Why or why not?
3. How interested are you and others in your church in knowing what the Bible teaches about finances?
4. What are your thoughts about spending one month annually addressing in sermons the topic of stewardship?
5. What is the basic teaching of the Bible on stewardship?
6. Do you believe that most congregations generally want to know what the Bible teaches about money? Why or why not?
7. Do you agree with the author's definition of stewardship? Why or why not?
8. Do you agree with the author's view that the pastor is responsible for leading and directing the church's finances? Why or why not? Does the Bible teach this? Explain.
9. Did you find the section on building and analyzing the budget helpful? Why or why not? What was the most helpful?
10. Did you find the section on raising finances helpful? Why or why not? Will this help you raise funding for the new church? Explain.

APPENDIX A

Spiritual Gifts Inventory

Directions

1. For each of the following 55 statements on spiritual gifts, check the box that best identifies the extent to which the statement describes you.
2. Do not answer on the basis of what you wish were true or what another says might be true, but on the basis of what, to your knowledge, is true of you.

Questions

	Never 1	Rarely 2	Sometimes 3	Often 4	Always 5
1. I enjoy working with others in determining ministry goals and objectives.	☐	☐	☐	☐	☐
2. I prefer to be involved in new ministries.	☐	☐	☐	☐	☐
3. I delight in telling lost people about what Christ has done for them.	☐	☐	☐	☐	☐

	Never 1	Rarely 2	Sometimes 3	Often 4	Always 5
4. It bothers me that some people are hurting and discouraged.	☐	☐	☐	☐	☐
5. I have a strong ability to see what needs to be done and believe that God will do it.	☐	☐	☐	☐	☐
6. I love to give a significant portion of my resources to God's work.	☐	☐	☐	☐	☐
7. I have a strong capacity to recognize practical needs and to do something about them.	☐	☐	☐	☐	☐
8. I have a clear vision for the direction of a ministry.	☐	☐	☐	☐	☐
9. I always feel compassion for those in difficult situations.	☐	☐	☐	☐	☐
10. I have a strong desire to nurture God's people.	☐	☐	☐	☐	☐
11. I spend a significant portion of my time each week studying the Bible.	☐	☐	☐	☐	☐
12. I am motivated to design plans to accomplish ministry goals.	☐	☐	☐	☐	☐
13. I prefer to create my own ministry problems than to inherit others.	☐	☐	☐	☐	☐
14. I have a strong attraction to lost people.	☐	☐	☐	☐	☐
15. I am very concerned that more people are not serving the Lord.	☐	☐	☐	☐	☐
16. I have a strong capacity to trust God for the difficult things in life.	☐	☐	☐	☐	☐
17. I am eager to support ministries financially that are accomplishing significant things for God.	☐	☐	☐	☐	☐
18. I enjoy helping people meet their practical needs.	☐	☐	☐	☐	☐
19. I find that I have a strong capacity to attract followers to my ministry.	☐	☐	☐	☐	☐
20. I am motivated to sympathize with those in the midst of a crisis.	☐	☐	☐	☐	☐
21. I am at my best when leading and shepherding a small group of believers.	☐	☐	☐	☐	☐

	Never 1	Rarely 2	Sometimes 3	Often 4	Always 5
22. I have strong insight into the Bible and how it applies to people's lives.	☐	☐	☐	☐	☐
23. I feel significant when developing budgets.	☐	☐	☐	☐	☐
24. I am motivated to minister in places where no one else has ministered.	☐	☐	☐	☐	☐
25. I find that I get along well with unsaved people.	☐	☐	☐	☐	☐
26. I have a strong desire to encourage Christians to mature in Christ.	☐	☐	☐	☐	☐
27. I delight in the truth that God accomplishes things that seem impossible to most people.	☐	☐	☐	☐	☐
28. God has greatly blessed me with life's provisions to help others.	☐	☐	☐	☐	☐
29. I enjoy making personal sacrifices to help others.	☐	☐	☐	☐	☐
30. I prefer to lead people more than to follow them.	☐	☐	☐	☐	☐
31. I delight in extending a hand to those in difficulty.	☐	☐	☐	☐	☐
32. I enjoy showing attention to those who are in need of care and concern.	☐	☐	☐	☐	☐
33. I am motivated to present God's truth to people so they can better understand the Bible.	☐	☐	☐	☐	☐
34. I am at my best when creating an organizational structure for a plan.	☐	☐	☐	☐	☐
35. I am definitely a self-starter with a pioneer spirit.	☐	☐	☐	☐	☐
36. I derive extreme satisfaction when lost people accept Christ.	☐	☐	☐	☐	☐
37. I have been effective in inspiring believers to a stronger faith.	☐	☐	☐	☐	☐
38. I am convinced that God is going to accomplish something special through my ministry.	☐	☐	☐	☐	☐
39. I am convinced that all I have belongs to God.	☐	☐	☐	☐	☐

	Never 1	Rarely 2	Sometimes 3	Often 4	Always 5
40. I work best when I serve others behind the scenes.	☐	☐	☐	☐	☐
41. If I am not careful, I have a tendency to dominate people and situations.	☐	☐	☐	☐	☐
42. I am a born burden-bearer.	☐	☐	☐	☐	☐
43. I have a deep desire to protect Christians from people and beliefs that may harm them.	☐	☐	☐	☐	☐
44. I am deeply committed to biblical truth and people's need to know and understand it.	☐	☐	☐	☐	☐
45. I delight in staffing a particular ministry structure.	☐	☐	☐	☐	☐
46. I am challenged by a big vision to accomplish what some believe is impossible.	☐	☐	☐	☐	☐
47. I feel a deep compassion for people who are without Christ.	☐	☐	☐	☐	☐
48. I have the ability to say the right things to people who are experiencing discouragement.	☐	☐	☐	☐	☐
49. I am rarely surprised when God turns seeming obstacles into opportunities for ministry.	☐	☐	☐	☐	☐
50. I feel good when I have the opportunity to give from my abundance to people with genuine needs.	☐	☐	☐	☐	☐
51. I have a strong capacity to serve people.	☐	☐	☐	☐	☐
52. I am motivated to be proactive, not passive, in my ministry for Christ.	☐	☐	☐	☐	☐
53. I have the ability to feel the pain of others who are suffering.	☐	☐	☐	☐	☐
54. I get excited about helping new Christians grow to maturity in Christ.	☐	☐	☐	☐	☐
55. Whenever I teach a Bible class, the size of the group increases in number.	☐	☐	☐	☐	☐

Instructions for Scoring

1. Place the number (1–5) from each of your answers on the line corresponding to the question number.
2. Add the numbers horizontally and place the total for each row in the space before each gift.

1. ___ 12. ___ 23. ___ 34. ___ 45. ___ _____ Administration

2. ___ 13. ___ 24. ___ 35. ___ 46. ___ _____ Apostleship

3. ___ 14. ___ 25. ___ 36. ___ 47. ___ _____ Evangelism

4. ___ 15. ___ 26. ___ 37. ___ 48. ___ _____ Encouragement

5. ___ 16. ___ 27. ___ 38. ___ 49. ___ _____ Faith

6. ___ 17. ___ 28. ___ 39. ___ 50. ___ _____ Giving

7. ___ 18. ___ 29. ___ 40. ___ 51. ___ _____ Helps

8. ___ 19. ___ 30. ___ 41. ___ 52. ___ _____ Leadership

9. ___ 20. ___ 31. ___ 42. ___ 53. ___ _____ Mercy

10. ___ 21. ___ 32. ___ 43. ___ 54. ___ _____ Pastor

11. ___ 22. ___ 33. ___ 44. ___ 55. ___ _____ Teacher

Instructions for Determining Your Spiritual Gifts

1. Place the names of your five highest-scoring gifts in the spaces below under Spiritual Gifts Inventory.
2. Place the names of any other gifts that are not identified in this inventory yet are present in your life under Other Spiritual Gifts.

Spiritual Gifts Inventory	Other Spiritual Gifts
1. _____	_____
2. _____	_____
3. _____	_____
4. _____	_____
5. _____	_____

Instructions for Determining Your Gift-Mix and Gift-Cluster

1. To determine your gift-mix, place the names of the five gifts (listed above under Spiritual Gifts Inventory) in descending order in the spaces below.
2. To determine if you have a gift-cluster, decide if the first gift or another gift in your mix is dominant and supported by the other gifts. If this is the case, place it in the center space under the title Gift-Cluster and place the other gifts in the spaces surrounding it.

Gift-Mix

_____

_____

_____

_____

_____

Gift-Cluster

APPENDIX B

Passion Audit

Directions

Answer each of the following questions as best you can.

1. Do you have a burning conviction that a particular ministry is the place where God wants you to serve him? If so, what is it?

2. Does your spiritual gift, gift-mix, or gift-cluster (see appendix A) point to a particular ministry? If so, what is it?

3. Do you have a burning, gut-level desire to reach a particular group of people or involve yourself in a certain ministry? If so, what people or what ministry?

4. Do you have a strong desire to pursue a particular issue as your ministry (for example, pro-life issues, poverty, child abuse victims)? Does the issue stir you emotionally?

5. Does the thought of pursuing a particular subject (for example, apologetics, cults, theology, the law, leadership, the arts) excite you?

6. If God were to appear before you and grant you one wish for your ministry for the rest of your life, what would it be?

7. What ministry opportunities do you care deeply and feel strongly about?

8. What do you dream about doing for the Savior?

9. During your free moments, what in terms of ministry do you find yourself doing naturally?

10. What do you really want to do with the rest of your life?

Prayerfully and carefully review your answers to the above questions. As you consider your answers, what do you think your passion or passions might be? Ask someone else who knows you well if he or she agrees. Write your passion(s) below:

APPENDIX C

Temperament Indicator 1

Directions

Read the four terms listed across each row. Then rank each characteristic for how well it describes you in a ministry or work-related situation. Number 4 is most like you, and number 1 is least like you. In each row use numbers 1–4. When you are finished, total the number in each column and write that number in the blank provided below that column. The column with the highest score is your temperament.

1. ___ Direct	___ Popular	___ Loyal	___ Analytical
2. ___ Decisive	___ Outgoing	___ Dependable	___ Logical
3. ___ Controlling	___ Expressive	___ Steady	___ Thorough
4. ___ Competent	___ Influential	___ Responsible	___ Skeptical
5. ___ Blunt	___ Enthusiastic	___ Sensible	___ Compliant
6. ___ Competitive	___ Persuasive	___ Cooperative	___ Serious
7. ___ Callous	___ Impulsive	___ Submissive	___ Accurate
8. ___ Volatile	___ Manipulative	___ Conforming	___ Picky
9. ___ Persistent	___ Personable	___ Harmonious	___ Creative
10. ___ Productive	___ Animated	___ Restrained	___ Fearful
11. ___ Self-reliant	___ Articulate	___ Predictable	___ Diplomatic
___ *Total* *(Doer)*	___ *Total* *(Influencer)*	___ *Total* *(Relator)*	___ *Total* *(Thinker)*

APPENDIX D

Temperament Indicator 2

Directions

As you take this indicator, please keep in mind that there are no correct or incorrect answers. Read each statement and circle the item (a or b) that best represents your preference in a ministry or work-related environment. Do not spend a lot of time thinking over your answers. Go with your first impulse.

1. When around other people, I am
   a) expressive
   b) quiet
2. I tend to
   a) dislike new problems
   b) like new problems
3. I make decisions based on my
   a) logic
   b) values
4. I prefer to work in a
   a) structured environment
   b) nonstructured environment
5. I feel more energetic after being
   a) around people
   b) away from people
6. I work best with
   a) facts
   b) ideas

7. People say I am
   a) impersonal
   b) a people-pleaser
8. My friends at work say I am very
   a) organized
   b) flexible
9. I get more work accomplished when I am
   a) with people
   b) by myself
10. I like to think about
    a) what is
    b) what could be
11. I admire
    a) strength
    b) compassion
12. I make decisions
    a) quickly
    b) slowly
13. I prefer
    a) variety and action
    b) focus and quiet
14. I like
    a) established ways to do things
    b) new ways to do things
15. I tend to be rather
    a) unemotional
    b) emotional
16. Most often I dislike
    a) carelessness with details
    b) complicated procedures
17. In my relationships I find that over time it is easy to
    a) keep up with people
    b) lose track of people
18. I enjoy skills that
    a) I have already learned and used
    b) are newly learned but unused
19. Sometimes I make decisions that
    a) hurt other people's feelings
    b) are too influenced by other people
20. When my circumstances change, I prefer to
    a) follow a good plan
    b) adapt to each new situation

21. In conversations I communicate
    a) freely and openly
    b) quietly and cautiously
22. In my work I tend to
    a) take time to be precise
    b) dislike taking time to be precise
23. I relate well to
    a) people like me
    b) most people
24. When working on a project, I do not
    a) like interruptions
    b) mind interruptions
25. Sometimes I find that I
    a) act first and ask questions later
    b) ask questions first and act later
26. I would describe my work style as
    a) steady with realistic expectations
    b) periodic with bursts of enthusiasm
27. At work I need
    a) fair treatment
    b) occasional praise
28. In a new job I prefer to know
    a) only what it takes to get it done
    b) all about it
29. In any job I am most interested in
    a) getting it done and the results
    b) the idea behind the job
30. I have found that I am
    a) patient with routine details
    b) impatient with routine details
31. When working with other people, I find it
    a) easy to correct them
    b) difficult to correct them
32. Once I have made a decision, I consider the case
    a) closed
    b) still open
33. I prefer
    a) lots of acquaintances
    b) a few good friends
34. I am more likely to trust my
    a) experiences
    b) inspirations

35. I consistently decide matters based on
    a) the facts in my head
    b) the feelings in my heart
36. I prefer to work
    a) in an established business
    b) as an entrepreneur

Instructions for Scoring

1. Place a check in the a or b box below to indicate how you answered each question.
2. Add the checks down each column and record the total for each column at the bottom.
3. The highest score for each pair indicates your temperament preference.
4. For each pair subtract the lower from the higher score to discover the difference in your preferences. A higher number indicates a clear choice or preference but does not indicate the measure of development. For example, a higher score for extroversion means that you prefer it over introversion. It does not mean that you are a strong extrovert.

	a	b		a	b		a	b		a	b
1	__	__	2	__	__	3	__	__	4	__	__
5	__	__	6	__	__	7	__	__	8	__	__
9	__	__	10	__	__	11	__	__	12	__	__
13	__	__	14	__	__	15	__	__	16	__	__
17	__	__	18	__	__	19	__	__	20	__	__
21	__	__	22	__	__	23	__	__	24	__	__
25	__	__	26	__	__	27	__	__	28	__	__
29	__	__	30	__	__	31	__	__	32	__	__
33	__	__	34	__	__	35	__	__	36	__	__
Total	__	__	Total	__	__	Total	__	__	Total	__	__
	E	I		S	N		T	F		J	P
	Extrovert	Introvert		Sensing	Intuition		Thinking	Feeling		Judgment	Perception

APPENDIX E

Leadership Style Inventory

Directions

Of the four statements on leadership style listed for each question (lettered A through D), check the one statement that is "most like me" and the one that is "least like me." You should have only one check in each column per question.

Sample:

	Most like me	Least like me
A. Needs difficult assignments.	A. _____ (+2)	A. _____ (−2)
B. Makes decisions emotionally.	B. _____ (+2)	B. _____ (−2)
C. Seeks identity with a group.	C. ✓ (+2)	C. _____ (−2)
D. Emphasizes quality control.	D. _____ (+2)	D. ✓ (−2)

Answer on the basis of what you believe is true of you, not on the basis of what you desire or hope is true. As you answer the questions, it will be helpful to consider your past experience as well as how you see yourself leading in your current or a future ministry context (church, parachurch, or ministry). Go with your first impression. Resist the temptation to analyze each or any response in detail.

Suggestions for responding: You should not worry about how you score on this inventory. This is not a test that you pass or fail, and there is no best or preferred leadership style. Sometimes it's helpful to have others who know you well (spouse, parent, team member, good friend) take the inventory about you. You may want to take this inventory to discover what leadership style is best for your church or parachurch ministry. Should this be the case, change "most like me" to "most like us" and "least like me" to "least like us."

Check the reason you're taking this inventory:

_____ To discover my leadership style
_____ To help another discover his or her leadership style
_____ To discover the best leadership style for my ministry's context (church, parachurch, or ministry)

		Most like me	Least like me
Q1	A. Loves a challenge.	A. _____ (+2)	A. _____ (−2)
	B. Spends time with people.	B. _____ (+2)	B. _____ (−2)
	C. Behaves in a predictable manner.	C. _____ (+2)	C. _____ (−2)
	D. Sets high ministry standards.	D. _____ (+2)	D. _____ (−2)

		Most like me	Least like me
Q2	A. Focuses on the details.	A. _____ (+2)	A. _____ (−2)
	B. Likes to start things.	B. _____ (+2)	B. _____ (−2)
	C. Motivates people.	C. _____ (+2)	C. _____ (−2)
	D. Shows patience with people.	D. _____ (+2)	D. _____ (−2)

		Most like me	Least like me
Q3	A. Develops deep friendships.	A. _____ (+2)	A. _____ (−2)
	B. Desires that people do quality work.	B. _____ (+2)	B. _____ (−2)
	C. Makes decisions quickly.	C. _____ (+2)	C. _____ (−2)
	D. Has lots of friends.	D. _____ (+2)	D. _____ (−2)

		Most like me	Least like me
Q4	A. Communicates with enthusiasm.	A. _____ (+2)	A. _____ (−2)
	B. Enjoys helping people.	B. _____ (+2)	B. _____ (−2)
	C. Thinks analytically.	C. _____ (+2)	C. _____ (−2)
	D. Challenges the status quo.	D. _____ (+2)	D. _____ (−2)

		Most like me	Least like me
Q5	A. Leads with authority.	A. _____ (+2)	A. _____ (−2)
	B. Displays optimism in ministry.	B. _____ (+2)	B. _____ (−2)
	C. Helps others feel comfortable in a group.	C. _____ (+2)	C. _____ (−2)
	D. Insists on accuracy of facts.	D. _____ (+2)	D. _____ (−2)

		Most like me	Least like me

Q6	A. Thinks systematically.	A. _____ (+2)	A. _____ (−2)
	B. Sets lofty goals.	B. _____ (+2)	B. _____ (−2)
	C. Treats others fairly.	C. _____ (+2)	C. _____ (−2)
	D. Prefers to minister with a team.	D. _____ (+2)	D. _____ (−2)

		Most like me	Least like me
Q7	A. Prefers a predictable routine.	A. _____ (+2)	A. _____ (−2)
	B. Evaluates programs well.	B. _____ (+2)	B. _____ (−2)
	C. Likes direct answers to questions.	C. _____ (+2)	C. _____ (−2)
	D. Loves to entertain people.	D. _____ (+2)	D. _____ (−2)

		Most like me	Least like me
Q8	A. Expresses self freely.	A. _____ (+2)	A. _____ (−2)
	B. Delights in sincere appreciation.	B. _____ (+2)	B. _____ (−2)
	C. Values quality and accuracy.	C. _____ (+2)	C. _____ (−2)
	D. Looks for new and varied activities.	D. _____ (+2)	D. _____ (−2)

		Most like me	Least like me
Q9	A. Solves problems well.	A. _____ (+2)	A. _____ (−2)
	B. Likes to "think out loud."	B. _____ (+2)	B. _____ (−2)
	C. Places a premium on keeping promises.	C. _____ (+2)	C. _____ (−2)
	D. Enjoys opportunities to display expertise.	D. _____ (+2)	D. _____ (−2)

		Most like me	Least like me
Q10	A. Needs to know what's expected.	A. _____ (+2)	A. _____ (−2)
	B. Pursues variety in ministry.	B. _____ (+2)	B. _____ (−2)
	C. Enjoys inspiring people to do great things.	C. _____ (+2)	C. _____ (−2)
	D. Listens well to others.	D. _____ (+2)	D. _____ (−2)

		Most like me	Least like me
Q11	A. Demonstrates great patience with people.	A. _____ (+2)	A. _____ (−2)
	B. Shows displeasure over poor performance.	B. _____ (+2)	B. _____ (−2)
	C. Makes his/her perspective clear to others.	C. _____ (+2)	C. _____ (−2)
	D. Expects good things from people.	D. _____ (+2)	D. _____ (−2)

		Most like me	Least like me
Q12	A. Presents ideas in compelling ways.	A. _____ (+2)	A. _____ (−2)
	B. Shows loyalty to those over him/her.	B. _____ (+2)	B. _____ (−2)
	C. Displays strong self-discipline in work.	C. _____ (+2)	C. _____ (−2)
	D. Believes in individual accomplishment.	D. _____ (+2)	D. _____ (−2)

	Most like me	Least like me

Q13 A. Is direct with people.
B. Enjoys being with people.
C. Has a calming influence on others.
D. Relates to people intellectually.

A. _____ (+2) A. _____ (−2)
B. _____ (+2) B. _____ (−2)
C. _____ (+2) C. _____ (−2)
D. _____ (+2) D. _____ (−2)

	Most like me	Least like me

Q14 A. Asks "why" questions.
B. Likes to get results.
C. Is a persuasive communicator.
D. Exhibits a strong empathy for others.

A. _____ (+2) A. _____ (−2)
B. _____ (+2) B. _____ (−2)
C. _____ (+2) C. _____ (−2)
D. _____ (+2) D. _____ (−2)

	Most like me	Least like me

Q15 A. Helps group members get along.
B. Encourages others to think deeply.
C. Shows persistence in pursuing goals.
D. Relates well to people emotionally.

A. _____ (+2) A. _____ (−2)
B. _____ (+2) B. _____ (−2)
C. _____ (+2) C. _____ (−2)
D. _____ (+2) D. _____ (−2)

	Most like me	Least like me

Q16 A. Enjoys expressing himself/herself.
B. Cooperates well to accomplish tasks.
C. Utilizes strong problem-solving skills.
D. Takes the initiative with people.

A. _____ (+2) A. _____ (−2)
B. _____ (+2) B. _____ (−2)
C. _____ (+2) C. _____ (−2)
D. _____ (+2) D. _____ (−2)

	Most like me	Least like me

Q17 A. Leads with strength.
B. Enjoys interacting with people.
C. Helps others feel comfortable.
D. Follows directions carefully.

A. _____ (+2) A. _____ (−2)
B. _____ (+2) B. _____ (−2)
C. _____ (+2) C. _____ (−2)
D. _____ (+2) D. _____ (−2)

	Most like me	Least like me

Q18 A. Wants explanations and answers.
B. Prefers practical experience.
C. Relates well to other people.
D. Enjoys serving other people.

A. _____ (+2) A. _____ (−2)
B. _____ (+2) B. _____ (−2)
C. _____ (+2) C. _____ (−2)
D. _____ (+2) D. _____ (−2)

	Most like me	Least like me

Q19 A. Supports group decisions.
B. Strives to improve situations.
C. Gravitates naturally to leadership positions.
D. Exhibits an ability to speak spontaneously.

A. _____ (+2) A. _____ (−2)
B. _____ (+2) B. _____ (−2)
C. _____ (+2) C. _____ (−2)
D. _____ (+2) D. _____ (−2)

		Most like me	Least like me

Q20	A. Encourages people's ideas.	A. _____ (+2)	A. _____ (−2)
	B. Cares about how change affects people.	B. _____ (+2)	B. _____ (−2)
	C. Provides lots of facts and data.	C. _____ (+2)	C. _____ (−2)
	D. States convictions firmly.	D. _____ (+2)	D. _____ (−2)

		Most like me	Least like me
Q21	A. Confronts dissenters directly.	A. _____ (+2)	A. _____ (−2)
	B. Cultivates commitment in others.	B. _____ (+2)	B. _____ (−2)
	C. Strives diligently to get along with others.	C. _____ (+2)	C. _____ (−2)
	D. Emphasizes working conscientiously.	D. _____ (+2)	D. _____ (−2)

		Most like me	Least like me
Q22	A. Focuses attention on the finer points.	A. _____ (+2)	A. _____ (−2)
	B. Pursues high personal performance.	B. _____ (+2)	B. _____ (−2)
	C. Stimulates people around him/her.	C. _____ (+2)	C. _____ (−2)
	D. Is easy to work with.	D. _____ (+2)	D. _____ (−2)

		Most like me	Least like me
Q23	A. Avoids conflict.	A. _____ (+2)	A. _____ (−2)
	B. Values good regulations.	B. _____ (+2)	B. _____ (−2)
	C. Overcomes opposition.	C. _____ (+2)	C. _____ (−2)
	D. Influences people naturally.	D. _____ (+2)	D. _____ (−2)

		Most like me	Least like me
Q24	A. Generates much enthusiasm.	A. _____ (+2)	A. _____ (−2)
	B. Shows sensitivity toward people.	B. _____ (+2)	B. _____ (−2)
	C. Prefers to probe a matter deeply.	C. _____ (+2)	C. _____ (−2)
	D. Finds difficult tasks challenging.	D. _____ (+2)	D. _____ (−2)

		Most like me	Least like me
Q25	A. Takes charge instinctively.	A. _____ (+2)	A. _____ (−2)
	B. Works best through other people.	B. _____ (+2)	B. _____ (−2)
	C. Displays care for others.	C. _____ (+2)	C. _____ (−2)
	D. Provides expertise in a particular area.	D. _____ (+2)	D. _____ (−2)

Leadership Style Inventory Scoring

Instructions for Scoring the Inventory

1. Transfer the appropriate score for each checked statement on the Leadership Style Inventory to the scoring sheet below.

For example:

If on question **Q1** you checked that statement **A** was "least like me," transfer the point value of –2 to the appropriate blank on the scoring sheet, marked **A** beside question **Q1**. Likewise, transfer the point value of **+2** for the statement that was "most like me" to the appropriate blank on the Scoring Sheet.

2. Once all scoring information has been transferred from the Inventory to the scoring sheet, add up each column and place the total at the bottom of the sheet in the row marked Column Totals.

3. Note that adding the four column totals together should result in a sum of zero. If this is not the case, then either data has been inaccurately transferred from the Inventory to the scoring sheet or an error in addition has occurred. Please check your work.

Sample Inventory Questions

		Most like me		Least like me	
Q1	A. Loves a challenge.	A. _____	(+2)	A. ✓	(–2)
	B. Spends time with people.	B. _____	(+2)	B. _____	(–2)
	C. Behaves in a predictable manner.	C. ✓	(+2)	C. _____	(–2)
	D. Sets high ministry standards.	D. _____	(+2)	D. _____	(–2)
		Most like me		Least like me	
Q2	A. Focuses on the details.	A. _____	(+2)	A. _____	(–2)
	B. Likes to start things.	B. _____	(+2)	B. ✓	(–2)
	C. Motivates people.	C. _____	(+2)	C. _____	(–2)
	D. Shows patience with people.	D. ✓	(+2)	D. _____	(–2)

Sample Scoring Sheet

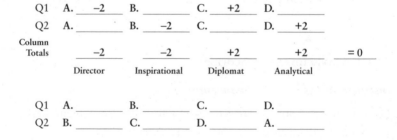

Q1	A. __–2__	B. _____	C. __+2__	D. _____		
Q2	A. _____	B. __–2__	C. _____	D. __+2__		
Column Totals	__–2__	__–2__	__+2__	__+2__	= 0
	Director	Inspirational	Diplomat	Analytical	

Q1	A. _____	B. _____	C. _____	D. _____
Q2	B. _____	C. _____	D. _____	A. _____

	Director	Inspirational	Diplomat	Analytical
Q3	C. _____	D. _____	A. _____	B. _____
Q4	D. _____	A. _____	B. _____	C. _____
Q5	A. _____	B. _____	C. _____	D. _____
Q6	B. _____	C. _____	D. _____	A. _____
Q7	C. _____	D. _____	A. _____	B. _____
Q8	D. _____	A. _____	B. _____	C. _____
Q9	A. _____	B. _____	C. _____	D. _____
Q10	B. _____	C. _____	D. _____	A. _____
Q11	C. _____	D. _____	A. _____	B. _____
Q12	D. _____	A. _____	B. _____	C. _____
Q13	A. _____	B. _____	C. _____	D. _____
Q14	B. _____	C. _____	D. _____	A. _____
Q15	C. _____	D. _____	A. _____	B. _____
Q16	D. _____	A. _____	B. _____	C. _____
Q17	A. _____	B. _____	C. _____	D. _____
Q18	B. _____	C. _____	D. _____	A. _____
Q19	C. _____	D. _____	A. _____	B. _____
Q20	D. _____	A. _____	B. _____	C. _____
Q21	A. _____	B. _____	C. _____	D. _____
Q22	B. _____	C. _____	D. _____	A. _____
Q23	C. _____	D. _____	A. _____	B. _____
Q24	D. _____	A. _____	B. _____	C. _____
Q25	A. _____	B. _____	C. _____	D. _____
Column Totals	_____	_____	_____	_____ = 0
	Director	Inspirational	Diplomat	Analytical

Identification of Leadership Style

Answer the following questions to identify your leadership style.

1. What is your primary or dominant style (the one with the highest score)?

   _____

2. What is your secondary style? _____

3. Does one of the two remaining styles also exert a noticeable impact on you? If so, which one? _____

4. According to this information, circle your leadership style in the following list (it will be the combination of your primary and secondary styles).

Director
Director-Inspirational
Director-Diplomat
Director-Analytical

Inspirational
Inspirational-Director
Inspirational-Diplomat
Inspirational-Analytical

Diplomat
Diplomat-Director
Diplomat-Inspirational
Diplomat-Analytical

Analytical
Analytical-Director
Analytical-Inspirational
Analytical-Diplomat

Complete the following: My leadership style is

_____.

Note: If a third style has a noticeable impact, you may want to place it in parentheses after your style. For example: Director-Inspirational (Analytical).

APPENDIX F

Men's Character Assessment for Leadership

Over the years, leaders have discovered that godly character is critical to effective ministry for Christ. However, no one is perfect, and all of us have our weaknesses and flaws as well as strengths. This character assessment is to help you determine your character strengths and weaknesses so that you can know where you are strong and where you need to develop and grow. The characteristics are found in 1 Timothy 3:1–7 and Titus 1:6–9.

Directions

Circle the number that best represents how you would rate yourself in each area.

1. I am "above reproach." I have a good reputation among people in general. I have done nothing that someone could use as an accusation against me.

   Weak   1   2   3   4   5   6   7   8   Strong

2. I am the "husband of one wife." If married, I have one wife and I am not physically or mentally promiscuous, for I am focused only on her.

   Weak   1   2   3   4   5   6   7   8   Strong

3. I am "temperate." I am a well-balanced person. I do not overdo my use of alcohol or any other activity. I am not excessive or given to extremes in beliefs or reactions.

Weak   1   2   3   4   5   6   7   8   Strong

4. I am "sensible." I show good judgment in life and have a proper perspective regarding myself and my abilities (I am humble).

Weak   1   2   3   4   5   6   7   8   Strong

5. I am "respectable." I conduct my life in an honorable way, and people have and show respect for me.

Weak   1   2   3   4   5   6   7   8   Strong

6. I am "hospitable." I use my residence as a place to serve and minister to Christians and non-Christians alike.

Weak   1   2   3   4   5   6   7   8   Strong

7. I am "able to teach." When I teach the Bible, I show an aptitude for handling the Scriptures with reasonable skill.

Weak   1   2   3   4   5   6   7   8   Strong

8. I am "not given to drunkenness." If I drink alcoholic beverages or indulge in other acceptable but potentially addictive practices, I do so in moderation.

Weak   1   2   3   4   5   6   7   8   Strong

9. I am "not violent." I am under control. I do not lose control to the point that I physically or verbally strike or cause damage to other people or their property.

Weak   1   2   3   4   5   6   7   8   Strong

10. I am "gentle." I am a kind, meek (not weak), forbearing person who does not insist on his rights or resort to violence.

Weak   1   2   3   4   5   6   7   8   Strong

11. I am "not quarrelsome." I am an uncontentious peacemaker who avoids hostile situations with people.

Weak   1   2   3   4   5   6   7   8   Strong

12. I am "not a lover of money." I am not in ministry for financial gain, but I seek first his righteousness, knowing that God will supply my needs.

Weak   1   2   3   4   5   6   7   8   Strong

13. I "manage my family well." If I am married and have a family, my children are believers who obey me with respect. People do not think my children are wild or disobedient.

Weak   1   2   3   4   5   6   7   8   Strong

14. I am "not a recent convert." I am not a new Christian who struggles constantly with pride and conceit.

Weak   1   2   3   4   5   6   7   8   Strong

15. I have "a good reputation with outsiders." Though lost people may not agree with my religious convictions, they still respect me as a person.

Weak   1   2   3   4   5   6   7   8   Strong

16. I am "not overbearing." I am not self-willed, stubborn, or arrogant.

Weak   1   2   3   4   5   6   7   8   Strong

17. I am "not quick-tempered." I am not inclined toward anger (an angry person) and I do not lose my temper quickly and easily.

Weak   1   2   3   4   5   6   7   8   Strong

18. I am "not pursuing dishonest gain." I am neither fond of nor involved in any wrongful practices that result in fraudulent gain.

Weak   1   2   3   4   5   6   7   8   Strong

19. I "love what is good." I love the things that honor God.

Weak   1   2   3   4   5   6   7   8   Strong

20. I am "upright." I live in accordance with the laws of God and man.

Weak   1   2   3   4   5   6   7   8   Strong

21. I am "holy." I am a devout person whose life is generally pleasing to God.

Weak   1   2   3   4   5   6   7   8   Strong

22. I "hold firmly to the faith." I understand, hold to, and attempt to conserve God's truth. I encourage others while refuting those who oppose the truth.

Weak   1   2   3   4   5   6   7   8   **Strong**

When you have completed this character assessment, note those characteristics that you gave the lowest rating (a 4 or below). These are to become the character goals or challenges that you focus on as you seek to grow and mature in the faith.

APPENDIX G

Women's Character Assessment
for Leadership

Over the years, leaders have discovered that godly character is critical to effective ministry for Christ. However, no one is perfect, and all of us have our weaknesses and flaws as well as strengths. This character assessment is to help you determine your character strengths and weaknesses so that you can know where you are strong and where you need to develop and grow. The characteristics are found in 1 Timothy 2:9–10; 3:11; Titus 2:3–5; and 1 Peter 3:1–4.

Directions: Circle the number that best represents how you would rate yourself in each area.

1. I am "worthy of respect." I find that most people who know me respect me and tend to honor me as a dignified person who is serious about spiritual things.

   Weak   1   2   3   4   5   6   7   8   Strong

2. I am not a "malicious talker." I do not slander people or gossip about them, whether believers or unbelievers.

   Weak   1   2   3   4   5   6   7   8   Strong

3. I am "temperate." I am a well-balanced person. I do not overdo my use of alcohol, etc. I am not excessive in my behavior or given to extremes in beliefs, etc.

Weak   1   2   3   4   5   6   7   8   Strong

4. I am "trustworthy in everything." The Lord and people find me to be a faithful person in everything.

Weak   1   2   3   4   5   6   7   8   Strong

5. I live "reverently." I have a deep respect for God and live in awe of him.

Weak   1   2   3   4   5   6   7   8   Strong

6. I am "not addicted to much wine." If I drink alcoholic beverages, I do so in moderation. I am not addicted to them.

Weak   1   2   3   4   5   6   7   8   Strong

7. I teach "what is good." I share with other women what God has taught me from his Word and from life in general.

Weak   1   2   3   4   5   6   7   8   Strong

8. I "love my husband." If I am married, I love my husband according to 1 Corinthians 13:4–8.

Weak   1   2   3   4   5   6   7   8   Strong

9. I "love my children." If I have children, I love them.

Weak   1   2   3   4   5   6   7   8   Strong

10. I am "self-controlled." I do not let other people or things run my life, and I am not a person of extremes or excessive behavior.

Weak   1   2   3   4   5   6   7   8   Strong

11. I am "pure." I am not involved emotionally or physically in sexual immorality.

Weak   1   2   3   4   5   6   7   8   Strong

12. I am "busy at home." If I am married, then I take care of my responsibilities at home.

Weak   1   2   3   4   5   6   7   8   Strong

13. I am "kind." I am essentially a good person.

    Weak   1   2   3   4   5   6   7   8   Strong

14. I am "subject to my husband." If I am married, I let my husband take responsibility for and lead our marriage, and I follow his leadership.

    Weak   1   2   3   4   5   6   7   8   Strong

15. I have "a gentle and quiet spirit." I am a mild, easygoing person who wins others over by a pure and reverent life more than by my words.

    Weak   1   2   3   4   5   6   7   8   Strong

16. I "dress modestly." I wear clothing that is decent and shows propriety.

    Weak   1   2   3   4   5   6   7   8   Strong

17. I "do good deeds." I do those things that are appropriate for women who profess to know and worship God.

    Weak   1   2   3   4   5   6   7   8   Strong

When you have completed this character assessment, note those characteristics that you gave the lowest rating (a 4 or below). You should develop the character goals to which you gave the lowest rating, focusing on one or two at a time.

Principles of Seeking Support

The Conversation

Eventually, visionary church planters will begin to contact potential supporters. Initially, this will be done by telephone, especially if the network is large. It is necessary to develop a phone message that will communicate the essential information pleasantly and concisely.[1] The following procedure is recommended:

1. *Determine the goals for the initial phone conversation.* You may have three goals for the first conversation. You want to inform the person of your vision and the fact that you are starting a church to implement this vision. You want to explain that you're developing a financial support team to help initially in accomplishing this ministry. Finally, ask for an appointment to give the person more information about the ministry and its costs.

   A possible variation of this would be to write a letter in which you explain your vision and ministry and the fact that you'll soon be following up the letter with a phone call to answer any questions. When you call, you would answer questions and explain that you're developing a support team to help start the church. Then you could ask for an appointment to give more information about the ministry and its costs.

2. *In the initial phone conversation, communicate the essential information the person needs to know regarding why you want to meet with him*

or her. Save most of the conversation for the time when you're together in person. Attempt to get as much personal time with him or her as possible. The better the person knows you, the greater the chance he or she will support you and your vision.

3. *Develop two phone conversations: one for people you know and another for people you don't know.* The following is a sample phone conversation designed by Dallas Seminary church planters for use with someone they don't know:

Hello, Mr./Mrs. _____. My name is _____. I'm a recent graduate of Dallas Seminary, and God has placed on my heart a significant vision to move to _____ and start a church for people who don't like church. Currently, I'm in the process of putting together a support team of people who might share this vision and desire to be a vital part of this ministry. _____ suggested that I call you because he/she thought you might be interested in what the Lord has put on my heart and learning more about a church designed to reach the unchurched. I'm not asking you to make any kind of commitment now. I would like to get together with you at your convenience to explain the ministry to you. Would that be possible? When would be a good time for you?

A phone conversation with someone you already know should be more personal. You should talk about whatever is appropriate, depending on the nature of your relationship. Include a brief discussion of your vision and how you came to adopt it. You may want to address the area of financial support in more detail than you would with someone you don't know. It's helpful to provide additional details and allow your friend to interact and ask more questions over the phone. Even if you know someone well, it adds a personal touch when you follow up and meet with him or her personally.

4. *Prepare an attractive, well-designed brochure.* You may want to send it to the people who desire to meet with you and to those who don't but show some interest in the church. In this brochure, demonstrate through your research and demographics why you're planting the church. Identify your target group and their need for the gospel. Present your core values, mission, vision, and strategy to accomplish the mission and vision. Using mini-biographical statements, introduce your team and explain their qualifications and what part they'll play in accomplishing the vision. Finally, include a brief but clear budget that presents your plans and financial needs. Make sure the document is visually attractive. If necessary, invest some time and sufficient funds in working with a

professional to develop the document. If you're not able to develop a quality brochure, it would be best not to use anything at all.

Should you send the brochure, include a personal handwritten note or letter explaining that you're forming a financial support team and you'll visit the recipient in a week or so to see if he or she has any questions and would like to become involved.

5. *When you meet with interested people, make sure they understand the vision.* Initially, after some introductory greetings and small talk, you should answer any questions they might have. And you'll want to ask a few questions yourself that focus on the vision, to determine if they understand it. Most likely, people who catch the vision will want to help in some way.

   One advantage American church planters often have over cross-cultural missionaries is that they need to raise support for a limited period of time, not for their lifetime. The idea is that the core group will grow and eventually take over the support of the church and its leaders. If this is your situation, you should make this clear to those with whom you meet because it allows them to make a short-term commitment, which is much more appealing than a long-term or lifetime commitment.

   In many cases, the core group should be able to take over the financial responsibility for the church plant anywhere from one to four or five years, depending on the financial abilities of the people who make up the core group and the number of people on the church-planting team. I worked with one Baby Boom core group consisting of nine couples. After they had caught a vision for reaching their unchurched friends, they committed at the beginning to provide enough funds to cover the planter-leader's expenses to get the church started.

6. *Finally, once you've established a support team, it's critical that you communicate with them regularly.* There are several ways to accomplish this. You could send your contacts a monthly letter to keep them informed as to the progress of the ministry. You could do the same with a more elaborate newsletter. If they live in the area, give them a phone call. Should you decide to use a mailer, consider including a self-addressed envelope. Remind them periodically that by making their check payable to the new church, the Internal Revenue Service will allow this as a deduction for them at the end of the year.

APPENDIX I

Is Pastoral Care the Primary Role
of the Pastor?

Over the past few years, God has allowed me not only to teach leadership at Dallas Seminary, but to minister in numerous churches and denominations as a consultant and trainer. As I work with various leaders, I've come across a fundamental assumption on which some base their pastoral paradigm. It's the assumption that the primary and foremost role of the pastor is to provide pastoral care for the congregation—to take care of the sheep. This expectation includes such hands-on care as visitation in the hospital and at home, counseling, and care during a crisis.

I challenge this assumption both biblically (exegetically) and practically. I believe that while pastoral care is a function of the pastorate, it's not the primary or the foremost role of the pastor. The primary responsibility of the pastor is to lead the congregation, which includes such things as teaching the Scriptures, propagating the mission, casting a vision, strategizing to accomplish the church's mission, and protecting the sheep from false teaching. I'll say more about this later.

First and foremost, the role of the pastor is to lead the congregation. Both the Old Testament and the New Testament use shepherd imagery for leaders, but a study of such passages reveals that this imagery refers to leadership more than pastoral care.

We begin with an examination of the shepherd metaphor in the Old Testament. While pastoral care may have been an aspect of what some leaders in the Old Testament did, their primary role was that of leadership. For example,

God and the prophets commonly used the term *shepherd* when referring to the political leaders of Israel and the nations (see 2 Sam. 7:7; Isa. 44:28; Jer. 25:34–38; and Ezek. 34:1–4). The emphasis here is clearly on them as leaders. In Psalm 78:70–72 the psalmist writes of David as Israel's shepherd. Is he referring here to David as the primary caregiver or leader of the nation? The answer is found in verse 72, where he uses parallelism. First, he says that David shepherded Israel "with integrity of heart." Then he follows with a parallel statement, "with skillful hands he led them." The latter term *led* explains the former *shepherded*. We see much the same in 2 Samuel 5:2, where the Israelites said to David, "And the LORD said to you, 'You will shepherd my people Israel, and you will become their ruler.'" Whether or not these leaders provided some type of pastoral care, the main thrust of what they did was to lead people.

The New Testament picks up on this imagery and uses it of the Savior, emphasizing specifically his leadership (John 10:1–6, 27). Then others such as Luke (Acts 20:28–29) and Peter (1 Peter 5:1–5) use it of the leaders in the church. These passages emphasize the role of the shepherd-leader as protector, overseer, and example to the flock.

Another point that relies less on shepherd imagery is found in Acts 6:1–7. The apostles and the early church found themselves in a difficult situation where one group of members was complaining that the other group was neglecting their widows—definitely a pastoral care situation. It's important to note how the apostles handled this concern. They delegated the pastoral care situation (the care of the widows) to others rather than do it themselves. And the reason is most important: "We will turn this responsibility over to them and will give our attention to prayer and the ministry of the word" (vv. 3–4). If pastoral care is the most important function, then why didn't they say so? Instead, they indicate that prayer and the ministry of the Word were most important.

There are several practical reasons we must be careful about overemphasizing the pastoral care side of a pastor's ministry.

1. Research teaches us that some pastors who are strong in pastoral care tend to resist healthy, necessary growth in their churches, because if the church adds more people through evangelism or some other means, then it grows too big for the pastor to be able to care for all the people. This would put an unreasonable demand on his time. He asks, "How can I visit and care for all these people that I love? There aren't enough hours in the day." Thus, often unconsciously, he resists healthy growth and the church stays small in size and fails to reach lost people.

2. Some in the church, often the older members, expect the pastor to visit them, particularly when they're in the hospital. If he fails to visit them for even a legitimate reason, they are often offended. This promotes the false idea that if the pastor doesn't visit you, you haven't been visited.

3. Others in the congregation may have gifts in the pastoral area (Eph. 4:11 applies to laypeople as well as pastoral leaders!) and often use these gifts when visiting some of these very same people in the hospital. However, still the same mistaken view prevails: if the pastor hasn't visited me, then I haven't been visited! This diminishes and even discourages this important ministry of the laity in the church.

4. Some ministries in the church are better at providing pastoral care than the pastor, who may not be gifted in this area. For example, one of the advantages of a small group ministry is that it provides hands-on pastoral care for its members. I recall visiting one of the ladies in my church who was in the hospital. When I arrived, I found several of the people in her small group there ministering to and caring for her. I suspect that I was more in their way than a help to her.

5. Finally, some churches are too large for the pastor to visit and offer pastoral care to all or even some of the members. So how can his role be primarily that of pastoral care? If it is, his congregation should demand that he visit everybody.

Based on the New Testament, I believe that other leadership functions are more important to the church than pastoral care. One of these is helping the church develop and adopt a passionate, compelling mission statement. The Savior gave the church its mission statement in Matthew 28:19–20, which is to make and mature disciples! This is what the church is to be about. The way to evaluate the effectiveness of the church is to look for its disciples. Do you want to know if your church is effective? Show us your disciples. While the Great Commission includes pastoral care, it's much broader than that.

You may wonder where this common view that equates the pastor's ministry primarily with hands-on pastoral care came from. I believe that it came from at least two sources—the biblical use of shepherd imagery and tradition. While Scripture uses shepherd imagery, shepherds did much more than just provide pastoral care for their sheep. The passages noted above demonstrate this and so does any good book on biblical customs. Consequently, this view is a misunderstanding of what shepherds did in biblical times. It assumes that a shepherd spent most of his day taking care of sheep. More accurately a shepherd was a sheep leader rather than a sheep caregiver.

Concerning the second source of this view—church tradition—an examination of church history reveals that in various historical periods, the church emphasized different roles for the pastor. During the Reformation, the Reformers emphasized the teaching of God's Word. However, in the 1600s the Puritans specifically stressed the role of pastor as a "physician of the soul." They believed that the pastor's primary role was that of the shepherd of souls. Much of the emphasis today on the pastor as caregiver comes from this emphasis.

While tradition may help today's pastor understand how the church has viewed the role of the pastor over the ages, we must draw our understanding from Scripture. If tradition contradicts the Bible, it's imperative that we not follow tradition.

The view that the pastor's primary responsibility is pastoral care becomes a problem if the pastor of a church pours most of his time into pastoral care and little, if any, into other areas, such as communicating and encouraging the church to pursue Jesus's mission for the church—the Great Commission. It is also wrong if people insist that the primary role of all pastors must be the pastoral care of the flock.

My purpose in writing this article isn't to diminish the importance of pastoral care but to put it in proper biblical perspective. At a time when pastoring a church is a leadership-intensive enterprise (Peter Drucker argues that leading a large church is one of the three most difficult professions in our culture), pastors must know what their biblical role is. I am convinced that the primary role is that of leader of the flock who at times provides pastoral care for the flock.

APPENDIX J

Church Core Values Audit

Directions

Using the scale below, circle the number that best expresses to what extent the following values are important to your church (actual values). Work your way through the list quickly, going with your first impression.

	1 Not Important	2 Somewhat Important	3 Important	4 Most Important
1. **Family:** The relationships between a husband and wife and their children	1	2	3	4
2. **Biblical instruction:** A familiarity with and desire to know the truths of Scripture	1	2	3	4
3. **World missions:** Spreading the gospel of Christ around the globe	1	2	3	4
4. **Encouragement:** Giving hope to people who at times need some hope	1	2	3	4
5. **Giving:** Providing a portion of one's finances to support the ministry	1	2	3	4
6. **Fellowship:** Relating to and spending time with others, especially people within the church	1	2	3	4
7. **Leadership:** A person's ability to influence others to pursue God's mission for the church	1	2	3	4
8. **Cultural relevance:** Communicating truth in a way that people who aren't like us understand	1	2	3	4

	1 Not Important	2 Somewhat Important	3 Important	4 Most Important
9. **Prayer:** Communicating with God	1	2	3	4
10. **Excellence:** Maintaining the highest ministry standards that bring glory to God	1	2	3	4
11. **Evangelism:** Telling others the Good News about Christ	1	2	3	4
12. **Team ministry:** A group of people ministering together	1	2	3	4
13. **Creativity:** Coming up with new ideas and ways of doing ministry	1	2	3	4
14. **Worship:** Attributing worth to God	1	2	3	4
15. **Cooperation:** The act of working together in the service of the Savior	1	2	3	4
16. **Ministry/service:** Christians actively involved and serving in the ministries of the church (a mobilized congregation)	1	2	3	4
17. **Obedience:** A willingness to do what God or others ask	1	2	3	4
18. **Innovation:** Making changes that promote the ministry as it serves Christ	1	2	3	4
19. **Initiative:** The willingness to take the first step or make the first move in a ministry situation	1	2	3	4
20. **Community:** The desire to reach out to the people who live within driving distance of the church (your Jerusalem)	1	2	3	4
21. **Other values:**	1	2	3	4

Note all the values that you rated with a 3 or 4. Rank these according to priority. The first six are your core values.

Personal Core Values Audit

Directions

Using the scale below, circle the number that best expresses to what extent the following values are important to you (actual values). Work your way through the list quickly, going with your first impression.

	1 Not Important	2 Somewhat Important	3 Important	4 Most Important
1. **Family:** The relationships between a husband and wife and their children	1	2	3	4
2. **Biblical instruction:** A familiarity with and desire to know the truths of Scripture	1	2	3	4
3. **World missions:** Spreading the gospel of Christ around the globe	1	2	3	4
4. **Encouragement:** Giving hope to people who at times need some hope	1	2	3	4
5. **Giving:** Providing a portion of one's finances to support the ministry	1	2	3	4
6. **Fellowship:** Relating to and spending time with others, especially people within the church	1	2	3	4
7. **Leadership:** A person's ability to influence others to pursue God's mission for the church	1	2	3	4
8. **Cultural relevance:** Communicating truth in a way that people who aren't like us understand	1	2	3	4

	1 Not Important	2 Somewhat Important	3 Important	4 Most Important
9. **Prayer:** Communicating with God	1	2	3	4
10. **Excellence:** Maintaining the highest ministry standards that bring glory to God	1	2	3	4
11. **Evangelism:** Telling others the Good News about Christ	1	2	3	4
12. **Team ministry:** A group of people ministering together	1	2	3	4
13. **Creativity:** Coming up with new ideas and ways of doing ministry	1	2	3	4
14. **Worship:** Attributing worth to God	1	2	3	4
15. **Cooperation:** The act of working together in the service of the Savior	1	2	3	4
16. **Ministry/service:** Christians actively involved and serving in the ministries of the church (a mobilized congregation)	1	2	3	4
17. **Obedience:** A willingness to do what God or others ask	1	2	3	4
18. **Innovation:** Making changes that promote the ministry as it serves Christ	1	2	3	4
19. **Initiative:** The willingness to take the first step or make the first move in a ministry situation	1	2	3	4
20. **Community:** The desire to reach out to the people who live within driving distance of the church (your Jerusalem)	1	2	3	4
21. **Other values:**	1	2	3	4

Note all the values that you rated with a 3 or 4. Rank these according to priority. The first six are your core values.

APPENDIX L

Sample Core Values Statement

Scripture

We believe that God's inerrant Word is our final authority for faith and practice (2 Tim. 3:16). This means that what we do is deeply theological. Therefore, we will use the Bible as the guide for our writing, consulting, training, and speaking ministries.

Church

We believe that Christ's church is the only hope for mankind (Matt. 16:18). Therefore, we have a passion to help churches—at home and abroad—discover and implement Christ's church-building process.

Leadership

We believe that leadership is the hope of the church (2 Tim. 2:2). Therefore, we serve primarily with those at staff and lay levels who have leadership gifts and abilities.

Great Commission

We are convinced that Christ's will and mission for His church is the Great Commission (Matt. 28:19–20). Therefore, we are committed to lead and equip churches to make and mature disciples at home and abroad.

Transformation

We believe that God's desire is to transform all His people into the likeness of His Son (Gal. 4:19; 5:22–23). This means that we challenge churches to change their forms but not their biblical functions to remain relevant to a lost and dying world (1 Chron. 12:32).

Creativity and Innovation

Our heavenly Father is a God of creativity (Genesis 1). Therefore, we challenge churches to be creative and innovative in what they do as they reach out to a lost and dying world while serving their constituents.

Excellence

Christians ultimately serve God, not men (Col. 3:23–24). Therefore, we seek to honor Him by maintaining a high standard of excellence in all our services for Him.

The Malphurs Group

Jesus's Command to Make Disciples

What did Jesus mean in Matthew 28:19–20 when he commanded his church to make disciples?

Perhaps the most important questions that a church and its leadership can ask are: What does God want us to do? What is our mandate or mission? What are our marching orders? The answer to all three questions isn't hard to find. More than two thousand years ago, the Savior predetermined the church's mission—it's the Great Commission, as found in such texts as Mark 16:15; Luke 24:46–49; John 20:21; and Matthew 28:19–20, where he says, "Make disciples." This commission raises several important questions, such as what is a disciple and what does it mean to make disciples?

If you asked ten different people in the church (including the pastoral staff) what a disciple is, you might get ten different answers. The same is true at a seminary. If the church is not clear on what Jesus meant, then it will be difficult for it to comply with his expressed will. For the church to understand what the Savior meant in Matthew 28:19–20, we must examine the main verb and its object "make disciples" and then the two participles that follow—"baptizing" and "teaching." What does all this mean?

"Make Disciples"

First, let's examine the main verb and its object: "make disciples." A common view is that a disciple is a committed believer. Thus a disciple is a believer, but a believer isn't necessarily a disciple. However, that's not how the New

Testament uses this term. I contend that the normative use of the term *disciple* (though there are some obvious exceptions[1]) is of one who is a convert to or a believer in Jesus Christ. Thus the Bible teaches that a disciple isn't necessarily a Christian who has made a deeper commitment to the Savior but simply a Christian. Committed Christians are committed disciples. Uncommitted Christians are uncommitted disciples. This is clearly how Luke uses the term *disciple* in the book of Acts and his Gospel. It is evident in passages such as the following: Acts 6:1–2, 7; 9:1, 26; 11:26; 14:21–22; 15:10; 18:23; 19:9. For example, Acts 6:7 tells us that God's Word kept spreading and the number of disciples continued to increase greatly in Jerusalem. Luke isn't telling us that the number of deeply committed believers was significantly increasing. He's telling his readers that the church was making numerous converts to the faith. In Acts 9:1 Luke writes that Saul (Paul) was "breathing out murderous threats against the Lord's disciples." It's most doubtful that Saul was threatening only the mature believers. He was persecuting as many believers as he could locate. A great example is Acts 14:21 where Luke says they "won a large number of disciples" in connection with evangelism. Here they preached the gospel and won or made a large number of disciples or converts, not mature or even growing Christians. (Note that the words "won a large number of disciples" is the one Greek word *mathateusantes*, the same word as in Matthew 28:19!) Disciples, then, were synonymous with believers. Virtually all scholars acknowledge this to be the case in Acts.

So is the command "make disciples" in Matthew 28:19 to be equated with evangelism? Before we can answer this question, we must also examine a second context. The first had to do with the use of the term *disciple* in the New Testament; the second has to do with the other Great Commission passages: Mark 16:15 and Luke 24:46–49 (with Acts 1:8). In Mark 16:15 Jesus commands the disciples, "Go into all the world and preach the good news to all creation." Here "preach" like "make disciples" is the main verb (an aorist imperative) preceded by another circumstantial participle of attendant circumstance translated "go." This is clearly a proactive command to do evangelism.

In Luke 24:46–48 we have much the same message with the gospel defined: "This is what is written: The Christ will suffer and rise from the dead on the third day, and repentance and forgiveness of sins will be preached in his name to all nations, beginning at Jerusalem. You are witnesses of these things." Jesus presents the gospel message and the necessity that his witnesses preach that gospel to all nations. In these two Great Commission passages, the emphasis is clearly on evangelism and missions.

Finally, John gives us the least information in his statement of the commission. In John 20:21–22 Jesus tells the disciples that he's sending them and provides them with the Holy Spirit in anticipation of Pentecost.

We must not stop here. There's a third context. Much of Jesus's teaching of the Twelve (who are believers, except for Judas) concerns discipleship or the need for the disciple to grow in Christ (Matt. 16:24–26; 20:26–28; Luke 9:23–25). For example, Matthew 16:24 says, "Then Jesus said to his disciples, 'If anyone would come after me, he must deny himself and take up his cross and follow me.'"

So how does this relate to the passages in Acts and the other commission passages in the Gospels? The answer is that the Great Commission has both an evangelism and an edification or spiritual growth component. To make a disciple, first one has to win a person (a nondisciple) to Christ. At that point he or she becomes a disciple. It doesn't stop there. Now this new disciple needs to grow or mature as a disciple, hence the edification component.

"Baptizing and Teaching"

Having studied the main verb and its object, "make disciples," we need to examine the two participles in Matthew 28:20—"baptizing" and "teaching." The interpretation of these will address whether "make disciples" involves both evangelism and edification. While there are two feasible interpretive options, the better one is that they are circumstantial (adverbial) participles of means.[2] The NIV has taken this interpretation: "Therefore go and *make disciples* of all nations, *baptizing* them in the name of the Father and of the Son and of the Holy Spirit, and *teaching* them to obey everything I have commanded you." Dan Wallace, a Greek scholar and professor of New Testament at Dallas Seminary, writes: "Finally, the other two participles *(baptizontes, didaskontes)* should not be taken as attendant circumstance. First, they do not fit the normal pattern for attendant circumstance participles (they are present tense and follow the main verb). And second, they obviously make good sense as participles of means; i.e., the *means* by which the disciples were to make disciples was to baptize and then to teach."[3] If this is the case, then the two participles provide us with the means or the *how* for growing the new disciples. The way the church makes disciples is by baptizing and teaching its people.

But what is the significance of baptism in the life of a new disciple (believer)? Baptism is mentioned eleven times in Acts (Acts 2:38; 8:12, 16, 36, 38; 9:18; 10:48; 16:15, 33; 19:5; 22:16). In every passage except one (19:5) it's used in close association with evangelism and immediately follows someone's conversion to Christ. Baptism was the public means or activity that identified the new disciple with Jesus.[4] Baptism was serious business, as it could mean rejection by one's parents and family, even resulting in the loss of one's life. As we have seen, it both implies or is closely associated with evangelism and was a public confession that one had become a disciple of Jesus. Thus Matthew includes evangelism in the context of disciple making.

And finally, what is the significance of *teaching*? Luke also addresses teaching in Acts (Acts 2:42; 5:25, 28; 15:35; 18:11; 28:31). Michael Wilkins summarizes this best when he says that "'teaching' introduces the activities by which the new disciple grows in discipleship."[5] The object of our teaching is obedience to Jesus's teaching. The emphasis on teaching isn't simply for the sake of knowledge. Effective teaching results in a transformed life or a maturing disciple/believer.

The Conclusion

The conclusion from the evidence above is that the two participles are best treated and translated as circumstantial participles of means. The term *make disciples (mathateusante)* is a clear reference to both evangelism (baptizing) and maturation (teaching). (Note again the use of *mathateusantes* in Acts 14:21 in the context of evangelism.) Mark and Luke emphasize the evangelism aspect of the Great Commission (and John the sending out of the disciples). Matthew emphasizes both evangelism and the need to grow disciples in their newfound faith, as he adds the need not only to baptize but to teach these new believers as well. According to other passages in the New Testament, the latter would lead the new converts to spiritual maturity (1 Cor. 3:1–4; Heb. 5:11–6:3). Therefore, the goal is for them to become mature disciples in time. This would result from a combination of being taught and obeying Jesus's commandments.

Jesus was clear about his intentions for his church. It wasn't just to teach or preach the Word, as important as those activities are. Nor was it evangelism alone, although the latter is emphasized as much as teaching. He expects his entire church (not simply a few passionate disciple makers) to move people from prebirth (unbelief) to the new birth (belief) and then to maturity. In fact, this is so important that we can measure a church's spiritual health and its ultimate success by its obedience to the Great Commission. It is fair to ask of every church's ministry how many people have become disciples (believers) and how many of these disciples are growing toward maturity. In short, it's imperative that every church make and mature disciples at home and abroad!

Note: I highly recommend Michael J. Wilkins's *Following the Master: A Biblical Theology of Discipleship* (Zondervan, 1992). Wilkins is professor of New Testament language and literature and dean of the faculty at the Talbot School of Theology, Biola University.

APPENDIX N

Sample Mission Statements

The following are mission statements that I've collected over the years. Some are great statements, some aren't so great, and some are included for the sake of levity. Regardless, they are here to help you understand better the mission concept and to come up with a mission statement that describes you and your planted church. I suggest that you read and critique them, using the information under The Development of the Mission Statement in chapter 6. Write down any that you like and think would fit your planted church.

"Our mission is to turn irreligious people into fully devoted followers of Christ."

"Our mission is to lead unchurched people to become fully devoted followers of Christ."

"Our mission is to grow people into completely committed Christ-followers."

"We exist to know Christ and make him known."

"Our mission is to present Christ as Savior and pursue Christ as Lord."

"Our mission is to provide the best opportunity for people to become fully devoted followers of Christ."

"We exist to lead all people into a life-changing, ever growing relationship with Christ."

"Our mission is to see people become fully developing followers of Christ."

"Our mission is to lead ordinary people to extraordinary life in Christ."

"Our mission is to follow and make followers of Christ."

"Our mission is to passionately follow and make followers of Christ."

"Our mission is that every man, woman, and child in Greater Austin hear the gospel from the lips of someone at Hill Country Bible Church."

"We exist to develop all people into fully functioning followers of Christ."

"Our mission is to lead people into a growing relationship with Christ."

"Our mission is to lead people into a growing relationship with Jesus Christ."

"Sharing Christ • Building Believers"

"Reach • Build • Release"

"Our mission is to connect the disconnected into a vital relationship with Jesus Christ."

"We exist to be used by God as he transforms people into disciples of Jesus Christ, here and around the world."

"Our mission is to meet people where they are and encourage them toward maturity in Christ."

"We exist to establish a church in Madrid that is radically devoted to God, relentlessly committed to authentic community, and remarkably passionate for lost people."

"We're a community of misfits transformed by Jesus to be a catalyst for loving people on the fringes of our culture."

APPENDIX O

Vision Audit

An important factor in developing a vision is your vision style. Your vision style is how you catch a vision.

Directions

From the choices a or b below, choose the one that best describes your preference.

1. I like courses that focus on
   a) fact
   b) theory
2. I prefer the company of
   a) realistic people
   b) imaginative people
3. People view me as
   a) a practical person
   b) an ingenious person
4. I like people best who
   a) prefer the "tried and true"
   b) come up with new ideas
5. People say that I am
   a) conventional
   b) unconventional

6. I like to pursue matters
   a) in the accepted way
   b) in my own unique way
7. I prefer
   a) facts
   b) ideas
8. I'm more comfortable with
   a) certainty
   b) theory
9. I like best
   a) building things
   b) inventing things
10. I am convinced that
   a) seeing is believing
   b) believing is seeing
11. I prefer
   a) the concrete
   b) the abstract
12. I am more comfortable with
   a) the known
   b) the unknown
13. I would prefer to be known as
   a) a realist
   b) a visionary
14. I like to think more about
   a) what is
   b) what could be
15. I'm more likely to trust
   a) my experience
   b) my intuition
16. I'm known as someone with
   a) common sense
   b) vision
17. I think it's more important to
   a) adjust to the facts
   b) see possibilities
18. I prefer to
   a) support established methods
   b) address unsolved problems

Interpretation

Total the number of As you circled. Then total the number of Bs you circled. Which is the greater number?

The Vision Catcher

If you circled more As than Bs, you're the type of leader who *catches* a vision by visiting another ministry and seeing it for yourself. You focus more on the present than the future.

Your vision style: *vision catcher*

The Vision Creator

If you circled more Bs than As, you're the type of leader who *creates* a vision in your head. You focus primarily on the future and are a natural visionary.

Your vision style: *vision creator*

Sample Vision Statements

Irving Bible Church

Our Dreams

About 10 years ago we developed a series of statements of what we dreamed IBC would become. The statements that follow have withstood the test of time and still reflect the heart of what is going on with IBC.

We dream of a church . . .

where the gospel is the underlying theme; where grace is accepted and extended; where the salvation of souls is the norm, not the exception; where love for people springs from love for God; where joy permeates the air; where people are one in spirit; where service is considered a privilege not a burden.

where people find real help, experience real change, and discover real answers; where marriages are healed and parents' hearts are turned toward their children; where destructive lifestyles, habits, addictions, and compulsions are forever jettisoned; where wasted lives are retrieved and new beginnings launched.

where God's Word is exalted in authority, studied with expectation, taught with relevance, heard with anticipation, and obeyed with passion; where the preaching is encouraging, positive, and practical.

where prayer is the undergirding and engulfing medium for all we do and for every initiative we take.

where people are free to attempt great things for God; where taking risks for his kingdom is an exalted virtue; where people have nothing to prove and therefore nothing to lose; where creativity and innovation are honored, not feared; where all kinds of people serve God in diverse ways with mutual love, encouragement, respect, and unity.

where people's hearts beat for God's work around the world; where impact is made on lives across the street and around the world; where short-term workers regularly go out to minister internationally and return with a world perspective.

where the challenge of nurturing new, cutting-edge ministries becomes reality; where past traditions form the foundations for launching new innovations, not the ball and chain to impede them; where hundreds of laymen and women are effectively trained and actually entrusted with the work of the ministry; where partnerships are formed by networking with other ministries to further the cause of Christ.

where children and youth are nurtured in the faith; where they are made strong in their ability to serve the Lord and stand for him in their world.

where God is worshiped joyfully and reverently; where the music is Christ-honoring and relevant; where worship is a significant event which encourages believers and transforms them into the triumphant army of God; where worship communicates to the visitor the greatness of our God, the joyfulness of the Christian life, and the emptiness of life without Jesus.

where the issues of our culture are seriously addressed; where the community expects to find a viewpoint both practical and godly, a viewpoint which must be taken seriously; where God's people take stands in the community that are courageous and compassionate.

where growth is not only welcomed, but anticipated as the norm; where the heartbeat of every person is for outreach and inclusion, not for comfortable complacency and seclusion.

Irving Bible Church
Irving, Texas

Village View Community Church

Our Vision

Our dream is to be a place known for its love, its worship of God, its service to its families, the discipling of its leaders, and its ability to reach others for Jesus and to see them become members of a local church fellowship.

Our dream is to be a place where the lost, hurting, and receptive can find love, acceptance, forgiveness, renewal, and healing.

Our dream is to be a place where people are encouraged to discover their spiritual gifts and use them in order to find fulfillment and fruitfulness in ministry and life.

Our dream is to be a loving fellowship of believers involved in small groups, serving and building relationships with one another, reaching the unchurched, sharing in ministry, discipled through the Bible, and worshiping God in our homes, church, and communities.

Our dream is to be a catalyst for the launching of new churches.

Our dream is to be a regional church for the tri-county area with beautiful yet simple facilities, a Bible School, Christian School, Christian Day Care, Youth and Senior Centers, Counseling Center, Catered and Assisted Living Facility, and Nursing Home to minister to the whole person: body, soul, and spirit and to be located on a piece of land that is peaceful, beautifully landscaped, and easily accessible.

Village View Community Church
The Villages
Summerfield, Florida

The Saddleback Vision

From Pastor Rick Warren's first sermon, March 30, 1980

It is the dream of a place where the hurting, the depressed, the frustrated, and the confused can find love, acceptance, help, hope, forgiveness, guidance, and encouragement.

It is the dream of sharing the Good News of Jesus Christ with the hundreds of thousands of residents in South Orange County.

It is the dream of welcoming 20,000 members into the fellowship of our church family—loving, learning, laughing, and living in harmony together.

It is the dream of equipping every believer for a significant ministry by helping them discover the gifts and talents God gave them. It is the dream of developing people to spiritual maturity through Bible studies, small groups, seminars, retreats, and a Bible school for our members.

It is the dream of sending out hundreds of career missionaries and church workers all around the world, and empowering every member for a personal life mission in the world.

It is the dream of sending our members by the thousands on short-term mission projects to every continent.

It is the dream of starting at least one new daughter church every year.

It is the dream of at least fifty acres of land, on which will be built a regional church for South Orange County—with beautiful, yet simple, facilities including a worship center seating thousands, a counseling and prayer center, classrooms for Bible studies and training lay ministers, and a recreation area. All of this will be designed to minister to the total person—spiritually, emotionally, and socially—and set in a peaceful inspiring garden landscape.

I stand before you today and state in confident assurance that these dreams will become reality. Why? Because they are inspired by God![1]

Saddleback Valley Community Church
Lake Forest, California

Forest Meadow Baptist Church

The vision of Forest Meadow Baptist Church is to provide for the needs of Lake Highlands' children and their families by providing lots of opportunities to experience creative, high-quality worship, discipleship, activities, and hands-on global missions involvement.

Our church is a Christian community that welcomes the mosaic of cultures living in our neighborhoods. Where needed, we establish culturally specific churches and ministries.

We are a multi-congregational church, meaning we offer services and discipleship in a variety of different languages and at numerous locations around the world. At our main campus on Church Road, we have services in English, Spanish, several Sudanese dialects, Bemba (Zambian), and Swahili. Our global missions vision is to share the love of Jesus Christ with all the peoples of the world, beginning here in Dallas and extending to the ends of the earth. We are working intensely with the Great Commission Initiative, and in a church planting ministry in Southern Sudan.

Forest Meadow Baptist Church
Dallas, Texas

Vision Statement

Clear Lake Community Church

CHILDREN'S PROGRAM

We envision children waking up parents on Sunday morning excited to go to church.

We see lots of smiles, glad to be in a place of belonging, welcomed again by a familiar face.

We see the fright of first time melted by an extra caring touch and loneliness replaced by laughter.

We see motivated volunteers, passionate about being with kids, gifted to teach, serve, and shepherd.

We see a facility which is "kid focused," that will facilitate learning and having fun for hundreds of kids.

We see a clean and attractive environment where excellence and creativity are immediately noticed.

We see concerned moms, relieved as they drop off their children, and dads without distraction, engaged in the service.

We envision a security process which builds confidence with parents.

We see physical care babies being cuddled and crawlers being chased.

We sense a foundation being laid where Sunday morning is an experience of God's love for the youngest baby to the oldest child, a time when seeds of faith can be planted and nurtured.

We hear cheers of older kids, and feel fun in the air as hundreds of kids celebrate and sing of the goodness of God; we hear the quietness of prayer.

We envision the stories of the Bible told in creative ways.

We see the look of conviction as the gospel penetrates a child's heart.

We see caring adults leading discussion and listening during small group time.

We dream of kids carrying Bibles and bringing friends.

We see whole families growing closer to God and each other through programs to motivate and equip parents.

In the next five years, we envision hundreds of kids choosing to be baptized and building a faith foundation that will lead to a lifetime of full devotion to Christ and multiplication of kingdom impact.

Will Mancini
Clear Lake Community Church
Houston, Texas

Notes

Introduction

1. David T. Olson, *The American Church in Crisis* (Grand Rapids: Zondervan, 2008), 28.
2. http://www.newsweek.com/id/192583/output/print.
3. Bruce McNicol, "Churches Die with Dignity," *Christianity Today* (Jan. 14, 1991), 69.

Chapter 2 Who Plants Churches?

1. Kent and Barbara Hughes, *Liberating Ministry from the Success Syndrome* (Wheaton, IL: Tyndale, 1988), 125.
2. Aubrey Malphurs, *Maximizing Your Effectiveness*, 2nd ed. (Grand Rapids: Baker, 2006), 107–9.

Chapter 3 How Much Will It Cost?

1. Valerie Calderon, "Taking the Guesswork Out of Church Planting," *Rev!* (Jan/Feb 2009), 28.

Chapter 4 What Are the Foundational Assumptions?

1. There are other hermeneutical principles as well as these. Should you wish to pursue them further, see my book *Doing Church* (Grand Rapids: Baker, 1999).
2. Francis A. Schaeffer, *The Church at the End of the Twentieth Century* (Wheaton, IL: Crossway Books, 1985), 68.
3. Aubrey Malphurs, *Planting Growing Churches* (Grand Rapids: Baker, 2004).

Chapter 5 What Drives a New Church?

1. Lyle E. Schaller, *Getting Things Done* (Nashville: Abingdon, 1987), 152.
2. James M. Kouzes and Barry Z. Posner, *The Leadership Challenge*, 4th ed. (San Francisco: Jossey-Bass, 1987), 62.
3. Aubrey Malphurs, *Values-Driven Leadership* (Grand Rapids: Baker, 1998).

Chapter 6 What Are New Churches Supposed to Do?

1. Peter F. Drucker, *Managing the Non-Profit Organization* (New York: Harper-Business, 1990), 3.
2. Ibid., 45.
3. Ibid., 3.

Chapter 7 What Kind of Church Will It Be?

1. Bill Hybels, *Courageous Leadership* (Grand Rapids: Zondervan, 2002), 46.
2. Ibid., 31.
3. Ibid., 50.
4. Ibid., 112.
5. Ibid., 113.
6. Marcus Buckingham, *One Thing You Need to Know* (New York: Free Press, 2008), 59.
7. John R. W. Stott, "What Makes Leadership Christian?" *Christianity Today*, August 1985, 24.

Chapter 9 Who Will Be Reached?

1. Helen Lee, "5 Kinds of Christians," *Christianity Today*, online http://www.christianitytoday.com/le/2007/fall/1.19.html?start=4, 1 October, 2007, 4.
2. Jim Collins, "The Good to Great Pastor," *Leadership*, Spring 2008, 48.
3. If you wish to pursue this further, you'll find my exegesis of Matthew 28:19–20 in appendix M.
4. Win Arn, "Average Driving Time to Church," *The Win Arn Growth Report* 1, no. 20.

Chapter 10 What Is the Goal?

1. Bob Gilliam, "Are Most Churches Intentionally Making Disciples? Findings from the Spiritual Journey Evaluation" (unpublished paper, circulated 29 March 1995), 1.
2. Ibid.
3. Ibid.
4. Greg L. Hawkins and Cally Parkinson, *Follow Me* (Chicago: The Willow Creek Association, 2008), 18–21.

Chapter 11 Who Will Implement the Goal?

1. Drucker, *Managing the Non-Profit Organization*, 145.

Chapter 12 Who Will Equip the Implementers?

1. Calderon, "Taking the Guesswork Out of Church Planting," 28.
2. Gary McIntosh, *Staff Your Church for Growth* (Grand Rapids: Baker, 2000), 52.
3. Drucker, *Managing the Non-Profit Organization*, 145.
4. Calderon, "Taking the Guesswork Out of Church Planting," 28.
5. McIntosh, *Staff Your Church for Growth*, 43.

6. Lyle E. Schaller, *The Multiple Staff and the Larger Church* (Nashville: Abingdon Press, 1980), 38.

7. Todd Rhoades, "Does Your Staff Know What You Expect from Them?" *Monday Morning Insight*, November 17, 2008. http://mondaymorninginsight.com/blog/post/does_your_staff_know_what_you_expect_of_them/.

8. Peter F. Drucker, *MBA in a Box* (New York: Crown Business, 2004), 192.

Chapter 14 What Will It Cost?

1. Dick Towner, "Money Management That Makes Sense," *Church Executive* (July 2005), http://www.churchexecutive.com/.

2. Calderon, "Taking the Guesswork Out of Church Planting," 28.

3. Aubrey Malphurs and Steve Stroope, *Money Matters in Church* (Grand Rapids: Baker, 2007).

4. Calderon, "Taking the Guesswork Out of Church Planting," 28.

5. Writing in *Christianity Today*, Rob Moll states, "The median annual giving for an American Christian is actually $200, just over half a percent of after-tax income." Rob Moll, "Scrooge Lives!" *Christianity Today* (December 5, 2008), 24.

6. While the average American allocates $26.86 per week (3.1 percent of adjusted gross income) toward charitable giving, according to the Social Capital Community Benchmark Survey, participants in Leadership Network's Generous Churches Leadership Community exceed that giving rate by 96 percent. Members of churches in that network give an average of $52.75 weekly (6.1 percent of adjusted gross income). Furthermore, giving rates among Generous Churches members continue to rise each year. Pat Springle, "The Genesis of Generosity," *Leadership Network Advance* (April 8, 2008), 1.

7. Moll, "Scrooge Lives!" 25.

Appendix H Principles of Seeking Support

1. Much of the following information was developed by my friend and former student Clayton Hayes.

Appendix M Jesus's Command to Make Disciples

1. Some exceptions are the disciples of Moses (John 9:28), the disciples of the Pharisees (Matt. 22:16; Mark 2:18), the disciples of John (Mark 2:18; John 1:35), and the disciples of Jesus who left him (John 6:60–66).

2. The second option is to treat them as circumstantial (adverbial) participles of attendant circumstance. If this is correct, then the participles *baptizing* and *teaching* express an idea not subordinate to as above but coordinate to or on a par with the main verb (make disciples). You would translate the main verb and the participles as a series of coordinate verbs, the mood of which is dictated by the main verb that in this case is imperative (aorist imperative). The verse would read: "Go, therefore, and *make disciples* of all nations, *baptize* them in the name of the Father and of the Son and of the Holy Spirit, and *teach* them to obey everything that I have commanded you." A former Dallas Seminary Greek professor, Philip Williams, takes this view in "Grammar Notes on the Noun and the Verb and Certain Other Items" (unpublished class

notes, which were used by Dr. Buist Fanning in his course Advanced Greek Grammar, 1977), 53–54. The conclusion here is that the passage addresses a series of separate, coordinate chronological acts or steps. The first is to go, which implies proactivity. The second is to make disciples. The third is to baptize those disciples, and the fourth is to teach them. However, I believe that Dan Wallace makes the better argument for these being circumstantial particples of means. While I don't believe that *baptizontes* and *didaskontes* are circumstantial participles of attendant circumstance, I do believe that the first participle in verse 19 (*poreuthentes*) is. It draws its mood from or is coordinate to the main verb (*mathateusate*), which is imperative. Jesus is commanding them to make disciples and to be proactive about it.

3. Daniel B. Wallace, *Greek Grammar beyond the Basics* (Grand Rapids: Zondervan, 1996), 645.

4. See Michael J. Wilkins, *Following the Master: A Biblical Theology of Discipleship* (Grand Rapids: Zondervan, 1992), 26.

5. Ibid, 189–90.

Appendix P Sample Vision Statements

1. Taken from *The Purpose Driven Church* by Rick Warren. Copyright 1995 by Rick Warren. Used by permission of Zondervan, www.zondervan.com.

General Index

Scripture Index

267

ALSO BY

AUBREY MALPHURS

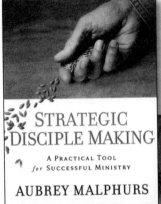

Strategic Disciple Making: A Practical Tool for Successful Ministry

9780801091964 • 192 pp.

Money Matters in Church: A Practical Guide for Leaders

9780801066276 • 224 pp.

A New Kind of Church: Understanding Models of Ministry for the 21st Century

9780801091896 • 208 pp.

BakerBooks
a division of Baker Publishing Group
www.BakerBooks.com